A Mother's Courage to Awaken

"Dr. Paula Petry shares her extremely personal and fascinating journey in *A Mother's Courage to Awaken,* a book that, regardless of your personal experiences or beliefs, is bound to resonate with some aspect of your life."

—Gloria Estefan

"Here is a story that touches every step—indeed, the very soul—of a life's honest journey. Moments of pain and joy and lifelong learning are captured beautifully. This is, above all, a story of love. What courage it took to tell this story."

—David Lawrence Jr., retired publisher of the *Miami Herald* and chair of The Children's Movement of Florida

"Paula's is a real story, inspiring in itself, but also a parable for the possibilities for each of us, at any stage of life, faced with any challenge, to create and renew."

—Marty Linsky, Harvard Kennedy School faculty and coauthor of *Leadership on the Line*

"Paula has mastered a love-centered regeneration process by embodying the power of the latent Divinity within us all. I am extremely proud of her path as a true healer."

—Reverend William Earle Cameron, retired Unity Minister and author of *SBNR Good God Renaissance*

"Paula's walkabout through this life will be familiar territory to many readers as we witness her journeys through love and loss, grief, and recovery, and the recreation of harmony in her soul and in her life. This book is good medicine."

—Hank Wesselman, PhD, anthropologist and author of *The Bowl of Light: Ancestral Wisdom from a Hawaiian Shaman, The Re-Enchantment,* and his Spiritwalker trilogy

"Authentic, Inspiring, and Transformative! Dr. Paula Petry leads us through her own journey and helps us discover our own in the process. Brilliantly written—weaving together a touch of science with personal exploration. This book will change your life."

—Larry Dossey, MD, *New York Times* bestselling author of *One Mind* and *Reinventing Medicine*

"Discover new meaning, purpose, deep healing, and contribution. This book will change your heart."

—Lori Fahey, CEO & president of The Family Café, Inc.

"A powerfully vulnerable and captivating book of self-discovery. It explores the all-encompassing struggles and joys of having a child with a disability and then finding a path back to the Light after unbearable loss."

—Leigh Kapps, PhD, Chief Operating Office, United Community Options of South Florida

"Here is an extraordinary story that eloquently chronicles a life of challenges with love, heartache, and spiritual transformation. This book will definitely touch your heart as you discover what it means to be 'resilient' and a 'spiritual warrior.' "

—Patricia Stauber, RN, LCSW, grief counselor and trauma specialist

"With her joyful sense of humor and humility, the author takes you on a ride that is both fulfilling and meaningful, and one that may leave you with many worthwhile questions."

—Eugene Ahn, MD

"This is an uplifting story of Paula's struggles with adversity and her ultimate success at building a rewarding and fulfilling life by becoming the person she wants and needs to be."

—Dr. Richard Urbano, retired professor, Vanderbilt University

A Mother's
Courage
to Awaken

A Mother's Courage to Awaken

Hope and Inspiration from My
Daughter's Journey in the Afterlife

Paula Petry, PhD

Coral Gables

For permission requests, please contact the publisher at:
Mango Publishing Group
2850 S Douglas Road, 2nd Floor
Coral Gables, FL 33134 USA
info@mango.bz

For special orders, quantity sales, course adoptions and corporate sales, please email the publisher at sales@mango.bz. For trade and wholesale sales, please contact Ingram Publisher Services at customer.service@ingramcontent.com or +1.800.509.4887.

A Mother's Courage to Awaken : Hope and Inspiration from My Daughter's Journey in the Afterlife

Library of Congress Cataloging-in-Publication number: 2020940926
ISBN: (print) 978-1-64250-417-0, (ebook) 978-1-64250-418-7
BISAC category code SEL010000, SELF-HELP / Death, Grief, Bereavement

Printed in the United States of America

Note: This publication is presented solely for informational, educational, and entertainment purposes. It is not intended to provide health advice and should not be relied upon as such. If expert assistance is required, the services of a professional should be sought. The publisher, the author, and their affiliated entities and individuals do not make any guarantees or other promises as to any results that may be obtained from using the content of this book. To the maximum extent permitted by law, the publisher, the author, and their affiliated entities and individuals disclaim any and all liability in the event any information contained in this book proves to be inaccurate, incomplete, or unreliable or results in any losses or harm. You, the reader, are responsible for your own choices, actions, and results.

For my children Alexandra and Jaime Lalinde
who keep showing me how to live life courageously.

Table of Contents

Foreword

Twenty-five hundred years ago in ancient Greece,
the great poet and tragedian Aeschylus wrote:

Drop by drop
Pain that cannot forget
Falls upon the heart
Until in our despair
Against our will
Comes wisdom
By the awful grace of God.

Paula's story is written in the spirit of Aeschylus. Her story is the story of humankind, a saga of pain, grief, trauma, disappointment, unyielding circumstances, unkind and uncaring people, and sorrow beyond bearing—through which the human spirit traverses without ceasing, never giving up, always persevering in hope against hope, faith beyond faith until, when the journey is done, we find ourselves mysteriously refined and purified through the intermingling of our suffering with our capacity to endure. Paula's story is thus all our stories and should be read as a microcosm of a larger journey we all take through the sacred path of suffering.

Chekhov, the passionate Russian poet of the nineteenth century, said, "Drop by drop we squeeze the slave out of ourselves." The beauty of Paula's book is that she describes each incident, each drop, with a painstaking exquisiteness that only a mother can express. Each incident from Alex's birth till Alex passed on to the next world is like a dewdrop, each refracting a different color and hue, each cascading upon our hearts until we are swept along in Paula's and Alex's journey and, with them, feel both piercing grief and the painstaking healing of love.

Paula's greatest act of courage was to not let Alex die in the hospital but to take Alex home to care for her and love her in her suffering. This courage is what defines our deepest humanity. It is a courage to be loving and compassionate whatever the cost, knowing that each human life is precious and sacred beyond reckoning. It is also the courage to simply keep going. It is one thing to decide. It is a completely different matter to persevere. Perseverance, no matter what the obstacle, is the true test of love.

The question that shouts from every page is why? Why are some children born deformed? Why does heartbreak happen to two people in love? Why are some condemned in complete innocence and others spared? Alex was clearly a beautiful and exquisitely sensitive child. Where did the deformity come from? Why Alex? Why was Jaime, the next born, spared?

Paula provides the answer to these imponderables as the book unfolds. There is ultimately only one answer to suffering—transformation. Suffering is not something to be understood rationally. It cannot be. There is no rational answer to Alex's suffering. Life is not an intellectual exercise. Life is a journey to be traversed, a drama to be enacted, a mystery to be lived. Life does not answer to our beck and call. Like Job, when confronted with suffering beyond reason, all we can do is submit to the destiny life dispenses and interact with it in a spirit of deep humility in order to purify our own souls and empower us to acts of compassion and tenderness for those around us.

The answer to every ultimate question is the same—how can this question, this situation, work its alchemical power within me to deepen my capacity to bring greater love into the world? As absurd as it may seem to the rational mind, the only true response to suffering is love, unconditional love. We are called to embrace all of life, whatever comes our way, and in that embrace to allow life to break us and rend us asunder, so that broken, in our despair, comes wisdom by the awful grace of God. This is what Alex and Paula embodied on behalf of us all.

Jim Garrison, PhD
President
Ubiquity University

Preface

ON JULY 5, 1996, I watched as my twelve-year-old daughter, Alex, was wheeled out of our home by the EMT responders, her struggle with spina bifida finally over. My grief, and guilt, led me on a quest, one for a deep understanding of who I am, why I am here, and what my suffering and my daughter's suffering meant to me as a woman, a mother, and a researcher. Through that quest, I made a journey back to my Self, that part of us that transcends our mind and body, the aspect of self that is connected to our divinity, where our wholeness resides. This is my story, a story about not giving up hope during the darkest hours of despair, but rather having faith that the divine light of love and beauty, Spirit itself, guides our path forward.

I believe there is a divine design for humanity and that it is linked to our innate ability to live a joy-filled and meaningful life. Searching for inner peace, I connected with reemerging ancient healing practices that are now fully supported by research as being effective in promoting positive emotional, mental, and physical health as well as spiritual well-being. These include shamanism, acupuncture, mantras, and other forms of energy medicine. I rediscovered the power of prayer, intention, and the imagination—our ability to direct our thoughts, to shape forms of energy to what we want rather than what we don't want. I found the empowering truth that our thought forms and beliefs shape the life we have, which gives us the glorious opportunity to create the life we want.

My life transformed from feeling victimized by circumstances and surrounded by dark forces into a bountiful life. I learned to deeply trust my own deaths and resurrections. By allowing both, my ability to love self and others was magnified. I found beauty even in the pains and struggles of life rather than brokenness, meaninglessness, cynicism,

and hatred. The many obstacles and hurdles I jumped over were a necessary part of my evolution. Whatever your journey, they are an essential part of yours, too.

This book was one of those obstacles. I tried many times to relinquish the task, the assignment seeming larger to me than who I perceived myself to be. But I kept showing up to the page, my beloved
Alex by my side. Our loved ones are always with us, just out of sight on
the other side of a thin veil. When the veil lifts through intention and
other means, we are together, again and always.

Through sharing my story, dear reader, I invite you to journey
along with me. My wish is that you, too, ultimately reclaim your Self
along the path to wholeness.

Prologue

What if you were sent here by something larger
Not against your will or wishes
But in alignment with your deepest longing
What if it was as simple as finding what you love
And letting it teach you how to live.
—Oriah "Mountain Dreamer" House

I STOOD IN FRONT OF THE door of the psychic medium's small cottage, feeling nervous but ready to face whatever was on its other side. My academic mind had turned off enough to do something irrational—to consult someone who thinks he can speak with the dead. My knee-jerk reaction of saying, "Sign me up" had come right after I heard, "He will be arriving on July 5, and his first appointment is at ten o'clock." The synchronicity was jolting, as was the memory. On a July 5 eleven years earlier, I watched as the Coral Gables Fire Rescue truck and the Miami-Dade county's coroner vehicle parked in my front yard and EMT workers wheeled my daughter's body out on a stretcher.

My anger, guilt, grief, and loss had subsided over the years, but the body memory from the trauma and the years of blaming myself were still there. I felt an ache in my chest and a pain in the pit of my stomach as I heard the date. The feeling of having done something wrong had left me sullen. When Alex died, people warned that life would never be the same. Why anyone would say a thing like a black cloud will always follow you was beyond me. However, I was inspired to not always live under a black cloud. Eleven years was a long time, though. Maybe they had been right.

Yes, there I stood outside a small white beach cottage in Pompano Beach, Florida, hopeful that a different life might lie across its threshold, a life once again filled with meaning and purpose. I wanted that fire in my belly again, as it had been in my early years when I formed a nonprofit to help other parents and advocated for children's right to a quality education and for public policies that empowered families. Those passions had faded with my daughter's death. Perhaps I no longer felt qualified to be that voice.

I was committed to showing up that day for my ten o'clock appointment. My car had broken down the night before, requiring a rental to drive the forty-five minutes north. I was not to be deterred. The love between my daughter and I was palpable, unique, and in the eyes of some, undeserved. At birth, doctors advised my then-husband and I to leave her at the hospital to die. We took her home instead. The part of me that already knew the future had chosen her name, Alexandra. I thought it sounded strong. She was and needed to be. The years falling in love with her were life changing. In fact, I can't imagine what my life would have been like without her. It was at her funeral that I realized I had gleaned all of life's important lessons simply by raising her, and as they closed her casket, I listed those lessons in a prayer that washed through me. Learning to love someone deeply was foremost, but Alexandra also brought me an appreciation for differences, the value of patience, and the importance of determination and empathy.

My yearning had been rekindled. I was hoping to be with this loving child. I was also ready to face her disappointment, to hear her scolding me, "How did you not realize my shunt wasn't working? I told you my head hurt." The remnants of guilt and remorse still percolated below the surface. Missing that night's clues haunted me. Her death did not make sense. The juxtaposition between the heroism in her life and the passivity in her death created a schism—one that I often filled with self-blame. I wanted to hear, "Mom, I still love you. It wasn't your fault."

I knew I was running out of options. Years of cognitive therapy and analysis had been helpful, but my guilt was deep-rooted. My daughter's birth and death triggered beliefs and patterns within me that I couldn't let go. I had spent twelve years trying to fix Alex, the name we called her, to no avail. Now, I, too, seemed unfixable. There was a seeking within me that seemed insatiable. Maybe this man from Georgia could help. Maybe he could give me the words I was so hoping to hear.

The door opened, and I saw a tall man with a kind face. I walked in, took a seat in the kitchen, and began sipping the herbal tea I was offered. Then I introduced myself.

"I have resigned from my longtime faculty position at the medical school and sold my house and have a few belongings. I don't have any questions about any of that. I came to commune with my daughter."

"I know, dear. She has been waiting for you," he said.

Others were there, too—you could say the room was packed. As he talked, I scribbled notes on my yellow pad, now rumpled with dried tears.

Memories of my younger brother Jim's death six years prior on Thanksgiving Day were also in those tears. The man knew my brother was dead. How was that possible? But it was Alex's presence for which I longed. And she was there. Scribbled on one of the pages are her words as he conveyed them to me.

"Mom, it was my time to go. I love you. Thank you."

He said she appeared to him as Dorothy from the Wizard of Oz.

"Mom, you are the Wizard. And remember the Wizard is fake."

I left in a swirl of mixed emotions and questions, but mostly a deep relief. My skin tingled and something inside me told me that it was Alex. I know you might think I was fooled—that psychic mediums aren't real and that we can't communicate with our loved ones after death. All I can say is that I felt something that day, something that told me the experience was real. Even so, I was left with the burning question of what she meant by saying I was the Wizard and that the Wizard was fake.

CHAPTER

1

A New Life

I MADE MY WAY WITH MY big belly into the obstetrician's office, located on a major throughway in Santo Domingo, the capitol of the Dominican Republic. After being weighed in and having my belly measured, the obstetrician arrived. She began, "Your ultrasound showed everything to be normal, but you are now two full weeks overdue. If you don't go into labor in the next two days, we will have to induce. Go home and take long walks. That will help." I so wanted everything to go perfectly. In preparation, I had read several books on the benefits of breastfeeding and how to raise a child with a high IQ. I followed her advice.

It was noon and blazing hot when I asked a friend whose husband also had an overseas bank assignment to accompany me on the walk. Eager to help, over she came. "Are you nervous? I sure would be. Foreign country and all," she asked as we headed out my front door. "No, not really. I thought a lot about having the baby in the United States, and I concluded that childbirth is just a natural part of life. How bad could it really be?" She didn't seem convinced and changed the topic. After an hour, we circled back to my house, hoping that the remedy had worked. She left wishing me luck. Over dinner with Jaime, I shared the ultrasound results and the doctor's recommendations. We were both new to babies. We went to bed hoping for good results.

Around eleven o'clock that night, the window air conditioning unit turned off. "Ugh, the electricity went out again. No water now, either. How can the city survive like this?" I mumbled. Although the bedroom quickly became uncomfortably hot, we fell back to sleep. Then, shortly after midnight, I realized that the rumbling in my tummy was the beginning of labor pains. By then we were hot and sticky. We began groping to find our clothes and the necessary items for my hospital stay. My contractions quickly strengthened, "I may deliver soon," I warned. "Where is the suitcase you packed for the hospital?" Jaime said. "In the closet, off to the right," I said. As he lifted it up, I heard, "But there is nothing in it." "No, open it up, I put the list of everything I will need inside. I couldn't put things inside that I still needed," I explained. His disgruntled response felt warranted. Later, it would bring us laughter.

My moans were loud, frantic, and frequent. We got dressed, decided the suitcase was not important, and left for the hospital—hoping to arrive before the baby. In this frenzied state, it hadn't occurred to me that a lack of electricity would be anything but an inconvenience. Seeing the near pitch-black hospital building, the ramifications of no electricity began to sink in. As we arrived, Jaime shared a bit of Colombian folklore, "You know, to be born on a night with no electricity is a sign of good luck." It didn't seem like it to me.

A sleepy-eyed guard met us at the entrance, a dim light hovering over him. "Buenas noches," he said, opening the door for us. The hospital's generator was sufficient to ensure the functioning of the emergency lighting system, but nothing else. At night, the hospital was only staffed with only nurses while the doctors were on call. After climbing up a long steep flight of stairs, we waited in the dull, gray, empty labor room for four hours until the obstetrician arrived.

My earlier fear of too fast of a delivery turned out to be unsupported. Now, after five hours of painful contractions, "You have dilated three centimeters," the obstetrician said as she adjusted my bed to a half-sitting position. The bed's rubberized mattress meant that, each time I moved, the corner of the sheet slipped off. The obstetrician would lean over and patiently place it back. She sat silently in a wooden chair next to me, reading much of the time. The excruciating back pain was relentless. Mid-morning, I received my first epidural, something else I had imagined I wouldn't need. "You may as well go get some rest," the doctor suggested to Jaime, after several hours had passed. He checked with me and I nodded okay. I was in an altered state, almost hyperventilating. His absence could not have made things any worse.

Sixteen hours later, I was wheeled into the delivery room. With a final push, at 4:05 p.m. according to the obstetrician's statement for the birth record, Alex was born. The exact time burrowed into my mind—as the tone of the obstetrician's voice when she announced the time revealed her concern, setting off a red alert. Something was wrong.

Jaime watched as Alex emerged from the birth canal. The red bulge on her back, her herniated spinal cord, and her turned right foot were visible. The pediatrician said something barely audible, "We will place her in an incubator until we can examine her foot." He brought her close to me, wrapped in a soft blanket with her little head peeking out. I could sense her softness and sweetness and wanted to hold her. Instead, she left with the pediatrician.

"Is there something wrong?"

Jaime placed his hand on mine. He knew but kept quiet. A heavy silence. The bubble of hope burst as, exhausted, I succumbed to sleep.

That evening, two male physicians came to my hospital room; one was our pediatrician and the other a neurosurgeon. My room was stark, with a twin bed, a metal nightstand, and exposed grey brick walls. I was lying in bed, Jaime seated next to me grimly, as the doctors explained, "Your daughter has a congenital birth defect. It is a severe form of spina bifida, myelomeningocele. She will have no feeling or movement in her legs, and if she lives, she will need surgery to prevent a swelling brain." They said a lot more words, ending with, "Do you understand what we said?" Jaime and I nodded our heads, too stunned and overwhelmed with sadness to speak.

But I understood enough. As they left, I turned toward the wall and curled up into an uncontrollable sobbing ball. My daughter had a severe something. She might die. All my dreams—gone.

Jaime went home that evening to get some sleep. There was no place for him to stay in the hospital. That evening, I had seizures. Per the nurse's description of my behavior over the telephone, my doctor prescribed an anti-anxiety medication. In the middle of the night, exhausted and medicated, I fell going into the bathroom, hitting my head as I collapsed on the floor. The next morning, I was seizing as my doctor entered the room. She immediately diagnosed eclampsia, a life-threatening condition. They had not detected my escalating blood pressure along with the other symptoms of preeclampsia: muscle aches, headaches, and vision changes. I needed an injection of a specific life-saving drug that the hospital did not have available. Shockingly, the physician handed Jaime a written prescription and said, "This drug is not easy to find. You may have to go to several pharmacies." Four pharmacies later, he was able to fill the prescription and buy the required needles to give the injection.

Over the next few days, the pediatrician and neurosurgeon met with us numerous times. Their words were filtered through their body language and tone of voice. "We can't tell you what to do. We do not recommend surgically closing her back. The opening is so large we will need to graft skin. That will raise the risk of an infection. If we don't surgically close her back, there is a high risk of meningitis. In several weeks, we will know if she will need a ventricular shunt, a tube that drains the cerebral fluid, so it does not accumulate in the brain." It was close to hopeless. If we left her in the hospital, she would die, yet they did not recommend doing what was needed to save her life. The outcome was dismal for both her and for us as a couple. She would suffer from mental retardation, as it was termed then, as well as being partially paralyzed. They also agreed that if she survived her first year of life, there was a 66 percent chance of death by the age of three due to kidney failure. The fact that that statistic came from a 1966 medical textbook did not deter the pediatrician from imparting the information—nor us from believing it to be so.

In 1984, there was no Google. The concept of doing research on your own health or medical condition was not something anyone knew how to do or even believed was necessary. Loyalty to the physician, for me, was like an insurance policy. Wandering off to get second and third opinions brought negative consequences. Of course, in the Dominican Republic, the specter of too many opinions was moot. There were only two neurosurgeons. In addition, they both had completed their neurosurgery fellowship in England. On a global scale, rates of spina bifida for people of British and Irish descent were among the highest in the world. This meant that before the 1960s, before the invention of the peritoneal shunt, the medical solution to a swelling brain (hydrocephalus) resulted in hospital wards filled with children like Alex who were there to die.

When I was stable enough to go home, Alex came with us. It was July 5, 1984. The incubator, a metal box with glass on the sides and a heat lamp glaring, looked barbaric and lifeless. If we didn't take her with us now, something told me we would never see her again. My mother, who had arrived to help, escorted me down the flight of stairs to the first-floor exit. I was weak and bruised. Jaime was desperately trying to hold himself and our family together. After almost losing his wife and child in a foreign country, he felt totally out of his depth. He had nowhere to turn, and I wasn't emotionally equipped to support anyone. His family and longtime friends were elsewhere, and communication via a home phone was not possible—we did not have one, as a personal telephone was a luxury item in the Dominican Republic, procured only with political muscle. This left us isolated at a time of great need.

The electricity was working when we arrived back home. Alex's bedroom had recently been painted aqua green, the hand-built mahogany crib waiting for her along with the quilted baby blanket I'd made and a needlepoint bear hanging on the wall. She was home, but the house felt empty. So did I.

During my mother's short stay, we arranged for Alex's baptism, her admission into the Catholic Church. I didn't resonate with the belief that it was required to enter heaven; however, I was pleased that her life was being acknowledged in some way other than through sympathy cards. What was left unspoken at the baptism among the family and friends who attended was the fact that we were preparing for Alex's death.

All the botched diagnoses and infections over the next two and a half months did not deter her brave, unwavering spirit. She had arrived and wanted to stay. Numbed by the shock and emotional upheavals, we did what had to be done just to survive. To prevent infection, we sterilized everything Alex touched. We boiled her diapers, bedsheets, clothes, and blankets in a huge pot on the stove, then ran them through a cycle in the washing machine and placed them in the dryer, and then we wrapped each item in a special brown paper and took it all to the autoclave at the hospital. We did that daily. Through word of mouth, I reached out to friends to find a chauffeur for trips to the hospital and networked for the political clout to obtain a telephone. While high-tech items were hard to come by, domestic help was available and inexpensive.

Alex's clothing wasn't the only thing I wanted to sterilize. I felt an awful sense of filth inside myself. Bearing a child with so many deformities triggered internalized negative beliefs about myself. I was convinced that I must have done something wrong or have something terribly wrong with me. When the doctors explained that spina bifida had a higher incidence among poor people in the countryside, the feeling got worse. I thought I had left "poor" behind when I married my sophisticated husband, but clearly I had not. Poverty stalked my mother's family and me, apparently. Images of my grandmother, who had been partially paralyzed in a car accident in her early thirties, widowed young and a mother of eight children, were part of my past, I thought.

It was the telephone call from my mother that seemed to seal our fate.

"We spoke with your Aunt Babe yesterday. Her first two babies didn't have hydrocephalus like we were told. They had the same birth defect as yours," she said.

My body went limp. I could feel the irritated tone in my mother's voice, as if to say, "They could have told us all sooner." When I inquired as to the babies' names, no one knew. Their births had taken place in the 1940s, and the little girls died before their first birthdays. Guilt, shame, and pain left my generation ignorant of potential genetic anomalies and susceptible to the same tragic emotional responses.

I took long showers, scrubbing and scrubbing myself with a washcloth. I wanted it all to just go away…down the drain. But only my hair washed away. With all the hormonal shifts and stress, my hair fell out in large clumps. At the end of my shower each day, the drain was clogged, but I lacked the energy to care. When my hair finally grew back in a year later, it was several shades darker. I didn't feel or look like myself.

On a day within a month of Alex's birth, she awoke with a high fever. Blood work indicated an infection, possibly of her cerebrospinal fluid, which put her at a high risk for meningitis: an infection of the meninges, which envelop the brain and the spinal cord that make up the central nervous system. Back at the pediatrician's office, he explained, "There is a drug trial underway at the community hospital. They are hoping it will increase the survival rate of patients with meningitis. It is the best shot we have, really."

The words "survival rate" made me light-headed and nauseous. Death was stalking us.

We were accepted into the drug trial, which simply entailed saying, "Yes." His instructions were shocking. "Take her to the hospital immediately. You will need to bring your own sheets, pillows, food, water, and necessary personal items. Don't delay." The drug trial required a twelve-day hospitalization with the medication given by an intravenous (IV) infusion. That hospital stay was horrendous and eye-opening. It explained what I learned many years later: In the Dominican Republic in 1984, 10 percent of all children under the age of five died.

Upon arrival, the pediatrician barked an order to a nurse, "Go find a suitable crib." I watched as they lowered the wooden staircase to the hospital's attic and carried down a dusty, half-painted, grayish white metal crib. I felt betrayed when I heard the pediatrician mumble half-heartedly, "Okay, clean it off." How could he approve such a rickety old thing? The sterilized crib sheets and clothes from home felt inconsequential. I lay her down on the bed, unable to allow the appropriate rage over the hospital conditions to well up inside of me. I was afraid that my rage would leave us completely abandoned, with no place to turn.

One afternoon while Alex slept, I saw a group of small black ants crawl past the window frame, along the floor, and up into her crib. Jumping to my feet, I stared in disbelief as the ants crept inside Alex's diaper. No call buttons or phones to request assistance were to be found. I ran out into the hallway and found a nurse. She was unmoved. "Your daughter must have some kind of bad juju that is attracting those ants," the nurse indicated as her head nodded toward the window. In fact, none of the nurses wanted to enter the room. If they needed to come in, they didn't stay long.

So, we hired our own nurse; qualifying as a nurse in the Dominican Republic meant you had an eighth-grade education and some hands-on training. We found her through an employment agency run by a woman in a poor area of Santo Domingo. We went there in the evening hours. Her office was low lit, dingy, and damp. It all felt terribly wrong. The heavyset women sitting behind her desk asked us questions, more curious about our bad luck than concerned with helping us. I was told, "I will let you know who I can find for you," as if they were doing us a favor with what seemed a 100 percent unemployment rate. We reluctantly hired one of her nurses. She was unkempt, had dirty fingernails, and slept most of the time. When I insisted on her staying awake when I was out of the room, she blurted out, "There is an evil force here. Either you and your husband caused this, or it is in her. And that is why none of the nurses want to come near this room." My mother-in-law was visiting at the time and was more than thrilled when I found the courage to fire the nurse. Going forward, I stayed in the room with the door closed. The physician thought that was a good idea.

On Saturday, the sixth day of the IV antibiotic treatment, two nurses came into our room with shocking news, "There are no more antibiotics. We gave her the last vial this morning." They were matter of fact. There was no surprise or apology, just a "for your information."

We panicked. Our pediatrician was spending the weekend at his farm in the mountains, with no telephone reception. We put in a distress call to the neurosurgeon, but he was going to be in surgery most of the day and unable to assist. He explained, "The medicine is kept in a marked cardboard box under a long table in the community hospital's emergency room area. I am in surgery all day. You will have to go get them." The only person we knew who had ever been to the community hospital was our chauffeur—he agreed to go. Heroically, he brought back ten vials of the trial antibiotic. Somehow, despite all of this, Alex survived the infection, and we returned home.

We were constantly reacting in those days, taking any necessary immediate steps to save Alex's life. But no long-term action to save her life was being pursued. My brother had called and urged me to seek medical advice in the United States. Two women from an American circle of women I was getting to know stopped by unannounced. We had barely begun to drink our tea when one of them leaned forward and said, "We own a private plane. We can take you to the United States immediately. Maybe they can do something." But I was so drained and had so little hope I declined.

During my mother-in-law's visit, she shared her point of view with her son after dinner one evening as they sat together on the back patio. I was in my bedroom, where I overheard the conversation. With few words, she let him know that she thought it best if Alex did not survive, "*Nina chiquita problema pequeña. Nina grande problema grande.*" Translated, it meant that things were only going to get worse for us as Alex grew older.

I could see no viable solution. I felt, horribly, that if Alex lived, my life would be impaired. And if she died, my heart would be irreversibly broken. There was no bearable way out. I tried to escape into the fairy-tale life I'd expected to have. I signed up for a French cooking class. During my first class, as we were learning how to make Chateaubriand,

I received a call from the nanny. "The baby has white liquid coming out of her incision." I bolted out the door and never returned.

We took Alex to a different hospital, one that was more modern, cleaner. The neurosurgeon removed her infected shunt and put her on ten days of IV antibiotics. After she came out of surgery, I asked the nurse if it was okay to give her the bottle. She said it was fine. Hungrily, Alex gulped down the milk. Then, I went outside to get some fresh air. As I exited the building, I ran into an acquaintance, someone I had first met poolside at a hotel where we were living when we first arrived in Santo Domingo. I remembered thinking that this mother was incredibly misguided that day to have allowed her twelve-year-old daughter to wear a bathing suit in public. As I had watched her daughter leave the lounge chair and walk to the pool, I could see a massive scar running down her back and leg, her crooked spine, and her irregular, clumsy gait. Her mother's doting and loving eyes clearly couldn't see the brokenness of her daughter's body. I thought, "What could this mother be thinking?!"

Now, standing outside in the dreadful heat of Santo Domingo, this mother became an ally. Emphatically, she said, "Take your daughter to the States immediately. We are still living with our own regrets, as our daughter was born outside of our country, Germany. There was irreparable harm before we sought good medical care." I felt she was right.

When I returned to the hospital room, I found that Alex had aspirated on her formula. They had taken her to an emergency room, and Jaime and I hurried toward the door marked '*Sala de Emergencia, No Entre.*'

The doctor, ashen, stepped out from the shadows of the long corridor and slowly walked toward us. We walked toward him. The air felt thick and my legs were heavy. My stride was in rhythm with the physician's, and I could sense his despair. As my heart sank, the Lord's Prayer rushed through me. I did not go searching for that prayer from the archives of my mind—it just suddenly appeared. I didn't tell anyone at the time. It ended as quickly as it had begun. I didn't know how to interpret its meaning until many years later. It meant we were not alone.

"Things are very grave," the doctor said as we met mid-corridor. "We will know more in twenty-four hours." As things stood, Alex had meningitis and no shunts to release the growing pressure on her brain, and now she had contracted pneumonia from the aspirated milk. Our pediatrician arrived a few hours later. He looked at me and stated, "Feeding her after surgery was a very stupid thing to do."

I turned away, furious, but without mentioning the nurse. This was my first child—my first *everything* it felt like. I didn't know better. My anger caught in my throat as I once again silently screamed.

As we waited for news, I sorted our mail. I found a thick, legal-sized envelope in the stack. It was from a friend in Chicago. I hadn't been in touch with her in several years, but somehow, through the grapevine, she had learned of Alex's birth. I was stunned as I read her three-page handwritten letter. In the neatest of penmanship, she had written five names, each with their medical specialty and their telephone numbers; they were all part of a medical specialty clinic for children with spina bifida located ninety miles from where I grew up. It was the Children's Memorial Hospital.

While reading the letter, I recalled that day's earlier conversation with the German mother. And I thought about the Lord's Prayer in the emergency room corridor. The universe had gotten my attention. I was ready to take decisive action.

That afternoon, I firmly stated my position. Jaime was hesitant, but listened and agreed we needed to get out of there. We asked the neurosurgeon to set up Alex's transfer of care as soon as possible. Meanwhile, we scrambled to get Alex a passport through the American embassy. Her tiny, two-by-two-inch, black-and-white passport photo captured her striking beauty. Her eyes were large and soulful.

Three days later, as I left that hospital for the last time, I was given one more opportunity to change my mind. The neurosurgeon appeared in the doorway of Alex's room. Semi-blocking my way, he said, "Even if she were my daughter, I would not do this. This will ruin your life and your marriage."

What he didn't know is that I had already crossed the threshold of indecision. Taking Alex to the United States for proper care was the right thing to do, regardless of the outcome. There was no alternative. I squeezed by the doctor, pulling Alex into my chest and holding her tightly.

Our arrival at the hospital in Chicago was comparable to waking from a nightmare and landing in a resort. Life went from black-and-white to full color. Like Dorothy arriving in the Land of Oz. But here there were no Munchkins; instead, there was the comfort of beeping machines, call buttons, a nursing station with nurses in clean uniforms copiously entering notes, hubbub in the hallways, freshly painted walls, soothing pieces of art, and yes, even stable electricity and running water. It was a paradise of health care.

If modern technology was the Munchkins, the neurosurgeon represented the Wizard. In our two-hour consult, he gave us the most up-to-date statistics about Alex's chances of survival, ability to walk, cognitive abilities, the risk of kidney failure, and a battery of other information. The statistics differed enormously from what we were told in the Dominican Republic. We had been told that she had a 20 percent chance of survival, with no chance of walking. Instead, it was an 80 percent chance of living a normal life, including walking with the assistance of braces and a walker. We were so relieved. We felt something that we hadn't before: hope.

After a few days, Jaime had to return to the Dominican Republic (or "DR"), and I moved to the Ronald McDonald House, a beautifully restored home, a few blocks from the children's hospital. I stayed there for one month, each day visiting Alex in the hospital, getting stronger. It was difficult to hold her, and I didn't insist—I sat beside her instead. I met with the hospital social worker several times for emotional relief. One day, she asked if I would like to meet with other mothers who also had children with spina bifida, and I readily agreed.

On the day of their visit, I was anxious. I picked out my favorite pair of khaki pants and a nice white blouse to wear. I had my own bathroom at the Ronald McDonald house, so I primped a little without anyone noticing or needing the mirror. Caring about my appearance had seemed empty in the wake of everything that had happened, but I now felt lighter and more hopeful. My groove was returning, and my appearance had always been important to me.

We visited as Alex slept. The mothers were amazingly like me. They were from Chicago, and I was raised in Rockford, Illinois, only ninety miles west. Their Midwestern accent felt familiar, as did their simple and genuine kindness. The two mothers had met when their daughters were young, through an organization called the National Spina Bifida Association of America.

In our sharing, we discovered that our three daughters all had the same lesion level, T-12, thoracic level, the twelfth vertebra. This meant that the development of their spinal columns was disrupted in utero at the same vertebrae, around the mid-section close to the waistline. Without the vertebrae of the spinal column properly fused together, the spinal cord herniated, thus the large red ball on Alex's back at the time of her birth. They shared photos. One mother explained, "My husband adapted that bicycle for her, it has hand controls. And see her here. She is using her braces and walker to get around. It is slow, so she doesn't use them much, but she can." I not only heard their words. I felt their happiness. I did not sense shame, remorse, or regrets in the stories they told.

Meeting those two mothers was empowering. I felt more equipped to make the necessary decisions on my daughter's behalf. Alex could lead a good life, and I could lead a good life with her. If those mothers could do it, so could I. It seemed so simple, yet spurred a profound change within me: I woke up with more energy, put on makeup, and began making plans for a future together.

The time came for us to return to the Dominican Republic. Upon arrival, I sought out a new pediatrician, neurosurgeon, and nanny. Believing that we deserved better made it so.

Concerned about Alex's cognitive development, a friend suggested I contact a colleague, a child psychologist. He was delightful; young and optimistic, he fit my new requirements for practitioners. I observed as he administered the Battelle Developmental Inventory simply by asking Alex to do things with the objects he brought. After an hour's time, he announced, "Your daughter is within the normal range of development." I wanted to hug him. As he worked with her, I took mental notes on how I too could optimize her development. Noticing my interest, he asked, "Would you like a copy of my findings? The chart will show you what to work on next." It was like getting a copy of the test ahead of time, a cheat sheet. I was thrilled. Little did I realize how unique that was, i.e., a practitioner handing a mother their professional tool, trusting her ability to use it appropriately. I would later be instrumental in formulating public policy to promote such full disclosure and strong parent/professional partnerships.

However beautiful and cognitively normal Alex was, she also obviously had a physical disability. Her legs could not move. Her scalp was shaved on her right side from her shunt surgeries. Her head's larger than normal circumference drew attention. But as she and I created a new normal together, that all faded into the background. This was, however, not true for the outside world, including my Lamaze instructor. I had finished an errand downtown and was walking back to my car, carrying Alex. I recognized her as we reached the intersection. Full of pride, I showed her my beautiful daughter. She looked bewildered. Perhaps wanting me to get a grip on my horrendous circumstances, she said, "I am inviting some other mothers from your class and their babies to attend my new class of expecting mothers." Misreading her intention, I said, "Would you like for me to come and bring Alex?" She looked stricken and readily declined my offer. I had already become the mother who told me to go to States, who had taken her daughter to the pool, not seeing her scars but rather her inner beauty.

We were bonding. As I spent my energies supporting Alex, I was supported by her in turn. I had a reason to wake up every day, and I felt alive in a new way. I worked to be a good mother because she needed me to. That was part of our plan together for this lifetime. I would rally to be my best self for her. Her vibrancy and stubbornness helped me over the bigger hurdles. She rallied to be her best self, too.

Despite my best efforts, Alex's health became more complicated. Her first urinary tract infection, at nine months old, was unsettling, recalling the statistic of early death due to kidney failure stated at birth. Fortuitously, Jaime had a business trip to Miami. I scheduled an appointment with a pediatric urologist at the University of Miami to learn more about how to protect her kidneys. It was there, in a fifteen-minute consult, that I learned about neurogenic bladders, the lack of bladder control due to a brain, spinal cord, or nerve problem. In the stark cold exam room, I tried to absorb the kind physician's explanation of how to drain her urine using a sterilized catheter—five times a day, every day, for the rest of her life. But the life-altering significance of the forever need of a diaper created emotional static; I could hear only every other syllable clearly.

Feeling once again over our heads in a foreign country, Jaime requested a transfer back to the United States from the bank that employed him. On July 5, 1985, we landed in Miami, again hoping for a new, normal life for Alex.

The Lioness Within

W E ARRIVED IN MIAMI IN the extreme heat of the summer. Alex had just turned one year old. She was strikingly beautiful, with large blue-gray eyes, almond-colored skin, blonde hair, and an endearing smile. Fragile and feminine, she exuded warmth and kindness with little effort. She lived on my hip much of the day as her own little legs would never be able to sustain her.

I hoped Miami would be a good place for us to live. Its warm climate was amenable to Alex's future wheelchair and other necessary devices. Her health and well-being were woven into every thought and decision, a pattern that would last for decades.

Our first month, while we searched for a house, we lived in a hotel suite in downtown Miami provided by the bank Jaime worked for. Our looming health expenses and my limited ability to work narrowed our options, so we ultimately settled in Kendall, a modest and growing area of shops, malls, and housing developments; a community that resonated much more with me than Jaime. We purchased a modest 1,100 square foot townhouse in a housing development. Our belongings, shipped from the Dominican Republic, arrived in time for our move into our new home. Although we no longer had a chauffeur, maid, or upscale home, this felt right to me. I was glad to be back in the US.

After meeting the two mothers at the Children's Hospital in Chicago, I knew where to look for resources and information. Shortly after getting settled, I called the local Spina Bifida Association. I learned that through its county Department of Health and Rehabilitative Services, the state of Florida provided early intervention programs for children with developmental disabilities. I wasted no time in completing all the required documents. However, our county's department was in turmoil, and I was met with delay after delay. Many telephone calls later, I sent my first letter to a governmental official. It was effective. Alex was soon enrolled in an early intervention program, and it was there I began to meet other mothers.

Through other parents, I learned that more of everything—including early intervention programs, therapies, specialists, and pediatricians—was available in Miami compared to the Dominican Republic, but the dilemma was similar. The world of disability remained hidden from the public eye. An underground network of providers existed but had to be accessed through the medical system, who were often uninformed. As my emotional fog lifted, I sensed the need for parents to coalesce, to break through the shame, guilt, and fear that paralyzed us.

In February 1986, I was invited to participate in a community-wide meeting to discuss the value of parent-to-parent types of support organizations. When I expressed my amazement at the invitation, the social worker at the early intervention program looked me straight in the eyes and said, "You have a lion within you, but you just don't know it." I was baffled by her observation but looked forward to the opportunity to attend the meeting.

The meeting was held at Miami's downtown Omni Hotel. I wore a beautiful white linen suit, one that I had purchased for our planned jet-set life in the DR. The fact that over fifty people attended surprised me. I didn't know there were so many people who cared about our children. The organizer, Susan Duwa, was a social worker from United Cerebral Palsy in Panama City, Florida. She caught my eye immediately. Her long white free-flowing curls matched her sixties style, a long flowing skirt and loose-fitting blouse. A fireball, she orchestrated the large group with vigor.

"Parents will meet in the room to the left. Providers please remain in this room," Susan began, after the general meeting introduction. The social worker who'd invited me remained in the room with Susan, and I walked into a room with fewer people. We were all mothers who easily spoke about the lack of services, funding, and information. More difficult was revealing our shattered dreams. "We were told to leave our daughter in the hospital to die," I began. "My boy is five years old and is blind. What's his future going to look like?" shared another. "My daughter has seizures all day long. I feel so helpless," shared another.

"Our son screams most hours of the day. No one knows what to do." "My daughter ate half of a can of Crisco in the middle of the night, I now lock her into her room at bedtime. We are overwhelmed." Around the room we went, sharing our heartfelt disappointments and struggles. At the end of the hour, we all enthusiastically supported the idea of parents helping other parents cope and adapt to this unfamiliar and challenging world.

As we joined up with the larger group, I noticed Odalys, the social worker with whom I had arrived, in a dispute with one of the other professionals. "That figures, I am friends with the rebels," I thought. They were nose-to-nose, wide-eyed, and their shoulders were flung back. I thought someone might have to intervene at any moment. I asked her about it later. "Paula, we can't let professionals run the show. They don't understand our needs the same way we do ourselves." Her dual role as a parent of a child with special needs and a professional in the field of disability gave her a unique perspective. I began to learn what that was about. Underlying the differences, I came to believe, was parents' love for their children and thus their greater sense of urgency, an urgency that was not subdued by administrative constraints, bureaucratic norms, and the perceived lack of resources. Yes, love and urgency are what fueled our creativity and ingenuity, our ability to mobilize others and say, "Why not?" when we heard, "No."

As the professionals continued to debate how the support group should begin, three of us got started with one. "Paula, can you come to a meeting next week? We are going to discuss our next steps." My "Yes" was not a difficult decision, and it was pivotal to my life. Those meetings became my lifeline. I knew so little about the world the other two women had conquered. I felt my daughter's life depended on my ability to become proficient as they had. As a young mother, my go-to guides and mentors, i.e., mothers, aunts, friends with young children, and even at times physicians, were often ill-equipped to provide quality advice.

Susan guided us long-distance. "I think you guys are ready to hold your first support parent training," said Susan.

"I do too, but they don't feel equipped," I replied.

"You guys are overthinking it. It's been a year of planning. You just have to begin."

We did. Susan and the two social workers facilitated the workshop. I sat in the front row, excited with the possibilities. When instructed, we introduced ourselves to the person to our right. "My name is Iliana Hernandez. I am a banker, married, and we have one daughter, Adriana. She was born with a rare genetic syndrome, Trisomy 13. She has already way surpassed her supposed six days of life." Her words didn't strike me as much as her physical glow and enthusiasm. "I want to help other Hispanic families. They are lost in a sea of dead-end telephone calls, legal documents they don't understand, and these waiting lists. They need help."

We teamed up. Wherever Iliana and I went, we met other parents desperate to find quality services for their sons and daughters: parents of children who were being mislabeled, neglected, isolated, and too often, psychologically and physically abused.

"Paula, there is no good information out there, what are we going to do? Parents don't know anything! I spoke with a parent yesterday whose child was locked into a closet at school by his teacher," Iliana said.

"I think we should start our own newsletter and include information about our legal rights, medical specialists, therapists, recreational programs, and support and advocacy organizations." Iliana concurred.

"That's it. We can't count on doctors, teachers, and therapists to share the information." With that, we began our News You Can Use newsletter. Typically, I wrote it first in English and then Iliana did a Spanish version. It was finalized using each of our manual typewriters.

It's hard to imagine, but no service directory in any form, paper, electronic, or even just hotline telephone numbers, existed. More importantly, parents had no access to each other, except in waiting rooms and parking lots. We began to meet those parents. Iliana worked full time, and her daughter's services were provided in their home, so much of her work was by phone in the evening. My life was quite different. I could meet parents wherever Alex went: at school, clinics, and hospitals mostly. It was in this way that I met and formed our first Board of Trustees.

"You're late picking up Alex, Mrs. Lalinde," said my daughter's preschool teacher. Shifting her gaze to the woman sitting to her right, she said, "Do you know Mrs. Kathy Feldman?"

"No, I don't," I replied, as I was invited to sit down next to her. She and the preschool teacher resumed their conversation.

"Allen is doing very well in class," the teacher reassured her. "You can't imagine what it has taken to get Allen this far. He's had multiple hospitalizations and surgeries; he has a chromosomal disorder and has extra X and Y chromosomes," Kathy said, looking at me.

Though we had not met before, as parents of children with disabilities, we shared our stories openly. We each understood that we were forging our way in a world that did not understand who we were, why we were there, or what we and our children needed.

Kathy Feldman worked for the bankruptcy court and moved in social circles that the rest of us didn't. She made the perfect treasurer as well as ably fundraising for our annual Christmas party.

"I can ask one of the federal judges to be Santa Claus. I even have someone in mind, and I can check into where we can get donated toys," Kathy offered.

By our third Christmas party, over one hundred parents and children came, most of them living far below poverty level. We held it at the Scottish Rite Temple. There were hundreds of toys, a banquet style meal, holiday music, and of course the judge dressed up as Santa. It was deeply satisfying to be part of this growing organization that was helping so many people.

Opportunities to talk about Parent to Parent of Miami kept surfacing.

"Paula, would you like to do a series of parent presentations for our preschool parents?" asked the director of the public school system's handicapped preschool programs. She was a fireball and strived to create high quality services for young children with disabilities. I said yes to everything in those days. It was there in an elementary school library that I met Ven and Chris Sequenzia. The two larger-than-life parents were stuffed into the library's pint-size chairs, articulating their concerns:

"Parents helping parents is all good, but we are facing a crisis situation with our daughter Amy. The classroom is overcrowded, and the teachers don't know what to do with her," said Ven.

"That is why we need to organize and be one strong voice for our children," I said.

"Our daughter was diagnosed with autism, with an IQ of twenty according to a team of specialists. When asked about the cause, we didn't get any straight answers," Ven said.

"Frigid mother is all I heard," said Chris. "Since she can't speak, we are really wondering if the IQ score is accurate."

Good point, I thought. Importantly, later assessments found Amy to have an IQ in the normal range. However, I didn't know anything about autism then—few people did—in high contrast to today, when one in sixty-eight children (one in 42 boys and one in 189 girls) are within the autism spectrum, affecting most families in some way.

"We hold monthly meetings in South Dade, why don't you attend?" I suggested.

"That's another thing. Everything is located south. That's an hour drive for us," Ven said.

Ven and Chris did attend our meetings, became members of our Board of Trustees, and organized parents in the northern part of the county. Chris's law firm filed our 501(C) 3 papers, making our support group officially not-for-profit. Ven was in the printing business and helped print and disseminate our News You Can Use newsletter. He became one of the leading advocates for children with autism in Florida.

By 1987, two short years after moving to Miami, I was up to my eyeballs in commitments. My home phone number became our parent referral telephone line. Bea Moss, a longtime journalist for the *Miami Herald* newspaper, interviewed me for an article in the Neighbors section. The day it published, I received thirty-four phone calls. Parents with sons and daughters with every type of disability and of every age called to offer their support and guidance and to ask for help. One call from an aging mother remains with me.

"I am so glad you are doing this. We didn't have anyone to guide us in the beginning. I was hoping you could help find someone we could trust to take care of our twenty-eight-year-old daughter for a few hours. We have never left her alone in all these years."

Her daughter was nonverbal and severely physically impaired. She and her husband had never gone out of the house alone together. I recognized that I was totally unqualified to give this aging parent advice. I also knew my generation of parents had to pave new roads and a new consciousness. I promised to look for someone. Fortunately, with our small home, the twelve-foot cord of our phone reached the dining room, the bathroom, and the entrance to the bedrooms, making it possible for me to multi-task. As there were no state-funded disability programs to provide quality respite care and no other programs in place, I was unable to assist that mother.

Jaime's bank salary was modest, and I needed to generate an income. Too often I was totally broke, arriving at the bank barely in time to deposit checks from our health insurance company before my written checks hit my account. My life was one big juggling act. Susan Duwa hired me as a part-time assistant to support other volunteer chapter leaders throughout Florida after I turned down a more lucrative offer working for the school system's bilingual education program. Full-time work seemed undoable. Alex's health was too precarious. In addition, I loved Susan's dynamic energy. I worked from home, but before long, I secured donated office space through the school system. There I met Dr. Carole Abbott, a school psychologist, who became a longtime colleague and friend. She invited me to attend a newly formed local council designed to improve services for infants and toddlers with disabilities. Saying no never entered my mind.

1987 was a year of emotional dips and pleasant surprises. Being pregnant brought excitement, hope, and panic. I was referred to the high-risk clinic affiliated with the University of Miami's medical school, located at our community hospital, Jackson Memorial. From there, I was referred to a geneticist who worked at the University of Miami's Mailman Center for Child Development, a place that I would come to intimately know years later. As we sat across from the geneticist, I silently assessed her words and body language for additional clues to determine how worried I should be. "I see that your alpha-fetoprotein blood test was negative, which is good news. Do you plan on having an amniocentesis? We do know there is a genetic component to spina bifida," she said as she completed our family trees. After her explanations, I asked the clarifying question most on my heart.

"Are you saying that the chances of having another child with spina bifida are greater once you have had one child?" Her response gave me chills.

"Yes, a slight increase." Then I thought, "It can't be greater than 100 percent," recognizing I was batting one for one. Life was scary and unfair. I left worried.

Now pregnant, I knew I must quit smoking again. It was a habit I had acquired as a teenager working at an amusement park where I had easy access to cigarettes. It seemed Alex thought it was time to quit again, too. During a general medical check-up, I told the doctor, "I am feeling fine except I have a lot of body aches. I am allergic to mold and dust, so perhaps that is the reason."

Alex, who was then two years old, was sitting on the floor to the left of the doctor's examination table. The stroller was wider than the exam room's door, and I couldn't leave her out in the hallway. There was no place else for her to safely sit.

"It could be your smoking that is causing your aches. You know smoking is also a health hazard," he said, glancing over toward Alex to indicate the importance of quitting. I followed his gaze to find Alex sitting there comfortably with one of my cigarettes hanging out of her mouth. She had a cute yellow summer jumper on, exposing her frail and beautifully golden-brown body in contrast to her strong will. The doctor rolled his eyes in a "say no more" gesture. I called my mother when I got home, and we had a big laugh.

Alex was like that—she knew everything that was going on. Her heart pulled her forward, not her brain. She also tried hard, learning to do what other children do automatically. "She doesn't have the right physical therapist. She should already be walking," explained the therapist I was interviewing. Strapping Alex into her RGO braces three times a week and watch her struggle to walk with her little walker down the wide hospital corridor was full of both hope and disappointment for both of us. I had learned all about reciprocating gait orthosis (RCO): when it had come into existence, how it was made, the best orthotist, and certainly its cost. My brain was full of these new and unwanted facts, but my heart did not know what to do with them. Moving her body along with the weight of the braces by using only her tiny arms, the arms of a two-and-a-half-year-old, was physically tough. "So, you really think she can walk?" I replied. "Of course," he reassured. I wanted it to be true. "Okay, please come to the house next week and we will give it a try." Alex loved this kind gentle man. Within a week's time, she was proudly shifting her hips and holding on to her walker so that her little legs moved forward. She was walking, albeit very slowly.

I got her a scooter that year; it was a wide green plastic seat with five wheels, low to the ground, that was powered by a back-and-forth movement of the handlebars as it moved. It was work, but she took to it easily. Outside, on the sidewalks in our neighborhood, she could move fast. There were two young girls across the street who would come out and play with her. Alex was like their little doll. They would invite her over to visit, brush her hair, and play with dolls together.

"I won't be taking a child with a disability home from the hospital," I warned the obstetrician during one of my visits. "So, we may need a back-up plan." He glanced up from writing his patient notes with a slightly bewildered look.

"You will see, everything will be fine," he reassured me. It was still too scary to hope very much. However, the day of my first ultrasound was a turning point. My mother was with me as the technician swirled the cold gel on my protruding abdomen. We watched the image appear on the screen. "Everything looks as expected," says the technician. My mother and I shared a look of joyful relief.

Worry lessened also with the tour of the hospital's maternity unit, thanks to the instructors of our Lamaze class. We suited up in white gowns and a face mask to prevent the spread of germs as we entered the empty operating room.

"Everyone have their face masks on? We can't go in until you do," the instructor said. "Talk about maintaining a sterile environment," I thought. "This pregnancy is different." That thought soothed me.

The high level of medical care and conditions resulted in a memory flashback from the Dominican Republic. It was ninety degrees. We were standing in the parking lot of the neurosurgeon's office complex. The neurosurgeon pulled up in his sports car, parked, and walked over to us.

"No need to come and wait inside the clinic. It is no doubt packed. Did you bring the needles?" he asked.

He swabbed the top of Alex's fontanelle, the soft spot on a baby's head where the skull bones haven't finished growing and fusing together, with alcohol and inserted the needle to extract her accumulating cerebral fluid. With Alex still screaming, we got back in our car, trying to feel grateful that he'd saved us some time. Yes, this pregnancy will be different, I reassured myself as I scanned all the equipment in the operating room.

Our son Jaime Nicholas was born on July 3 at 11:25 a.m. He was born with a mighty cry, lots of black hair, and four moving limbs. I gave a sigh of relief when I heard his Apgar score of 7, which meant he was perfectly healthy. Under careful medical watch, I rested and recovered. Jaime was wheeled into my room in a bassinet the following day, and I delightfully began breastfeeding. I felt an inner peace, the kind that only comes with motherhood. The hospital days flew by. I rested, breastfed, rested and breastfed. On the fourth day, we went home together. I sat in the back seat holding our new baby. Jaime turned off the car's AC in case it was too drafty and drove twenty miles per hour home.

When we arrived, Alex was sitting on her bed with open arms, ready to receive her little brother. I placed him next to her and she began lightly touching his forehead, in a kind of caressing, gentle, soft, and motherly way. My mother stayed for a few days, helping with the meals and laundry. As Jaime grew, Alex continued to be motherly, keeping her eye on him even when they were not interacting with each other. They soon became inseparable. How I folded Jaime into my already merciless schedule I hardly recall. I hired sitters and live-in housekeepers and pushed down on my own internal gas pedal.

I was clearly overwhelmed. Alex had already had eleven surgeries, multiple developmental evaluations, and physical and occupational therapies at the children's hospital several times a week and had been fitted several times for a complex standing apparatus which allowed her to walk very short distances. Jaime was as speedy as Alex was slow. He was agile and had a good golf swing by the age of two. Watching the contrast brought joy and pain.

My pedal-to-the-metal daily life never let up, and my marriage was disintegrating. The fairytale life we had both signed up for did not exist. The adjustment was difficult for both of us. Jaime's interest in disability politics and my struggles was as paltry as my interest in Latin American politics and his banking woes. His political ambitions back in his home country of Colombia were eclipsed by a reality that was much less inspiring, i.e., middle America, modest income, a second child, and a daughter with a physical disability that absorbed much of our income, as well as most of my time and attention. Most importantly, we were both emotionally and physically exhausted by day's end, with no mutually enjoyable common ground to bring us together as a couple. Instead of addressing those realities, I formed deep friendships with other parents and dedicated myself to those from whom I felt appreciation.

In addition, I—and our daughter's disability—came between him and his aspirations.

"Miami only thinks it is the banking capital of the world, but it isn't. It is a small town, and I can't move up here," he bemoaned. Having had a taste of the banking industry in New York City and all his various responsibilities in the DR, in Florida he was feeling stuck.

"We have lived in Chicago, Puerto Rico, Santo Domingo, and Miami in less than five years, I don't want to move again. You don't know what it takes to keep Alex healthy, and I finally have some friends."

He didn't let up, "There is an opening in London, we could go live there."

"You go to London," I said.

Nothing seemed to ever satisfy him. I had unconsciously given up trying. And vice versa.

A few years later he did take a position in New York City in the hopes I would move there with the children. Pushing a wheelchair in Manhattan seemed daunting, and the alternative living options in New Jersey felt cold and isolating. He came back after six months. Alex wrote about it in her school portfolio, with the title, "A Friendly Welcome Home.":

> *Welcome home Daddy. I hope you are happy with me at home. Now we are happy because you are home now. Stay home now, Please! Thank you very Much.*
>
> *Love, Alex Lalinde and Jaime and Paula.*

She so loved her family.

Venturing to relocate to *any* place with all of Alex's needs was incomprehensible to me. What I also knew was that living with Jaime was a lonely endeavor, wherever we were. His alliances were with his work and himself. My own issues with intimacy complicated matters. His materialistic orientation, once shared, was no longer equally important to me. Our worlds had grown apart. I was scared, lonely, angry, and frustrated. I needed help.

In June 1988, after much searching for the right person, I made an appointment with psychologist Dr. Rose Morgan. As I mentally prepared, I recalled my only other experience with a psychologist. I had just become engaged to my present husband. I was extremely anxious as to whether this was the right man for me. The male psychologist listened and toward the end of the session said, "Perhaps you are not in love with him." I panicked. I had said no to other men, hoping this one would be different. I made the mistake of repeating this insight to my fiancé. He was alarmed, "You should never go to see that psychologist again. What does he know?" I called off the engagement for six months. I never did return to that psychologist.

The day arrived. "You can sit out here at this desk and fill out this required paperwork," began Dr. Morgan. I completed the mental health questionnaire and other medical forms. The atmosphere felt cold and clinical. As I sat across from her, I wished I were her. In fact, I wanted to have most anyone else's life but my own. She was well-spoken, well-dressed, and had clear boundaries; she was not very warm but seemed capable. She listened to my fears about my children dying. My fragile sense of self and lack of feeling safe were no doubt recorded on her notepad. At the end, we discussed how we would go forward.

"I can't afford coming here every week. I am so stretched financially," I explained.

"You really need to be here weekly to make progress. I don't see patients less than once a week. Know that as you get better, so will your finances," she said.

And so, every week I sat across from her for fifty minutes, trying to lessen the horrific grip of grief and fear on my life. As promised, my inner life calmed and my outer life expanded with new opportunities.

Twenty-eight families from across the country, including ours, were invited to an international conference in Washington, DC, on family-centered care practices. I was ecstatic, while Jaime had little interest in attending. Additionally, our son was only two months old, making it difficult to travel with him or leave him behind. In the end, Jaime stayed with our live-in housekeeper and my husband came with me for two days.

Surgeon General C. Everett Koop was the keynote speaker. It was the debut of family-centered care practices, captured in the new monograph, the Red Book. The practices emphasized the family as a constant in the child's life, collaboration between practitioners and families, full disclosure of information, cultural competency, and mutual respect. This approach had been written into the legislation passed zero to three under IDEA, requiring states to adopt this approach if they chose to participate in the legislation, which was attached to federal dollars.

At an outdoor gathering, Alex, Jaime, Susan, the director of our county's preschool disability program, and I gathered around Dr. Koop for a photo. For me, the photo, the Red Book, and the presentations at the conference meant that Washington cared about our children. I saw an advocacy future for myself and resources and services for Alex. Another highlight was meeting Terri Urbano, PhD. Sitting next to each other on a circular-shaped bench in the hotel's atrium, we discovered we were both from Miami. She was part of the nursing faculty at the Mailman Center for Child Development at the University of Miami. I sensed a depth of knowledge, character, and genuine kindness. We shared our enthusiasm for the Red Book's debut. Walking away after our short exchange, I thought, now there is a nice woman. These were exciting times for me, being with people who believed in the same ideals.

What became clear was that families perceived the family-centered care approach as specified in the federal legislation, Part H of IDEA, as the answer to our challenges. Florida, however, was undecided as to its participation in this law. A governor-appointed council, Florida Interagency Coordinating Council for Infants and Toddlers (FICCIT), was charged with figuring out how to structure the implementation of these services. I, along with two other parents, was invited to participate on this council. Since Florida was receiving millions of planning dollars, parents organized and requested that some of those planning dollars support increased parent participation. Our request was granted. I became the chair of what we called the *Parent Resource Organization*: young warriors all, and all naive enough to believe that we could convince the Florida legislature to increase its investment in Florida's most vulnerable children.

3

Broken Boundaries, Broken Trust

I WAS BORN ON AUGUST 11, 1953, in La Crosse, Wisconsin. I was what is now termed an empathic child. I tended to feel the emotions of those around me more intensely than others, which made a harsh environment more traumatic. My older brother, Jeff, was 20 months old when I was born. He sought attention in all the wrong ways. By age five, he was notably mischievous, rebellious, and clever. On his first day of kindergarten, he slipped out and was back home before my mother. She found him hiding behind the oil drum outside. She was dumbstruck. At a younger age yet, while still in his crib, he pasted all the postage stamps to the wall and did the same with the contents of his diaper on another day. These stories would just be funny family stories, as they were, but my sense is that my mother came unglued each time, resulting in spankings that became less and less effective as my brother slowly detached from authority.

A memory from my own experience is the time when Jeff, at about six years old, filled a brown paper bag with dead rats and mice and handed it forward to our Grandma Ames sitting in the front seat of the car. Known to be deathly afraid of mice, my Grandma screeched when she opened the bag. My Great Uncle Jerry, who was driving, slammed on the car brakes, jumped out, dragged Jeff out of the back seat, and spanked him hard. Then Uncle Jerry sat my brother down hard on the back seat next to me. I froze. I had never seen my uncle lose his temper, and it seemed like an unjust thing to do over some dead rats. I felt sorry for Jeff and guilty that he had it worse than I did. In these situations, I would often assume some fault as well, as if I could have prevented it in some way. The more Jeff caused trouble, the more I hid my feelings and strove to please.

Jeff's basic temperament, i.e., restless, moody, and high energy, was unfortunate, as my parents were young and possessed little tolerance or desire to be dealing with a challenging child. It was 1951. My mother had become pregnant at sixteen, and my grandmother, Clara, made sure she wasn't left unwed and scorned as numbers of other women in that era were. My father, Jim, was twenty, a carpenter, living at home with his parents, Marcella and Carl. Clara met them with one simple demand: that Jim and her daughter be married. On May 25, 1951, my mother waited for my father out in front of her house, suitcase in hand. They married at the courthouse with my Aunt Jean and Uncle Lyle as witnesses. They moved into an apartment above my father's parents' home, and they became parents in December of 1951—an unwanted responsibility for both of them. Resentment set in.

Jeff sought my dad's attention, but there was an early dislike. "Jim, you need to pay more attention to him," scolded my Grandmother Petry. The friction was something others noticed but never spoke about. My mother felt sorry for Jeff and overcompensated at times, fueling his already intrusive behavior. By the time I was born, my mother was in no mood for another unruly child. There was an attitude of almost lost hope of controlling Jeff's behavior, so I would need to toe the line. My brother and I each had what the other didn't in our personality, which created an interdependency that endured beyond the time when it was useful.

His rebellious adventurousness created a lot of excitement for me but also trouble. Our endeavors had fallen into a recognizable pattern by an early age: Jeff came up with the plan. It would have something wonky about it, how I was to personally benefit would be unclear, things would end abruptly, and I would be surprised by the outcome. One such incident was our greeting card scandal. I was ten years old. Less than a mile from our house was the main drag lined with small general goods stores, a Milk-A-Rama, and a small grocery store. One of the stores, shabby as it was, sold greeting cards; and they allowed children to sell them and make a profit. My mother strictly prohibited us from doing it. Without much consideration for her stern warning, Jeff negotiated a deal with the store owner. My role, which my brother presented to me as pretty small and insignificant, therefore limiting my profits, was to actually sell the cards. So I did.

My Schwinn bicycle helped me cover more territory. All was going swimmingly well until, "Mrs. Petry, Paula dropped by my greeting cards yesterday. I would like to exchange them," said one of my buyers. Moments after she had left our house, I came barreling home on my bicycle after a good day of sales to find my mother waiting for me in the front yard waving the box of cards in the air, "What did I tell you about this? Get in the house." She was furious and made us stop selling the cards. I am sure there was more to the punishment, but don't recall. Jeff did not flinch about the loss of the card business; he was numb to their efforts to control him. With little love and no trust, they were left powerless.

Another joint project started at about the same age. "Paula, if you start selling your Girl Scout cookies today, before everyone else, you'll sell the most," Jeff said. Easily convinced to do most anything he suggested, off we went door-to-door. I approached the house, easily made the sale, and carefully recorded each sale in the provided ledger. It was fun having my brother along, which I thought was a bit generous of his time. When we got back home, the booming sales fell flat when Jeff with his gleeful mischievous grin announced, "Paula sold her Girl Scout cookies before she was supposed to. What happened to Girl Scout honor," as he mocked me for being part of the group and breaking my pledge. My mother with a look of horror, "Call everyone right now and tell them what you have done. You should be ashamed of yourself." My brother went unscathed. I was considered naive and easily duped to have listened to him, which was true. However, his role as an older brother would not have been overlooked in other families and cultures. Particularly on my mother's side of the family, males were often perceived as weak and not given the role of protector.

In 1959, my younger brother Jim was born. I remember staying at my cousin Denise's house while my mother was in the hospital. They lived in the nicest house of all my thirty-one first cousins. My Aunt Ruth was kind to me, making Swedish pancakes for breakfast and speaking nicely. She was showing me how to make a bed when she said, "You have a baby brother, Paula." I remember being disappointed that it was not a girl. I no doubt felt there were already enough males in the house.

My brother Jim became my father's favorite child. They looked like each other, tall with blonde hair and straight thin bodies. Growing up, they shared a love of sports, particularly basketball. Jim also had my father's learning challenges; school was a struggle, and I sometimes helped him with homework. With Jim's birth, I was displaced as my father's favorite. Jeff was my mother's pet, so there I was, the middle child and the only girl, with no place to go. Sandwiched in between, I had to have been jealous of Jim, and I later recalled a time when I slapped him hard across his face repeatedly; he was only six years old but wouldn't do what I said. He didn't cry, but I could see the hurt of betrayal in his eyes. It still saddens me when I remember what was done to us, what we did to each other. It was a bit like the Wild Wild West. My dad even bought us boxing gloves for Christmas one year.

Unlike all his other friends, my brother Jeff was still alive in his mid-twenties. Since he knew the home building business well, having learned it from my father, Jeff dove in and became an ambitious risk-taker. He carved out a big role for himself and became the third largest home builder in the state of Illinois and the largest residential builder in Williston, North Dakota, during the oil boom in 2010.

Our basic differences have continued. At one point, he owned nine hundred rental properties while I lived in a 310-square-foot condo by choice. He is as imprudent as I am mindful. He is short-tempered, much like my mother. He focuses on people's shortcomings, prefers isolation, and is skilled at bullying. I was voted the kindest person in my high school class and was on the homecoming and prom courts, and the school administration created a new 'Civic Service' award category for me. I share only cautiously about myself and am more likely to be the victim or rescuer than a bully.

However different we seemed, our strengths and weaknesses came from the same source. We represented two sides of the same coin. We were both seeking something we never got as children: to be noticed, loved, and appreciated for just being us; just to feel worthy. We both lost essential parts of ourselves that we strove to regain, my brother through an accumulation of riches, though for me it was more about badges of recognition. While Jeff's loss of self led to his struggle with addictive substances and amassing wealth, mine led to an exhausting life of geographic relocations, honors, degrees, projects, creating surrogate families, and living too often through other people's dreams rather than my own.

My brother's contradictions made it difficult for me to see the inherent traps in doing things with him. He is family-oriented, as is the mafia, and generous to those he feels called to help—which is usually when doing so will solve one of his myriad of problems, but not always; there was the time he loaned a cousin $50,000 so she could get an appropriate divorce settlement, which she did, millions and millions, so the story went. She was one of the few who ended up on the long end of the stick with him. What appeared to be generosity at the onset was often snarled with complicating details that were never discussed. Our business dealings fell mostly into this category.

Jeff and I remained close into adulthood, although our married lives made our visits infrequent and short. His second wife, with whom he had five children, was cold-hearted and calculating. My folks stayed away, and my life was in Miami with my own family.

For me, I felt there was no safe ground to stand on. I feared letting my impulses get out of control. If I spoke my mind freely, I risked being ridiculed. If I was too kind, I was a sucker. If I was assertive, I might get in trouble. The overall impact was I learned to show up not freely and as I am, but cautiously and as everyone wanted me to be. When I did speak up, it was abrupt, unexpected, and too direct—as it was the last time I saw Jim.

It was 2001 and Jim and I, along with my mom and dad, were all helping Jeff move into his exquisite vacation home overlooking San Jose Valley in Costa Rica. I helped Jeff find the realtor, translate documents, hire the staff, and shop for much of the furniture. My brother and I were both divorced, and spending time together felt right. It was a big fun project for me.

That week in Costa Rica with Jim, however, was tense. He drank a lot, which meant he was loud, often till the wee hours of the morning. A friend of his came for a few days to help with the unpacking, electrical work, and hanging heavy objects and so on. It was the way they denigrated women that set me off. Most of my brother Jim's actions left me irritated.

When the inside work was mostly handled, Jim and his friend went off sightseeing, a foreshadowing of what was to come. "So, where did you guys go in the end?" I asked upon their return. Jim explained, "We got a bunch of beer and took a taxi heading up toward the volcano. Can you believe they sell wooden caskets along the highway? We got out and laid down in every one of them." He laughed the whole time he was telling the story, as did his friend. "So how was the volcano?" I asked. He said, "We didn't make it that far. We just turned back after a while." What an ugly American story, I thought. As much as I wanted to, now, as an adult, I just couldn't relate to any part of his personality or life. He had been twelve years old when I went to college. He was almost invisible in our family dynamic, except for his warm relationship with my father.

Jim's Costa Rica plan was downright scary. "What do you mean Jim wants to move here with Pat and the girls?" I said to Jeff. He said, "Yah, but I can't have him staying here. He will be up to no good. I want to get away from all that." I said, "Well, maybe he wants to clean up his life. Get a fresh start."

"Paula, don't even go there. That is not Jim. I've seen it. It is really bad."

"Perhaps you are right."

Jim left the next day to return to the States. As the taxi arrived, I sat down next to him. For a flash of a second, I noticed that he seemed pleased that I had come to sit with him. If I had paused to absorb that, I might not have proceeded. But I had a plan in my head, and present moments didn't count. I said, "I don't ever plan on being here at the same time with you again." He shrugged his shoulders in a bit of confusion and sadness, got up, and walked out the door. Regrettably, that was my last communication with my brother.

What does a child do to feel safe and loved in the absence of having those experiences within her own family? She creates protective illusions, pretends not to see what is going on, blames herself rather than others, and feels shame and guilt without even realizing it. Her feelings at any given moment become almost inaccessible. Unconsciously, she seeks what she never had, and the results are always the same.

4

Taking Charge:
Tallahassee, Florida,
The Governor's Chambers

I FELT HONORED TO BE INCLUDED in the meeting with Governor Lawton Chiles to talk about Florida's position on Part H of IDEA. I admired him. "Walkin' Lawton" he was called, for having walked the length of Florida during one of his early campaigns. He fought doggedly for legislation that supported vulnerable populations, particularly mothers and their young children. He was on our side.

There were four of us, two researchers from Florida State University, the Chair of the Florida Interagency Coordinating Council for Infants and Toddlers (FICCIT), and me. Governor Chiles's assistant led us into his private chambers.

"He will be with you shortly," she said, as she closed the door behind her. When he arrived, he gave us a wide, friendly smile that spoke to his willingness to listen. He sat down at the head of his conference room table. In his relaxed, Southern-sounding drawl, he opened with a personal story and then nodded to let us know it was time for business.

"Our longitudinal study is complete. We can now say unequivocally that providing early intervention services for infants and toddlers at risk and/or born with a disability reduces the need for more complex and expensive services later. It will in fact save millions of taxpayers' dollars," said the FSU researcher. Governor Chiles looked pleased. We each added our reasons for supporting the Part H of IDEA legislation. Mine, as instructed, was short.

"Parents across the state are organized and ready to support this legislation. You can count on us." He seemed pleased with our support. He gave us his advice on how to proceed and thanked us for all our work.

I emerged from the meeting aware of the power of both the individual and collective voice. I felt heard, strong, and confident in what I was doing. That night back in the hotel room, I called home to check in with the kids. My husband answered the telephone.

"How's everything?" I said. "I got to meet with the Governor today. He is supportive of the legislation, so it may actually have a chance."

"The kids are here wanting to say hello." Jaime's tone was sullen. The kids were too young to understand the importance of the meeting but joined me in my enthusiasm. Alex, particularly, loved when I got excited. We were the same in that way. From Jaime's perspective, he had been assigned the low-status role of a nanny and resented it. I went to bed conflicted and lonely in my victory—as, most likely, was he.

When the legislative session began, the Parent Resource Organization carried out what we called the Snicker Bar campaign—early intervention for infants and toddlers born with a disability is not to be snickered at. The opinion on the street was that there was no way the Florida legislators would agree to this legislation. They saw it as another runaway entitlement program. It was early spring, 1992. Drawing on the statewide network of parent-to-parent support groups that had formed over the years, we began to fax parent leaders with specific action steps—which involved inundating our state legislature with letters, faxes, and phone calls. On a given day, fifty families traveled to the capitol with their children to deliver the message. We met in the capitol building to be briefed. I ran the meeting, and clearly the lion within me was out of her cage. I spoke and people listened. After the briefing, everyone dispersed throughout the capitol with fact sheets, a bag of wrapped baby snicker bars, and their young children–along with their walkers, wheelchairs, and ventilators.

Not everyone could travel due to their child's vulnerable condition. Even more lacked the financial resources. For those parents, their support for the bill, along with their anger and sense of being abandoned by those charged with protecting them, was expressed in other ways. For example, the mother of a baby born prematurely sent a box of preemie diapers to the Senate Office building. Each of the twenty-five diapers had an unwrapped Baby Ruth candy bar carefully placed inside, representing parents' dissatisfaction with the level of governmental support. In myriad ways, some unplanned, we got the legislators' attention.

Alex, who was now five years old, participated. She was in her element. She loved people and easily captured the heart of anyone moving slowly enough to notice her. At one point, I turned to find Alex conversing with Senator Al Gutman. He had unsuspectingly walked off an elevator and met her. She was wearing one of her favorite dresses, white with polka dots, and a rounded collar. Her blonde hair, blue eyes, and sparkling smile held his attention for several minutes. Her wheelchair was as petite as she was, making it easy for her to navigate. On that day, while Alex captured the senator's heart, parents set out to appeal to his logic and his decision-making mind.

I returned to the Capitol several times during that legislative session to meet with key legislators. The parent voice was important. As parents, we were perceived to have no financial interests. Rather, we were consumers with an educated opinion. Parents throughout the state had become well-organized, continually sending faxes and making phone calls. The extent to which this was effective became clear during a meeting with a senior staff member of the Senate Finance Committee. I was with two respected longtime child advocates and was seated directly across from the senior staff member. At a particular moment in our conversation, respect and trust eclipsed threats and power plays; it was a moment when my incessant doubts ceased to exist, my heart opened, and the importance of our mission was clear.

"Give us one year. If this bill is not revenue neutral (meaning that no additional state revenue would be needed to fund it), parents will no longer fight you," I said. He perceived my sincerity and looked relieved.

On April 1, 1992, the legislation passed. Florida would join other states to participate in what is currently Part C of the Individuals with Disabilities Act (IDEA). The FICCIT council held a celebratory gathering. I was given a plaque and heralded as an important advocate. We had achieved what everyone said was impossible. Florida now had access to an additional twenty-million-dollar federal grant which brought with it a commitment to family-centered practices. This meant early intervention programs for young children with disabilities would need to comply with new standards, giving families more decision-making power.

Soon after, I received a telephone call from one of Florida's top disability lobbyists. She wanted to reflect on our win and thank me. I took the call in my bedroom; the lights were off, and I was whispering. After the call, instead of running into the living room and having a high-five moment with my husband, I sat in the dark, feeling I had done something wrong. It was an old familiar feeling—one I knew from childhood. In my home, my ambitions and successes had to fly under the radar of a jealous mother and a brother who was like a hungry ghost: His share was never large enough. The phone conversation also reminded me of the social worker's observation six years earlier, "You have a lion inside of you." Yes, there was a lion inside of me, but when she roared, even though she won, I wanted to run back into the cage.

Jaime didn't know what to do with my evolving self. The early days of focusing on his aspirations evaporated as I pursued my own goals. The rules governing our marriage had been unavoidably rewritten by Alex's birth, a fact that had gone mostly unrecognized by both of us. Whatever my endeavors, his response was, "That is not good enough for you," or "That person is not quite right, you can do better," or "Don't invest your time in that." I was too easily dissuaded from pursuing opportunities and friendships.

I had a true passion for anthropology; when that fell away, my other pursuits were less satisfying. Instead, I had then focused on his ambitions, with hopes of them being satisfying for both of us. From helping him translate his master's thesis due to language barriers to moving to the Dominican Republic, his pursuits were our pursuits. Those days were now gone, and our marriage was slipping away with them. Instead of mutually supporting each other's dreams, we competed and felt bad when the other did well.

During those years, a little marriage glue was provided by my parents' winter visits. They would rent a place nearby and would often dine with us. My folks loved golf as much as Jaime did. Although they didn't play on the weekends because the prices were higher, they did love to commiserate with Jaime about their sand traps and water dunks and cheer on their birdies and rare hole-in-ones. My dad and Jaime genuinely liked each other.

The other person for whom my father genuinely felt closeness, and there were few, was Alex. He admired her spunk and her natural ability to help others feel comfortable, including him. "Grandpa, I can beat you in arm wrestling. Want to see?" He'd smile and put his elbow on the table, lower arm extended upward, palm open. "Okay,

I'm ready, show me your stuff." Jaime would be in close, watching to see who'd win.

Alex, proud of her upper body strength, would then assume the same position. She was serious in the endeavor, gritting her teeth and grunting with the strain of holding her arm erect. At the same time, she was not too surprised or disappointed when she would lose. A big roar of laughter would complete the exchange. My dad was a shy man. As such, he appreciated her love of being an 'onstage' presence.

One year, my dad built a deck off the side of our townhouse. It added to our 1,200 square foot home and was a perfect space for Alex and her brother to play outdoors. "Come hear us sing, Grandpa." We all went out to enjoy the show and the cool winter air. There she was with her shiny pink plastic microphone belting out a song, and Jaime, up on the bench/ledge strumming on his silver plastic guitar. Their lively performance came to an abrupt halt when Jaime stepped too far backward and disappeared. His moans as he hit the ground traveled through the airwaves. Alex rolled over and looked down, "Are you okay?" Captured on video no less, that unforgettable moment became etched on our funny bones.

As Jaime and I grew apart and my life was more and more stretched, my parents' visits at some point became more strain than help. My mother didn't think I should be working outside of the home, and her attitude seemed to say, "You cooked your own goose." Then one winter, she shared, "Each year your marriage situation is getting worse."

"No kidding!" I replied. Left unsaid was my disappointment that my mother didn't offer to babysit and perhaps give us a weekend off together, cook us dinner every now and then, or lend us some money to lighten the financial strain. I wanted to scream, "Do something!" Their visits were both enjoyable and an additional caretaking responsibility.

My life revolved around my children and my work of advocating fervently for what I saw so many families needed: a nurturing and caring environment where they would be heard and respected. My soul, too, hungered for exactly that. In lieu of partner support in my marriage, I built a community of support around me. I folded my children up in it. I found meaning and purpose in my life through my daughter and my efforts to create a world where she, too, could live a purpose-filled life. My life mattered; if not to my husband, then at least to those I was helping.

We began holding parent support trainings at one of the local hospitals. At our first one, six mothers attended. I didn't plan on taking the children along, but our babysitter canceled at the last minute. Jaime sat remarkably quiet, drawing. Alex, however, wheeled her chair right up next to me, ready to speak to the group. It took me a while to figure out that she rightly saw herself an expert on the topic as well. "Alex, would you like to say something?" I said. She didn't hesitate.

"I am Alex Lalinde and I have spina bifida. That is my brother, Jaime," she said, pointing off to her right. "He is a real pest sometimes." This was followed by a big laugh, in rhythm with her shoulders moving up and down; everyone laughed with her. Jaime glanced up from his drawing and then returned his gaze to his paper. These experiences gave me hope of us teaching together when she got older.

As much as the spring of 1992 brought hope and vitality, our summer that year brought destruction. On Sunday, August 23, what had been a tropical storm was reclassified as a hurricane as it moved north and westward toward Miami. It was the first one of the season, and it was named Andrew: Hurricane Andrew.

In the absence of destructive hurricanes over the previous three decades, Miamians had developed a false sense of security, believing that the hurricane would once again dissolve into the Atlantic Ocean as so many others had done. But as Andrew pushed in our direction, we prepared in earnest. News channels were informing people where they could still find plywood, bottled water, batteries, and canned goods. Hurricane coverage focused on the vulnerabilities of our coastal communities and downtown Miami. Living inland gave our community a sense of safety that proved to be misguided.

With a sense of growing worry gnawing at me, I procured several plastic gallons of water, filled up our bathtub, made sure a battery-operated radio was on hand, and stocked our cupboards with canned goods along with plenty of peanut butter, bread, and cereals. We taped our windows to prevent shattered glass from entering our home, ruling out the need for plywood over the windows. We lived inland, outside the projected path of the hurricane.

By afternoon, I was increasingly anxious. The air was thick and still. My anxiety sent me out for a walk around four o'clock. A block away, I found a neighbor hastily loading up his car with sleeping bags, sacks of groceries, and gallons of water. He was taking his family to a shelter. "Better safe than sorry," he said as he turned toward his house for his next load of essentials. "Good idea," I thought.

I returned home and woke up my resting husband and insisted that we go to the nearby shelter. He resisted, but it was fruitless. With my escalating anxieties continuing to rise, staying at home wasn't an option. Within an hour, we were on our way to Miami Killian High School, a few miles southeast of our home. Along with the four of us, our neighbor's two-year-old son and her Mexican housekeeper, Maria, who spoke no English, rode to the shelter in our car. The little boy's mother was on a business trip and like many, couldn't return.

The six of us arrived at the shelter with pillows, blankets, continence supplies for Alex, a bag of food, and a jug of water. Jaime was five years old, and he carried the gallon of water. On Alex's lap was a bag of groceries that she encircled with her arms as I pushed her wheelchair. Maria carried the little boy, and my husband toted the rest. There was not a breath of wind, and the sultry heat of the day and the drop in barometric pressure left us lethargic.

Once inside, we were directed to the auditorium for instructions. A woman on stage belted out instructions. "Bottles of water and snack foods are on the back tables. You will stay down here until seven o'clock, when we will proceed upstairs to find sleeping quarters." No one seemed much interested in the food and water. People were intent on settling into their own space and keeping abreast of the storm's development via our local news channel. Around seven o'clock, we took the school's elevator to the second floor. Alex and Jaime felt privileged as they noticed everyone else lugging their things up the double flight of stairs.

Our classroom had no windows or furniture. We spread out in the far-left corner of the empty room with our blankets and pillows. I lifted Alex down out of her wheelchair onto the blanket. She was unusually quiet, a sign she was worried. Another sign of worry was the frequency of her questions. "How long are we going to be here? Are we sleeping here? What about breakfast?" My husband wanted to be anywhere but this place and quietly exuded resentment that I'd insisted on coming here. Maria the housekeeper was no doubt grateful. Jaime played with the two-year-old boy. The space was organized, one family occupied each corner.

At around nine o'clock, an old woman was helped into our room by one of the organizers. She was just over five feet tall, walked stiffly, and carried a small brown cloth suitcase made from burlap with bronze clasps, a 1940s style. She placed the suitcase beside her in the very center of the room. She removed her top layer, a heavy black woolen coat which served as her bedding. There were many more layers underneath the coat. She brought with her a stench, the sweat on top of sweat of homelessness, that settled as she laid down. The room felt complete, the four corners and the homeless woman in the center. I felt safe in this large group and safe having someone else in charge. Who that someone was I had no idea; it just wasn't my husband nor me. Whatever was about to happen was beyond us.

No one spoke as we all cocooned in for the night. The only light came from the promised television in one of the classroom's corners. Meteorologist and weatherman Bryan Norcross's calm steady voice was a sharp contrast to the images of high-speed winds heading inland, in our direction. At one point, there was a loud crack and the television went black. As the room went dark, so did my mind, I drifted off to sleep. I had gotten everyone to safety, and that was all I had in me.

In the middle of the night, I made my way through the dimly lit hallways to go to the bathroom. On my way back, two organizers, their voices pitched low so as not to alarm anyone, said, "That couple was fortunate to arrive when they did. Crazy coming here in a canoe." I thought, "How is that possible? We are miles inland."

I went back into the classroom and fell into a deep sleep. Suddenly, before dawn, I was aroused by a sound that I surmised had something to do with the roof. It only lasted a few seconds: metal scraping on metal, followed by a thud onto the outside wall. Indeed, it was the roof.

At daybreak, I left the classroom, turned right, and looked out through the shattered glass window of the second-floor corridor, I absorbed the horrific damage the hurricane had done to our city. Trees were uprooted, electricity poles ripped out of the ground, homes were flattened, and roofs were absent; the inside walls of condominiums were exposed, their exterior walls collapsed. Back in the classroom, families were stirring, digging into their grocery bags and coolers for their Fruit Loops, Captain Crunch, and milk. Barely anyone spoke.

I took Jaime to the bathroom. "Mom, I want to see, I want to see," he begged, so I would lift him up to look out the broken window.

After a moment's glance, he turned around and dug his head into my shoulder. Someone on the other end of a bullhorn intoned, "Pick up your belongings, do not leave any valuables behind, and move to the library. Pick up your belongings, do not leave any valuables behind, and move to the library." Over and over we heard that message as we packed our things. The homeless woman who had taken center stage the night before moved slowly. I resonated with her in some way. We lined up with our scant belongings and one by one, entered the library, the designated safe space in this very compromised school building. Within a short time, we were asked to line up again and file out of the building. We carried Alex down the stairs, and instead of following the hundreds of people to the portable trailers, we headed to our car, risking the downed electrical wires. Jaime had had enough, and I was happy to follow behind.

The drive home was disorienting. Wide-eyed and foggy-brained, with the children unusually quiet, we edged our way through the downed trees and other heavy debris on the streets. All the normal landmarks had been altered—with no street signs, uprooted trees, and missing mailboxes, it was difficult just to navigate. Two miles and thirty minutes later, we arrived in our neighborhood. "My car's trunk looks popped open," Jaime complained, as if it were my fault. "And it looks like we lost a few roof tiles. Looks like that's it, though," he finished as we hesitantly opened the front door. Alex looked truly relieved to be home as she popped a wheelie to get over the front door's lip. Jaime ran into each room, making sure everything was okay. He came back beaming.

The inside of our home was unaltered, in sharp contrast to the outside world. The house felt sad and empty, like the sadness one feels when a family visit comes to an end and you stand alone at the door waving goodbye. Healthy sadness comes and goes, but this was deeper. All my layers of grief had been activated. That is the nature of grief.

I babysat friends' children and did their laundry so they could go to work. The kids enjoyed having the company. Once the roads were cleared sufficiently, Jaime returned to work at the bank downtown. Scenes of the Cuban singer Gloria Estefan filled our television screens as she doggedly assisted the community by distributing water and food supplies in the area most devastated, Homestead. I wanted to be her, out helping lots of people. Instead, I was homebound with two young children of my own and other children whose parents were needed at the hospital.

Two scenes best capture Andrew's destructive force. One was on Ingraham Highway, where a large black tugboat rested, blocks from the ocean. The second scene was from a car trip I took with the children into Homestead several months after Andrew hit. I surrounded myself with pain in those days, a reflection of my own inner life. That day I felt the pain of the twisted, broken, fallen trees. In a West African tradition for grief, the grieving widow or mother travels into the forest and removes a small piece of bark from a tree. Healing from grief is measured in tree time—as the tree heals, so does she. In 1992, part of me was still emotionally adjusting to the loss of the idealized child.

1992 was an important year for other reasons. Jaime was to start kindergarten in the fall at Calusa Elementary School, a lovely and fully accessible school ten minutes from our home. Although he'd had a great preschool experience, he was ready for more structured learning. Since Jaime's new school was physically accessible, I hoped Alex and Jaime could both attend that school. My attempt to achieve that aim was eye-opening—and ended up being a lesson in not trying to fly solo.

IDEA, enacted in 1979, for the first time gave school-aged children with disabilities access to a free and appropriate education. According to IDEA's wording, it was to occur in the "least restrictive environment." The intention of Connecticut Senator Lowell Weicker, Jr., and the other crafters of the bill was to ensure children with disabilities could attend school and be integrated with their peers in regular education classrooms. In Florida, as in many other states, school districts disregarded the fine print and proceeded to build segregated schools and/or designate entire sections of a school building for the handicapped, as they were called. The classrooms even had signage on the door frames, e.g., Mentally Retarded, Blind, and Deaf, etc., so no one would get lost, I guess. Although this was not in alignment with the original intention of the law, parents were expected to feel thankful that their children were even allowed to go to school. If they didn't, they were easily bullied and intimidated, especially first-generation immigrant parents and low-income families. I sat in meetings with principals slamming their fists on their desk and declaring, "We don't take those handicapped children at our school." However, with the disability movement in the 80s and 90s, parents became more informed as court cases were settled in favor of inclusive settings, implementing successful classroom models from progressive well-funded states, and research demonstrating the emotional and cognitive benefits of inclusive environments.

Being part of Parent to Parent of Miami gave us access to this information, which both raised our expectations and often increased our frustration, as in my case. Alex's classrooms at Tropical Elementary were in a separate wing of a 1950s school building. The bathrooms were not accessible; the doorways were narrow and had a high sill, making them difficult to enter with a wheelchair unassisted. Above some of the doors, the stigmatizing categorical labels still hung. When the honor roll students' grades were posted for everyone to see, children with disabilities, who made up one-third of the entire school population, were excluded. Not one single child was integrated into the regular education classrooms, not even for lunch or music. It enraged me on most days. Moving Alex to an inclusive setting was an admirable goal.

I began by first meeting with the school principal at Calusa Elementary. She was welcoming and open to having Alex as a student. The transfer would require district funds and permission, which meant I had to request an IEP (Individualized Education Plan) meeting at the district level to get approval. I did.

When Jaime and I arrived at the IEP meeting, held downtown at the district office, there were twenty-five administrators and teachers sitting around the conference room table. The meeting was three hours long with no resolution. The following meetings were similar. In total, we put ourselves through fifteen hours of excruciating meetings. Their arguments against an inclusive school placement were lame: "We don't feel you really understand your daughter's complex needs;" and, "It is best during her early years for her to be around other children with disabilities to help her feel better about herself;" and, "It's best for her to receive her therapies at school, and there are no therapists at that school." They requested the attendance of the principal of Calusa Elementary School, and then they convinced her that she was incapable of meeting Alex's needs.

I was screaming inside and so angry that it was difficult to speak at times. I felt as if I were back in the Dominican Republic with doctors telling us to leave Alex in the hospital to die. During the last meeting, Jaime read aloud our request, citing the law and the research that supported inclusive settings. He concluded, "This is our beautiful daughter. She is a very social person, who loves being around all kinds of children, and already is integrated into our family and community. All we want is the chance to try. We are willing to accept defeat if it does not work." We were denied—denied access to her neighborhood school by decision-makers, all representing other marginalized minority groups, including religious and ethnic communities. We clearly needed a lawyer.

That night was the only time I called Dr. Morgan, my therapist, outside office hours. I sobbed uncontrollably, full of rage and disappointment, primarily with myself. I felt helpless, disappointed, and angry that all our efforts had been for naught: all for naught, making tremendous strides and efforts only to face disappointment in the end. We had the option of filing for a due process hearing, but the legal costs deterred me. Alex completed third and fourth grade at Tropical Elementary, where she was integrated into music, lunch, and physical education. She was the only pupil in her class with an IQ in the normal range. However, her teacher, Cathy Orlando, was skilled, compassionate, and supportive of both Alex and me.

Several months later, I got a phone call.

"They just fired the Director of Exceptional Student Education," said John.

"What! That is unheard of, what happened?" The Director had been instrumental in blocking our campaign to mainstream Alex.

"No one is saying too much, but I did hear that the way she handled your case contributed to it." John added, "You know, most people around that table were silently on your side."

I felt a little better knowing that. However, our children never attended the same schools.

CHAPTER

5

Dreams Fulfilled

WITH MIAMI'S HOUSING IN UPHEAVAL after Hurricane Andrew, we got the itch to move. Jaime wanted to live closer to downtown to reduce his commute. I began house-hunting, but we couldn't agree on price and location. I was leaning toward a more modest home, as I saw divorce looming. However, after months of searching, the day we found a lovely three-bedroom ranch house on a tree-lined street in south Coral Gables, I caved. Financially, we were now very stretched.

Our 1994 move to Coral Gables legitimately reopened the school placement can of worms. By now, both Alex and Jaime fit the criteria for special education; Alex, due to her physical and learning challenges, and Jaime, because he met the criteria for the gifted program as a child with an intelligence quotient greater than 120, diagnosed at the end of kindergarten.

Fortunately, I had become quite savvy and had made peace with everyone at Alex's school. My prior act of heroism of sorts had in an odd way gained me the favor of the principal. Alex's third and fourth grade teacher was excellent, and there was mutual respect. It all created a springboard effect for Alex starting at our neighborhood school. Sunset Elementary did not have a gifted program, so Jaime's school was different.

The actual IEP meeting for Alex's placement was at Tropical Elementary and involved only five people meeting around a small circular table. In attendance were the acting principal of Sunset Elementary, the principal of another segregated school, Alex's current teacher and current assistant principal, and me. Placed on the table in front of the assistant principal was a blank Individualized Education Plan (IEP). The meeting began very cordially. Alex's teacher talked about her progress and the facts that Alex was on grade level, worked hard, and showed continued achievement on her standardized tests. The teacher had brought examples of her work.

I was then asked to share our reasons for requesting Sunset Elementary school. Again I calmly explained, "We have moved to that part of the city. If Alex goes to Sunset Elementary, only three miles from our home, she will not have the stress of a long bus ride and will have more time for homework and physical therapy. Also, we know research demonstrates that children show an increase in self-esteem when they attend school with their typical peers and are more well-adjusted as adults. Children on our block go to this school, and as you all know, the law provides for programs in the least restrictive environment." Remarkably, I felt little resistance. No doubt, the decision had already been made ahead of time.

This whole time, the acting principal of Sunset Elementary had been quietly sitting. I am sure he was waiting for the moment when someone would put the kibosh on my request. When no one else did, he made his own attempt: Suddenly turning and looking directly at me, he asked, "Why would anyone want two pushy parents like you and your husband and a child with so many problems in their school?"

I am not sure who said what next. By that time, I knew my request was going to be approved, so I remained quiet. The current assistant principal deflected his comment by putting her attention on the actual IEP document. "How do we indicate the new school on the IEP?" After that, the necessary regional and district approvals came quickly. Alex was assigned a full-time one-on-one aide and the necessary nursing services. Victory!—or so I thought. When the end of summer rolled around, I sent a letter to the *new* principal saying that we looked forward to meeting her. A few days later, I received a call from the district administrator, who told me, "The principal just called, and she's upset. She was wondering what had happened while she was out. Can you and Alex meet me at the school tomorrow? We can talk it through with her directly." I replied, "Of course, good idea."

Together with the bristly principal, we walked around the school to identify accessibility issues. Alex was her chatty cheerful self, and I decided to take the same approach.

"Thank you for taking the time to meet with us," I began.

"Well, it is important that Alex have a successful school year. We must adequately plan for that. Let's start down this corridor, toward the fifth-grade classrooms," she said. Alex pushed herself, showing how she could maneuver on her own. As we entered what would be Alex's classroom, I noticed the narrow door into the bathroom.

"This is fairly new construction. I'm surprised it is not up to code," I said.

"Several things are being renovated over the summer, and it should be ready. But you will notice that the walkway around the inside perimeter of the classrooms is not continuous. I don't see any way Alex could go up and down those stairs."

"What is in that other half of the building?" the district administrator asked. "Those are the classrooms for the international language programs. Alex will be in our home school program."

We continued to troubleshoot potential physical and programmatic accessibility issues as we circled back to her office. There, the district administrator assured the principal that Alex would have a full-time aide and nursing services for her bathroom needs, paid for out of district funds.

At her desk, Alex went over to sit alongside her, checking out the small objects on its surface. "Is this your pen? Can I touch this? Who is in the photo?" She loved to engage with people by asking questions. It was a perhaps coping mechanism due to her difficulty with language processing. The principal, seeing that we were not a looming legal threat and came with financial support from the district office, offered practical solutions to the accessibility issues. Where there's a will, there is always a way.

Truthfully, I am not sure how much Alex really cared about the school choice. She cared because I cared. She trusted that I knew best for her. I had been intervening on her behalf since the first days of her life. I believe there was a part of her deep down that knew our success was not being measured by perceived wins and losses but rather by the degree to which we were aligned with what we believed was right—aligned with what we had set out to achieve together in this lifetime. She also knew the battles I fought on her behalf were also mine; getting people to respect her was connected to my struggle to respect myself. Her father also benefited from her emotional acuity; she understood his vulnerabilities and looked past them. She gave us both the gift of her unconditional love as well as someone to love unconditionally.

It is difficult to fully convey the strength of the love between a parent and their child with special needs—a love I had seen and been moved by that day poolside in the Dominican Republic. It is captured in such a doting mother's look, expressing a complete focus on her child's well-being, who they are, and how they are at that very moment; an adoring look that conveys there is nothing that is being taken for granted, not the wobbly walk toward the pool, the ability to bend forward and to sit on the pool deck, the ability to lower oneself into the water and paddle around to feel the water's coolness, nor the very freedom to move. Nothing is taken for granted, each movement or uttered word or sentence exists as a tiny miracle long after it has transpired. It is a love that is built upon heartaches and conquests. It is a love that propels parents to work tirelessly for not only their own child, but for countless others. For this love, we forfeit income, leisure time, time with our spouses and our other children, and sometimes our health. We endure one stressful encounter after another, pushing back the status quo again and again.

The love I had for both my children was the high-octane fuel for my own personal growth. Advocating for Alex's health and educational needs was the way I engaged with life, giving my own existence purpose and meaning. I learned that we expand by doing, not by reading, planning, or hoping for something, but rather by living it—by being in the arena slugging it out. Yes, I was often bruised by defeat and disappointment, but I got back up. I needed to for my family.

Meanwhile, what had begun with three women and biweekly meetings, had blossomed into a formidable organization, Parent to Parent of Miami, Inc. The thirty-one parent referrals the first year tripled the next year—and the next. Dozens of parents were trained to provide peer support to families who had a child not unlike their own. As the organization grew, so did the know-how of the members of its board of trustees, which expanded the group's mission to include more advocacy, particularly on school-related issues. We joined the task forces and advisory groups for the systems of care that served our children: hospitals, early intervention programs, human service organizations, the public school system, and universities, providing an articulate and knowledgeable parent perspective which undoubtedly reshaped, expanded, and improved services. With funding from the March of

Dimes, the US Department of Education Office of Special Education Programs, and our local Children's Trust, we hired paid staff, including our first formidable director, Isabel Garcia, who continues in this role today, along with twelve staff members. They now serve over three thousand families each year.

I was no different than the other board members. As my knowledge grew, so did my opportunities to create programmatic change. My legislative advocacy work in Tallahassee had won me favor with Dr. Robert Stempfel, the director of the Mailman Center for Child Development within the Department of Pediatrics at the University of Miami's Medical School. Shortly after our move to Coral Gables, I received a telephone call from one of his faculty members, Dr. Terri Urbano, the kind woman I had met in Washington, DC, years earlier. She talked with me about the Center's restructuring and their plans to create a new faculty position. She was hoping I was interested. I was. On February 2, 1994, I began as Terri's assistant.

"Paula, we have this office for you. It's not very big, but don't worry, all this is changing. Now, as the Director of Training, I will have better control of programmatic decisions and budget." At that time, women gaining titles and power in a medical school was not the norm, nor easy. "Why don't you start by reading over last year's progress report to the Administration on Developmental Disabilities? We will meet early afternoon and I'll explain more," she said.

My enthusiasm and willingness to learn and be supportive was just what Terri needed. The twelve-member faculty committee she now chaired was not used to much oversight. "It's like herding cats, so you have to be persistent," she would say. But the struggles seemed to carry a price, as two years later, Terri was diagnosed with cancer. I stepped into her role as much as I was able until she returned seven months later. It was a good preparation for her ultimate resignation a year later, when I would be promoted into her position.

My new faculty position at the medical school was ideal. The Mailman Center's mission was to provide training, service, and research to support children with disabilities and their families. It had a prestigious beginning, having been founded in 1970 through legislation and funding designated by President John F. Kennedy's administration. Eunice Shriver, President Kennedy's sister, is said to have personally crafted the legislation, helping to ensure children with disabilities would receive appropriate care and services. Family-centered practices were part of the Center's funding mandate. Terri and I began to create new training initiatives to fold those practices into the training programs for pediatric residents and interns from other disciplines.

The position felt right, even though I often hobbled into Dr. Morgan's office, wishing I were someone else or filled with regret and disappointment. With her help, I removed one prison bar after another, slowly making my escape from my mental torture chamber. One of the prison bars had to do with my relationship with money.

"I am so miserable, but I don't see how I can get divorced. I can't afford my life even now. The bank closed my account last week—too many bounced checks." Her response gave me pause.

"Keeping yourself in the red may be a way to hold yourself back," she asserted.

"Back from what?" I inquired.

"What do you think?" she asked.

"From taking risks," I responded. No answer. I sat with my own reflection. Money as a form of self-restraint had not occurred to me. Was I keeping myself in debt to shackle myself to my marriage?

With that awareness came more questions and eventual resolution. What am I so afraid of? And why do I have such a need to suffer? I recognized how I used the cost of things as one of the primary criteria to make decisions. My heart's desire didn't weigh in as part of my choices as it should, in part because I didn't know myself well enough to do that. This left me indecisive and easily derailed. I also realized money represented safety and security. This kept entangling me in friendships, romantic relationships, and other situations that were unhealthy: I would forfeit my integrity and spirit for the sake of physical safety and needs. I now know that feeling safe is an inside job, experienced when one is aligned with one's own truth. I first had to figure out what that was.

With our move into the Gables, I hoped there would be children on our block.

"Hi, my name is Roy Helm, we see you just moved in," he said as he reached out to shake my hand. I was standing at the end of my driveway, and Roy was out for a walk. "Welcome to the neighborhood. Where did you move from?" I shared our Hurricane Andrew story, as people were still doing, and explained how we wanted to be closer to downtown.

"Oh, we understand that. I ride my bike to work, to avoid all that traffic," he said.

"We have two children and are hoping they will have friends here," I said. He lit up as he shared that they too had children, Mary and Jennings.

"In fact, we all go to the First United Church of Coral Gables, if you are looking for a church," he said.

"Really? I was baptized Methodist and have been wanting to join a church, so maybe we will just do that." We said goodbye and Roy went on with his walk.

On Sunday, Alex, Jaime, and my son and I went to church. The church became our home three times a week: Monday night children's choir, Wednesday night church dinner, and the Sunday service. Seeing my children together at church, in choir, musicals, and mission trips was what I loved the most. I reached out beyond my disability circles and made new friends.

The children's friendships in the neighborhood resulted in lemonade stands, car washes, pool parties, movie nights, birthday parties, tree climbing, boyfriend struggles, and just plain chats in the kids' rooms. I remember three incidents. The first was one of the few squabbles between Alex and Mary, her new best friend. It was over the new and very cute Argentine boy, Gonzalo, who had moved in next door to us. Unbeknownst to him, the girls engaged in a heated discussion as to who would "get him." Luckily for one of the two girls, a light bulb went off, and they decided the best solution was to ask him who he liked best. Eleven-year-old Alex did the asking. Gonzalo, quick on his mental feet, replied that he wasn't quite sure. Alex, in her relentless manner, retorted, "You have until tomorrow. Meet us both at my house at three." He showed up, and under duress, he gave his answer, "I choose Mary." He was quickly dismissed and Alex, not accepting full defeat, told Mary, "The next one is mine." These were priceless moments, moments for which I had been hoping, ones with neighborhood friends and a normal life in the suburbs. Like those two mothers with their twelve-year-old daughters in Chicago, my dreams for Alex were coming true.

The second incident was a bittersweet moment. Alex was a diehard romantic. She kept much of it inside, but her budding interest in boys was becoming evident. She loved romantic movies and listening to Mariah Carey and Gloria Estefan love songs, reflections of her own swelling heartstrings. It was on a Saturday in the early afternoon, and Jaime was off with his father. Alex and I were in her bedroom, organizing her closet. We weren't rushing to finish the task nor in a hurry to then go somewhere else. It was more like just being together, quiet time. In that space of quiet sharing, she asked me a heartfelt question. "Mom, do you think I will ever get married?"

Her tone and the thickness in the air indicated that she was braced for the truth, which is what she expected from me. I swallowed hard and said what any mother would, "Yes, I believe so."

Her second question, even more earnest and important than the first, was, "How will he carry me over the threshold with my wheelchair?" I paused slightly and then replied, "Well, you certainly will want to be carried across the threshold. He will just need to pick you up and leave the wheelchair behind."

She looked relieved. I wanted to bolt from the room but resisted for a few minutes. Then I ran into the bathroom and silently cried.

The third moment happened on the Saturday morning that Alex decided to perform for all the neighborhood children. As I walked into our living room, she was setting up her karaoke machine and microphone, having already moved the rattan dining room chairs to form audience seating. Our floors were tiled, and the light rattan chairs slid easily across them. Plus, her upper body strength was substantial as she had even won arm wrestling matches with her brother, Uncles Jeff and Jim, and her grandmother. During her preparations, she announced that she would be charging a two-dollar entrance fee. I suggested twenty-five cents. We had such a level of trust with each other that we then shared an instantaneous loving look whereby she deciphered that my suggestion was the right one. Six children showed up and settled themselves into the chairs Alex had set out for them. She wasn't quite ready, and they waited patiently. Suddenly, she blasted a Mariah Carey song and began to sing and dance. She had mastered moving to the Latin beat with shakes and wiggles of her upper body and her arms swaying in sync with the rest. Her ability to quickly turn her wheelchair added a bit of twisting and turning at unexpected moments. Hats, scarves, makeup, and costume jewelry were always a must.

The children drank lemonade, ate cookies, and had a good time. Alex was a magnet for fun. She loved people, and she loved to laugh,

sing and dance. She participated in a performing arts group for children with disabilities called the Genie's Workshop. They performed
once a year in a televised presentation. Her favorite pastime, though,
was watching the *I Love Lucy* and *Sabado Gigante* television shows on
Saturday nights in her bedroom while braiding her Barbie doll's hair.
The laughs from her room reached all the way into the living room as
we watched our own program or worked on a puzzle with Jaime.

Jaime and Alex were never too far away from each other. From
that first day when Alex held out her open arms to receive her little
brother home from the hospital, they were tight. Squabbles and rival-
ries happened of course as expected, but there was togetherness. They
had their ways with each other. Alex, unable to accomplish other forms
of revenge, often resorted to running over Jaime's bare feet 'by accident.' "Mom, Jaime hit me," she would holler. "Jaime, what are you
doing to your sister?" knowing that it would be slight.

At the same time, he often intervened on Alex's behalf, using his
verbal acuity to maneuver in and around the household rules, the few
that there were. Often in cahoots, their escapade at the Coral Gables
Youth Center was a good example. I arrived at the Youth Center's office
at the usual after-school care pick-up time. A staff member asked to
speak with me. She was visibly upset as she inquired why I kept for-
getting to give my daughter her after-school treat money. She said that
Alex had been asking her for money for weeks. She had already loaned
her $2.50, which didn't seem to be the core issue. She went on to
explain that when she'd asked Alex about getting paid back, Alex had
wheeled herself out of the office, saying, "I don't pay back my debts."

The staff person had cognitive limitations, but her ability to count
and her personal ethics were intact. Embarrassed, I made an excuse for
Alex's behavior, paid her debt, and marched off to find her. I found the
two siblings together, an unforgettable sight: Jaime was standing on Alex's
wheelchair, feeding the vending machine the virtually stolen coins. As I
approached, Jaime's bottle of soda tumbled down the machine. Furious,
I no doubt grounded them forever and reported them to their father,
who felt embarrassed as well. Even less of a disciplinarian than I, he said
something like, "Now Jaime, why would you do such a thing?"

Perhaps their tight connection created a stronger sense of security
in a home that had huge emotional cracks. The cracks were measured
by the degree to which we led separate lives and the lack of true inti-

macy between my husband and me. Our marriage was strained for
months; I slept in the spare bedroom. I declined my husband's invitation to travel with him and the children to Colombia.

"Oh, *now* you are being nice! You want me to go so I can take care
of the kids while you're with your family, no thanks!" Sadly, we had a
classic "rubber band syndrome" marriage. He moved toward me, and
then I moved away. When I moved toward him, he distanced himself.
It made for a lot of built-up sexual energy that exploded in frustrated
verbal outbursts.

"And remember what happened on our last trip" I added, recalling the night in Colombia when I had locked him out of the bedroom.
"And we should also remember your mother's good advice, 'Don't
come here when you are not getting along.' "

If anything, since that incident, our relationship had worsened.
As their plane lifted off from the Miami International Airport, I mostly
felt relief. I wished I had wanted to go, but I didn't. With my children
taken care of, I ventured off on my own trip. I telephoned my cousin
Denise, and we met in Savannah, Georgia, a place with history and
nearby beaches.

That Christmas, I hosted the Parent to Parent of Miami's holiday
party at our new home. Jaime shook everyone's hand very attentively as
he left to have dinner with clients. The only person not surprised was
me. My endeavors were not his. His world of high net worth clients
and wealthy South Americans was becoming more and more foreign to
me. The part of me that had once felt like a part of that world left to
build a community where I felt inspired, needed, and resourceful. My
success and Alex's future depended upon it.

6

Walls Begin to Crumble

TAPED TO MY OFFICE DOOR at work was the Children's Defense Fund logo that features a child's drawing of a purple boat on a swirly sea and the prayer, "Dear Lord, be good to me. The sea is so wide, and my boat is so small." No matter how much I resisted that vulnerability, my boat was getting smaller and smaller. Life at home with Alex and her health was challenging, and I felt that I was losing control of my marriage.

Although Alex was a bit quiet and shy at school, at home, she ruled the roost. She could be stubborn and argumentative. Our power struggles were usually about food, exercise, and her bathroom needs. "I will order your fish sandwich with tartar sauce, but you know we will have to scrape some of it off," I would say at the McDonald's drive-up window. Wails of protest would then come from the back seat while her brother Jaime whispered, "I'll give you some of mine." My concern wasn't so much nutrition as it was calories, the way we all thought in the 1990s. Mobility was already a challenge, and additional pounds would only make things worse. I could still lift her up off the floor into her wheelchair at eighty-five pounds, but I had reached my maximum.

The hardest and most exasperating thing was the every-five-hours regimen of draining her urine with a catheter. Alex resisted, slamming on her brakes when I would try to get her into the bathroom. Lack of compliance meant a potential urinary tract infection and a possible hospitalization for IV antibiotics. Her veins were tiny, which meant there would be multiple painful attempts to insert the IV. One of these occasions happened when I had left her alone while I went for a coffee with my brother-in-law who was visiting from Colombia. Stepping back off the elevator, I heard her screams all the way down the hall. The eight people surrounding her bed all looked sheepishly guilty when I ran into the room. Almost everyone exited as I entered. Alex was only five years old. Mothers were seen as obstacles to providing medical interventions, and I often had to insist on being in the room. I would sing in her ear and rub the top of her head. Alex quipped one time to a friend, "Moms are good for the good times and the bad."

By age six, she was independent as far as catheterizing (or 'cathing') herself; however, convincing her to go do it promptly often resulted in back-and-forth arguments between us like, "I don't want to, later maybe." "I know, but you have to!" When Mary was at the house, they would go into the bathroom together. I could hear them chatting away as Alex tended to her business. Mary was the compliant helper, she loved helping Alex.

Alex's bathroom needs at school were also challenging, but for other reasons. Her classroom had a bathroom, but the expected renovations did not occur, which meant her wheelchair did not fit through the bathroom door. Her noon time cathing, administered by a nurse, took place in the open classroom space while the other children were still at lunch. However, that plan wasn't working so well, which prompted the following phone call:

"Mrs. Lalinde, this is Jane, the director of the itinerant nursing agency that provides your daughter's services at Sunset Elementary." "Oh, hello, is there a problem?" I asked. "In our attempt to meet Alex's needs and provide services in a family-centered, child-friendly way, we would like your permission to make some adjustments. We would like Alex to be able to have lunch with the other children, and our suggestion is to provide Alex's cathing after lunch." A little confusedly, I inquired, "So where would you do that?" She explained, "We have gotten permission to build a private curtain space, and Alex would be cathed there once the nurse arrives, sometime after her lunch period." I was getting clearer, "Oh, so the nurse is unable to arrive on time and you need some flexibility. Where would this private curtain be located?" Then came the unbelievable reply, "Just outside of the bathroom area." Now I was totally clear, "So Alex would be cathed behind a curtain in the front of the room during class?" She affirmed a bit sheepishly, "Yes, but the curtain is full-length and provides complete privacy." I said, "I have been told that one of the boys is already referring to my daughter as the Green Machine, referring to Alex's green Depends undergarment. There has already been enough of a lack of privacy. Furthermore, what if Alex has had a bowel movement?" "Mrs. Lalinde, we are just trying to accommodate Alex's needs in the most child-centered fashion possible," she replied, apparently hoping that a mirroring of my customary words would camouflage the reality, a tactic I had become extremely skilled at detecting due to its widespread use. "I cannot give permission for such a thing. The answer is no." When I hung up, I held my head between my hands and wanted to cry or scream. Instead, I took a deep breath and recognized how far I had come in acquiring the ability to sort out truth and set limits.

A good solution was found; Alex's aide, who was a most wonderfully mature and capable woman, was trained to provide that service. That year, when Alex received the Most Courageous Student achievement award, we were proud and felt she deserved it. From what I learned, Alex could have also been given the award for being most kind. "From across the corridor, with the biggest smile, she would yell, "Hello, Mr. Gomez!" the school counselor said.

However, the next year meant new potential social challenges. Her aide would continue with her to Ponce de Leon Middle School, but the Green Machine comment left me saddened. "If only we could get rid of those Depends," I thought. I had heard about a new treatment at Children's Memorial Hospital in Chicago, where we had gone years earlier. They were using the functional electrical stimulation method, applying low-level electrical currents to the rectum, to improve bowel function for children with spina bifida. Could this be our answer? I made arrangements to spend two weeks at that clinic while Jaime stayed home and attended a baseball camp.

The trip to Chicago was the closest thing we were going to have to a vacation. Alex and I settled into the beautifully renovated Ronald McDonald House. The next day, we began our daily trips to the clinic for her one-hour treatment. I also scheduled appointments with the specialists.

Our first was with the orthopedic surgeon. Waiting for an hour was expected. What wasn't anticipated was the contrast between Alex and the other children in the waiting room. The children had more erect postures, better controlled weight, and their wheelchairs fitted them more precisely. "Would you like to receive a free wheelchair consult while you wait?" asked a young man with a bag of tools in his hand. After he provided several basic recommendations, I began to realize that although I strove to stay on top of Alex's care, it had been too much to keep up with. The contrast of my idealized persona and the actual reality hit me hard. My body got hot and I felt light-headed. "Mrs. Lalinde, you can go in now." As the orthopedic surgeon lifted Alex's blouse, which made me cringe as she was a budding almost-teenager, he was visibly shocked. "Her spine was never surgically closed?" he asked. I explained, "She was born in the Dominican Republic, and local hospital conditions meant there would have been a high risk of infection due to the need to graft her skin." He didn't respond. Looking at her x-rays, "She has a severe, 70 percent kyphosis, she will need back surgery." I asked, "What will that entail?" My knees got weak as I listened, "A section of her spine will be removed, and a titanium metal rod inserted—to straighten her back. If not, she will eventually lose her lung capacity; they could suddenly collapse. It's best to do the surgery in Miami. There is a good surgeon there." As he completed his examination, I explained, "We have been consulting an orthopedic surgeon twice a year, and at no time did he recommend surgery. With such widespread denial and neglect judgments on parents raising a child with a disability, I wanted to set the record straight.

I also made an appointment with the neurosurgeon, the one who had given us so much time when we arrived from the Dominican Republic. I had a choice to book either a private consultation or a visit during clinic hours. For the sake of what I perceived to be his convenience, I made the appointment during clinic hours. Later, I felt that decision had been unfortunate. He was rushed and a bit cold and distant. "I brought my daughter here when she was born. You were helpful. While we are here for the bowel treatment, I wanted to have Alex's shunt checked," I told him. A bit gruffly, he answered, "I don't order CAT scans frivolously. Does she have symptoms?" Headache, nausea, stiff neck, and lethargy were ticked off as he went down the list. "Not all the time. Headaches come and go, but it has been over ten years since it was changed," I said. "No, the symptoms would need to be continual." After checking her pupils, her arm strength, and her reflexes, he got up and ended the consultation. I left feeling unsettled. I realized that I had been expecting a 'welcome back' moment. Instead, I felt like we were foreigners trying to cash in on another country's goodies, their CAT scan machine. The consultation felt incomplete.

During that entire stay, I had a foreboding, a strong sense that we had lost control of Alex's health. She had taken a slide downhill without us realizing. After the neurological consultation, I questioned our decision to have Alex attend her neighborhood school, to mainstream her, in the parlance of special education, concerned that removing a layer of therapeutic protection had been misguided. Had we forfeited those other trained sets of eyes? Had our approach been wrong? Could we get her health back on track? Then I would tell myself that in fact we had been doing everything as prescribed—that her exercise therapist included Mary and the other neighborhood children in her workout, which made it fun. When that didn't help me feel better, I reminded myself of the many meetings I'd attended to establish a multidisciplinary spina bifida clinic in Miami that would raise the local level of care. That wasn't soothing either. "I should have continued to bring her here, what was I thinking? I said to myself. My internal warfare was exhausting when it kicked in.

Alone and unable to put words to my feelings, I went into emotional overwhelm. An alarm bell had gone off, a sense that something was terribly wrong. On a public phone at the Ronald McDonald House, I sobbed uncontrollably to my mother. In those same tears were a world of hurt for my dissolving marriage, the lost dreams, my disconnection from my family, and my disappointment with myself. I never did enough. Defeat haunted me as well as death.

My emotional turmoil spoke to a truth about disability, one that became clear during my participation in an executive leadership program at Harvard University. Marty Linsky. standing in front of the blackboard, told us, "The single biggest failure of leadership is to treat adaptive challenges, those requiring a change in beliefs, values, roles, and responsibilities, solely as if they were technical." My whole body reacted to that statement.

Albeit the spina bifida clinic in Chicago was far more experienced in addressing the children's technical issues, they too failed to incorporate the adaptive aspects of disability. There was one-way communication about the technical aspects of her physical health and disability, while simmering below the surface were the adaptive ones. Surgeries, special seats to support her weak torso, adaptive swimming gear to help her build upper body strength, medications to calm her neurogenic bladder, catheters, wheelchairs. and braces to help her move, all the technical solutions provided by child-focused specialists, left the parents struggling alone with the adaptive challenges that are critical for the family to thrive. A better approach had to exist, I thought.

While I was on the call with my mother, Alex was up in the common area, inviting all the other children and parents to her eleventh birthday party. I dried my tears and joined her. Two days later, on June 29, 1995, all the families in the house gathered around her. She beamed as we sang happy birthday and she blew out her candles. The heartstrings connecting her to the other children and mothers were palpable. Her tiny legs, big tummy, crooked spine, big green Depends diaper—all of her was loved. She was enough just as she was for so many people. I kept trying to fix her. When I wasn't fixing her, I was trying to change the world she was growing into. The bowel treatment was over. We returned to Miami, still in Depends, though hopefully for only a bit longer.

While I struggled with my guilt and sense of failure, Alex was accepting of her limitations. "Mom, it doesn't matter," she said putting her petite little hand over mine, as we sat at US I and Red Road, waiting for the light to turn green. She knew I was fighting back tears, having just left the endocrinologist's office after a visit to discuss growth hormones. "Her back is too unstable, and we don't know how the growth hormones would affect her," he explained. "But without them, she won't even be five feet tall," I lamented. He handed me research articles that seemed useless. I left defeated and scared for her future. She met all this with, "Mom, it doesn't matter," in a tone that expressed a profound knowing. It seemed that Alex was so broken in the traditional sense that it left her free to not strive for perfection. She felt that she was enough. For me, it took decades to even get close to that.

If the goal was to acquire patience and to learn to accept limitations and imperfection, I clearly was given the right situation. I would feel like I was handling things well, then I would lose patience and become overwhelmed. With spina bifida, nothing works as expected: bowel and bladder incontinence, lower limb paralysis, weak fine motor skills, learning disabilities, visual perceptual challenges due to pressure on the brain and posture, and the continual risks of a lethal shunt malfunction and meningitis. When one challenge ended, another began.

In early fall that year, I consulted the recommended Miami orthopedic surgeon. He too felt the surgery was required. As he left the consult, closing the door behind him, Alex began crying, begging me not to make her have this surgery. I tried to calm her by explaining we had not yet decided. "But I know you. You will make me do it," she said. I felt panic. This was the first surgery she would be able to weigh in on. "How do I respond to this?" I wondered. Thankfully, a well-trained pediatric nurse walked into the room, assessed the situation, and calmed Alex with her child-friendly explanation.

Alex and I were quiet as we drove home together. She didn't want the surgery yet knew it was inevitable, as she had said. Jaime later met the surgeon, and they seemed to click on the topic of Colombia. Their rapport that day calmed my worries, reassuring me that there would be a good surgical outcome. Determined that Alex would not miss school, in September of 1995, I asked that the surgery date be set for the following summer. The postponement was a surprise to the surgeon. Unknowingly, I had bought more time with my daughter.

While dealing with the realities of a major surgery for Alex, Jaime and I continued seeing a marriage counselor. In one of our early sessions, Dr. Gomez asked, "Do you feel that perhaps Jaime should have been able to protect you and Alex or could have prevented what happened?" I muddled through some response and then shared a story I had not told anyone. "If we had gone to the hospital, everything would be different. We could have prevented all of this." The counselor looked puzzled and invited me to share more. I began with, "Alex wasn't my first pregnancy." The rest came out in sobs, bits of rage, and an accusatory tone.

While we were living in New York City, waiting for Jaime's overseas assignment, I got pregnant. We were excited but didn't tell anyone, deciding to wait till I was three months along, which was not long from when we learned of the pregnancy. Then at three o'clock on a Friday afternoon, in the bathroom at the Lord & Taylor department store, I noticed spots of blood in my underwear. The doctor immediately returned my phone call and told me to go home and rest with my legs up and to call him if anything changed. I took a taxi back to the St. Moritz Hotel; our hotel room was one large square room filled with our seven big suitcases, everything we then owned.

When Jaime got back to the hotel, he found me with my legs up resting. I explained what had happened. "Are you sure you're not up to going? We already have the tickets, and the Clydesdale horses are world-famous, this may perhaps be our only chance." Importantly, a colleague and his wife were joining us.

As on other occasions, his whining convinced me to forgo any of my own good judgment as well as the doctor's. Before I knew it, now potentially late, we were running down Fifth Avenue to catch a bus to Madison Square Gardens. We found the couple and our seats and began to enjoy the show. An hour into the performance, my stomach began to rumble and then stop and then rumble again. I froze, unable to say anything. As I sat, distracted and in periodic pain, the prancing horses were ever more meaningless.

Finally, the performance was over, and the four of us joined thousands of others in exiting the building. I was wearing my cousin's winter coat, thankfully, as it absorbed some of the blood that was now running down my legs. It was only then that I whispered, "Something is wrong, I am bleeding." The four of us piled into a taxicab. I was last in, now silently sobbing. As the couple got out at their stop, I leaned forward, "Nice to meet you," as if nothing had happened and as if they hadn't noticed.

"Take us to the St. Moritz," Jaime said. In disbelief, I retorted, "No, we need to go to the hospital." The driver was confused as he headed up Eighth Avenue. "We need to go to the hotel for you to clean up first," Jaime argued. I asked the driver, "What is the closest hospital?" He said, "Columbia Presbyterian is the closest." That sounded fine to me. "Take us to the hotel," But Jaime insisted, repeating, "You need to get cleaned up." Unable to speak up for our child and my own body, I succumbed. Inside our hotel room, within moments, I felt pressure in my abdomen—then while sitting on the toilet, I heard a plop sound as the fetus fell into the commode. Jaime called the doctor. We got into a taxi and went to the emergency room at the nearby hospital. I felt sad and weak.

The next morning, tears ran down my cheeks as I slipped away under the effects of a general anesthetic for a necessary D&C procedure, while the doctor tried to comfort me. My perpetually late husband did not make it to the hospital on time. He was there when I came to. My questions about our baby's gender and why I'd had a miscarriage went unanswered, "Without the fetus, we don't know." We went home that same day. I don't remember talking about it again.

Later that week, I took my cousin's winter coat to the dry cleaners. I asked the attendant to please try to remove the stain. She was the only person who ever knew what probably had happened. Lonely, sad, and overwhelmed by the filth and noise of the city, I wanted to go home, but there was no turning back. My mother 's general response to my marriage woes, "You made your bed, now lie in it." I was sure it had to have been her mother's response too. Deserting the family had consequences, and marrying a foreigner had made it worse.

Dr. Gomez was clearly taken aback by the story. However, my rage and blame toward Jaime were met with a soft-toned comment, "Yes, and you were unable to take care of yourself." He was right, but I didn't understand why I couldn't. Then he turned to Jaime and said, "Get cleaned up first?" prompting him to explore his motivations. Jaime looked ashamed and didn't respond. Later, Dr. Gomez looked straight at me and in a puzzled tone asked me, "What did they do to you?" meaning my parents. I really had no idea.

So, in my mind, Alex's birth defect could have been prevented. With an analysis of the fetus, we would have known to take precautions and I would have had prenatal testing and would have traveled to the United States to give birth. I had no framework in which to understand Alex's birth other than Western medicine and psychology. In my awareness at the time, there was no 'meant to be,' divine time, God's gift, soul contracts, karma, or evolutionary journey of the soul from which to derive relief and richer life meaning. Nor did I have the ability to forgive, accept, nor fully appreciate what life gave me then.

Additionally, Alex's traumatic hospitalizations and surgeries as well as discriminatory school personnel and children kept the trauma activated. What happens to our children also happens to us as parents. Cognitive therapy once a week was never going to be enough.

Without having sufficiently worked through the trauma, forgiveness was improbable. In addition, Jaime and I kept expecting something the other person was unable to give. This pattern existed both inside and outside of our marriage. It was a pattern that fueled my advocacy efforts and had a role in my many disappointments with myself—my "all for naught" moments. Many years later, I did develop a greater ability to let go of expectations, or at least gained the awareness that expectations were causing my suffering. I worked hard to be present with what was really happening in the moment in my mind and body. Being aware of myself was a necessary component in my learning to speak up for myself.

CHAPTER

7

The Affair

M Y HUSBAND'S AFFAIR SHOULD NOT have come as such an emotional blow, but it did. "I want to talk about his late nights out," I said to Dr. Gomez. "What would you like to know about that?" he replied. Jaime was sitting to my left and without hesitating, I turned and said, "Are you having an affair?"

His answer was not convincing. It was a simple, "No." It wasn't a "No, I couldn't do that to you;" nor was it anything like, "No, our marriage is too important to lose. I want to make things better for us." Not even close. I asked again, and his longest answer was, "No, I am not. I know you think I am, but I am not."

The marriage counselor seemed to try to get me to accept his answer. In those moments, I appeared to accept Jaime's "No." However, his late nights at work and lack of interest and involvement in my life continued to leave me suspicious. We had been two ships passing in the night for a long time—a situation which had natural consequences.

On one fateful Saturday in January of 1996, I reached into his briefcase on the floor next to a small parsons table in the living room. I pulled out his MCI business telephone bill. With a pounding heart, I scanned the bill, unclear about what I was looking for. But there it was: repeated phone calls in the wee hours of the morning from Mexico, where he had traveled on business, to two phone numbers in Miami, neither of them ours. Trembling, I called each number. First, an answering machine with a woman's voicemail message. The voicemail belonging to the second line was Jaime's, a private line I knew nothing about.

In a rage of hurt and confusion, I drove to Rick and Terri's house. Terri wasn't home, and Rick tried to help me uncover more information about the phone numbers, to no avail. In a state of disbelief, I kept calling the two numbers and hanging up. The women's voice on the answering machine felt more real each time. The fact that Jaime was calling a woman at three o'clock in the morning could only mean one thing. I returned home, my psyche drastically altered.

When Jaime came home, he went on the offensive, waving his finger at me while accusing, "I know what you have been doing." His bulldog tone was unexpected. I jumped off the sofa, ran over, and started beating on him and yelling. "You bet I have been calling those numbers!" He replied, "You have no right to do that"—which meant I swung harder. At some point he admitted he was having an affair. That night, I cried myself to sleep.

I woke up in the morning with swollen eyes. Underneath all my pent-up rage and anger was sadness and remorse. My own fallibility became evident to me, as well as my deep desire to have a loving and committed marriage. Because of that and perhaps to prevent the onrush of even more pain, we attempted to reconcile.

A few days later, as I came out of the bathroom, Alex was at the breakfast table, drawing. "Let me see," I said. As she held up her drawing, "It is a butterfly. She wasn't going to live but then she changed." I wiped my tears as I walked into the kitchen. Parental discord is so painful for children. And my children were no different. Alex loved to love people. A divorce would have been devastating. And although we wanted our marriage to work, we had no idea of how to make that happen. Routines and patterns driven by faulty beliefs about ourselves and each other had gone unaddressed for almost two decades.

One thing I thought I could do was to be more attentive to the things that were important to him. So, I asked him if he would like me to iron his dress shirts like I used to, remembering a frequent quip, "You don't even iron my shirts anymore." He seemed a bit surprised by my offer.

Why I thought ironing those shirts would save my marriage I can't imagine. I dragged out my ironing board and iron, filled the iron with water so the steamer would work, and ironed his Colombian custom-made shirts. Within a week, without any explanation, he asked me to please stop. Perhaps he felt guilty or didn't want to owe me anything in return. Or perhaps the French Cleaners simply did it better. I felt hurt and confused at the time.

Much later, I realized we were two of a kind. The nice things we did for each other often went unnoticed. Our brains were hardwired for disappointment. We literally did not have a computer file folder for, "Things for which I am grateful." So, although we both did thoughtful things for the other, those incidents went unrecorded. "I love buying Paula nice jewelry, but she thinks it is just to show off." Jaime told our marriage counselor. "Oh, she has no ability to receive anything like that," he said without hesitation. At the time, I had no idea of the full meaning of his response—only a feeling inside that told me it was true. The consequence of our mutual inability to receive and feel grateful had a simple and profound impact: We slowly stopped doing nice things for each other.

Instead, we focused on disappointments and what the other person could do to improve themselves. "Paula is like a diamond in the rough," Jaime told the marriage counselor; a true enough statement. Aren't we all? But it was not endearing. It also meant that I was always in need of adjustment. I was too loud, or too quiet, or didn't look right after leaving a social event, where I had no doubt already felt inadequate.

"Did you notice how his wife dresses?" he asked.

I kept my thoughts to myself, protecting him and myself. "Oh, the woman wearing the thousand-dollar outfit—are you giving me the money to buy that outfit? We can hardly pay our mortgage."

In turn, I was waiting for the man who would protect and take care of us. The Paula who wanted to be a stay-at-home-mother volunteering for charity organizations—a kind of Mother Teresa with Evita Peron's bank account—was angry and disappointed. What happened, I wondered, to the man who said he wanted to be president of his country one day? "If that agreement had been kept, my life would be easier," I secretly thought. I was operating under so many delusions, and, most of the time, I was not even aware of my own self-deceit.

Jaime's ambition was proportional to my self-restraint. Marrying a man with such high aspirations gave me the illusion that I would be taken care of; what he couldn't give, I could buy. We'd met at a Cinco de Mayo party while we were both graduate students at the University of Illinois. The language and culture of the celebration of Mexico's Day of Independence were a magnet for us both. He was from South America, Colombia, and I had worked on an archeology project in

Mexico. Jaime was the most handsome man at the party, six feet tall with long, dark, curly hair and the tall, thin body type I liked. We talked, then danced, and I left intrigued. The next week, he attended a party at my house. I remember the pitter-pat moment I saw him walk in the door. Within a few months, I left for California to gather data for my master's thesis in bilingual education. I received long love letters as I turned down other potential suitors. We got engaged shortly after I returned.

While we were engaged, the reality of his tendency toward moodiness and conflict with authority figures, which included me, felt familiar and was unsettling. I postponed the engagement and felt relieved. My conflicted emotions continued, yet so did our relationship. His ambitions coupled with my own insecurities and self-constraints fueled a relationship that otherwise might not have survived. I remember contemplating the fact that although I was about to finish my master's degree, I wasn't sure if I could really support myself. My mother had worked outside of the home for only four days, at which time my father put an end to it due to his crippling jealousy. I had no role models to follow, and it felt daunting to try to be independent and gainfully employed. And it may well have been; I was walking through life wearing a blindfold with my hands tied behind my back. His romantic pursuit of me continued, and though I had conflicted feelings, I eventually said, "I do." We were married in a small United Methodist church near where I grew up.

Now here I was, decades later, with a new version of the same problem. Do I tackle life on my own or succumb to the ease and safety found in familiarity and the financial support of a husband? Forgoing my home and my ability to travel unencumbered was a lot to lose, not to mention the intermittent help with Alex's care. I knew the children would be devastated, and I wasn't sure Jaime would even stay in the United States given the chance to leave, which meant I couldn't really count on child support or alimony.

Perhaps more importantly, I had never experienced a love-filled marriage; I could not have known what I was missing. When the emotional dust settled, I did whatever was next to plan and do.

CHAPTER

8

Preparing and the Day

B Y SPRING OF 1996, WE were in the thick of preparation for Alex's June 27 surgery. Planning had become one of my talents, always trying to make sure things went as expected. Our consultation with the recommended orthopedic surgeon resulted in a referral to a pediatric plastic surgeon. The skin along her spine was thin, prohibiting the proper closure post-surgery. In March of 1996, the pediatric plastic surgeon inserted tissue expanders, one on each side of her spine at waist level. The two silicone bags each had a valve, and twice a week we met him at the hospital at two o'clock to begin filling them with the required saline solution. As the silicone bags expanded, so did Alex's skin. The process was to take three weeks. It took eleven weeks, wreaking havoc on my work responsibilities and her studies.

The plastic surgeon had a difficult personality, giving short answers to complicated questions and offering no flexibility with appointment times. At one visit, as the physician was prepping Alex for the saline injection, he asked, "Your husband works for Citibank, doesn't he?" I affirmed that he did. "I just got off my third call with them to fix something they are too stupid to figure out," he said. The more he talked, the more upset he became. Alex lay face down on top of an x-ray machine table, watching my reactions from the corner of her left eye. Suddenly, he raised his right hand with the syringe full of saline and with force aimed toward the valve's entrance stating, "This one is for Citibank." Alex cringed feeling the pressure from the driving force. The nurse assistant across from us was visibly shocked, as were we. No one acknowledged his abusive action. His task finished, he abruptly left the room.

"Are you okay, Alex?" I said.

"It's not our fault that the bank did that," she said a bit confused and almost crying.

I quietly inquired, but unfortunately for us, there were no other pediatric plastic surgeons suitable for the task. We returned the next week.

I preserved my silence to prevent a backlash that would endanger Alex's health, a not uncommon behavior for parents of children with disabilities. However, I still had an especially hard time speaking up for myself or my daughter, even when the person was right in front of me. I was sure remnants of a childhood where it was indeed not safe to speak the truth had caused this behavior. Ridicule was prevalent in my home, and there was no talking back, as it was described. I swallowed not only my words, but my feelings and self-pride. Pieces of myself got lost, along with the ability to remain connected to my feelings in the moment. Long after the other person had left the scene, I would feel the insult, the ridicule, or the deceit. By emotionally checking out, referred to as dissociation in psychology, I kept everyone safe from my inner rage—everyone except myself.

As I was aware of the emotional effects of hospitalization on young children, even though scant research on the subject existed at the time, I proposed the tissue expanders be removed on the same day as the rod surgery. Both surgeons concurred that it was a suitable plan. I felt heroic for having proposed it, saving Alex a two-day hospitalization and surgery. Due to Alex missing so much school for medical procedures, in that late spring, I helped her with her homework more than usual.

On evenings, snuggled into bed together, I read her literature assignments from her Prentice Hall Literature book out loud to her. "Where the Red Fern Grows" was one of our favorite stories. However, as it was her last reading assignment for the school year, it left an indelible mark on both of us. In "Tuck Everlasting" by Natalie Babbitt, we met Winnie Foster, a ten-year-old girl who, while wandering in the forest, stumbled upon and befriended the Tuck family. The family had drunk from a magic spring and were blessed and cursed with eternal life. We both appreciated Winnie's spunk and adventurous nature and how she so loved the Tuck family. As the ending neared, though, there was a palpable tension in the room. Unbeknownst to us, death was the story's central theme. Winnie's lessons about the hardships of eternal life and then death as a natural and necessary part of life were not lost on the two of us. We sobbed together at the story's end, where Tuck is seen standing in a graveyard, reading Winnie's tombstone.

"'So,' said Tuck to himself, 'Two years. She's been gone two years.' He stood up and looked around, embarrassed, trying to clear the lump from his throat. But there was no one to see him. The cemetery was quiet."

The book was a Final Gift,[1] a foreshadowing of a truth that was meant to be shared beforehand.

Three weeks before surgery, my car's electrical system went haywire. The repairs took longer than the mechanic anticipated, which left me in the lurch with no car. My car's entire electrical wiring system snaked around the debris on top of the mechanic's wooden workbench. I pleaded with him to finish the repairs, explaining my biweekly trips to the hospital and Alex's imminent surgery. In true Miami style, he shrugged and nodded in the direction of the snaked wires—not possible. However, my despair was palpable, so he offered me the use of his pickup truck. I said, "Yes." Getting Alex into the truck meant I had to lift her up, all ninety pounds of her, onto the front seat. Her wheelchair banged around in the back. Meanwhile, Jaime saw my dilemma as mine alone. I needed his signature to buy or lease a car. He was unwilling, and I was personally broke. No doubt, he was as well. We both saw the inevitable at our doorstep and were done trying to be happy together. He didn't want to invest another cent or drop of goodness, not even in this state of emergency, as I perceived it. I swore to myself that I would never be that broke again in my life. I kept learning life lessons the hard way.

Upon returning the pickup truck, the mechanic and owner of European Motors explained that my car's electrical problem was complicated and that he couldn't give me a realistic estimate of either time or cost to finish the repairs. Instead, he offered an equal trade, my Volvo station wagon for a much older one. I glanced over and spotted the gray, gas-guzzling, tank-sized station wagon, dulled from Miami's tropical sun. My disappointment was fleeting as I knew there were few to no other options. We struck a deal, and there on the spot, we signed off on

---

[1]   Callanan, M., Kelley, P. (1992). *Final Gifts: Understanding the Special Awareness, Needs, and Communications of the Dying*. New York: Simon & Schuster.

the car titles and I transferred my license plate. He got his pickup truck back, and I got a car within my budget, which was zero. As I drove off, I knew Jaime would really love the rumble seat, and he did.

On June 26, 1996, I felt ready for Alex's surgery set for the following morning. All our meticulous preparation and planning was complete. Alex's June 29 birthday had been celebrated in our home with her friends a month early so as not to miss it. The church had prayed for us the Sunday before, blood had been donated, and family and friends notified. Alex's skin was adequately stretched, my vacation days were secured, a friend had arrived from Tallahassee to help, and a family friend was ready to paint and decorate her room as a welcome-home surprise. Alex's brother Jaime was with our church group in North Carolina on a children's music trip. We spoke with him before bedtime. Alex got extra-long hugs from her father and I that night. We extended story time. I was anxious but ready for the surgery to be behind us. Exhausted, I fell into bed.

On the morning of June 27, Alex woke up with a 105-degree temperature. I was beside myself, confused, and unsure of what would happen next. I had no idea what the source of the fever could be. Her symptoms were unlike those she had with urinary tract infections. Nevertheless, after numerous phone calls, we left for the hospital.

The following seven days were tumultuous. The rod surgery was canceled, and the tissue expanders, the probable culprits of the fever, were surgically removed later that morning. Post-surgery, Alex had a headache that became severe. We kept her hospital room lights off to give her comfort. She spent three nights in the intensive care unit (ICU) for close monitoring. The hospital's neurosurgeon was called in, as our neurosurgeon had recently retired. A CAT scan of the brain suggested that her shunt was malfunctioning, and the accumulating cerebrospinal fluid in the brain was likely causing her severe headache. Because Alex was recuperating from the surgical removal of the tissue expanders, the neurosurgeon thought it best to wait. He explained that back-to-back surgeries carried an additional risk for a poor outcome. I simultaneously felt relieved and worried.

Jaime and I rotated shifts between hospital and home. A friend, Joanne Scaturro, flew in as planned to help during recovery. Emotionally, I was a bundle of nerves. It was hard to remain focused.

Without proper sleep, I couldn't function well. I was worried, *very* worried. Nothing was as it should be, and I couldn't get my legs firmly underneath me.

Our son Jaime had returned from his church trip and now spent days at the hospital. His small, pink, seashell wind chime, purchased for his sister at one of Florida's roadside stops, had made it back in one piece. He had held it in his hand for five hundred miles. His sister was pleased and proud. So was he.

On the nights Alex slept in the ICU, I slept in her empty hospital room. The third morning, I woke up a bit late and got some coffee before I went in to see her. When I entered, she gave me a questioning look, one conveying there had been a breach of trust caused by my leaving her alone for as long as I had. It was impossible to keep up with both her needs and my own. The nurses explained that the bed had been repositioned several times during the night to alleviate her headaches. Alex's skin color looked better and she was hungry, all good signs. I went to the cafeteria and got her a hamburger for lunch.

"I brought one of your favorite books, *Where the Sidewalk Ends*. Shall I read "The Crocodile's Toothache?" This brought only a slight smile to her face. I proceeded, but at the end, when the crocodile eats the dentist, her usual cackle was missing. I continued reading as we waited for the neurosurgeon.

He arrived around eleven o'clock, read the chart, and walked over to the foot of Alex's bed.

"I have signed an order to release her from the ICU," he said.

"You don't think we should get another CAT scan to make sure everything really is working?" I asked.

"The clinical signs of shunt malfunction are the most important. Her headache has subsided, and she looks better," he explained.

The scare was over—she didn't need a shunt revision after all. She was released from the ICU and went back to the surgical floor. I was both depleted and relieved.

Her brother sat on Alex's bed as they watched television together. That night, we gathered all around her: her father, myself, her brother, and my friend Joanne. When it was time to depart, Joanne said, "I can stay here tonight if you want to go home and get some rest, Paula." I glanced at Alex, who was silently asking me to stay with her. I wanted to stay. But I also sensed that Joanne wanted to stay.

"Oh, thanks, Joanne. I will take you up on your offer," I said, in my default pattern of deferring to and pleasing others.

The next morning Terri Urbano visited Alex in the hospital.

"I am still having headaches, but I don't want them to know. I want to go home," Alex shared with her.

"Alex, make sure you tell the doctor about your headaches," said Terri as she left. I hadn't arrived yet. When I did arrive, it was to discover that Alex had been released from the hospital. The social worker processing the discharge introduced herself to me.

"Hi, I'm the social worker in charge of your discharge papers," she said. "The doctor has ordered home wound care. However, due to the Fourth of July holiday, the nursing agency can't send out a nurse until Monday. The surgical sites where the tissue expanders were removed need to be cleaned in a special way."

I was too exhausted to argue. Alex wanted to go home. For me, this meant we were out of the scary woods and back to everyday living. Being left in the lurch was not new to me, and without even thinking about it, I assumed the responsibility of the absent nurse. Besides, at the time of Alex's birth, we had done her wound care ourselves, and I felt confident in my ability to do it. The social worker went over the prescription, an oral antibiotic for seven days. Alex had been on an IV antibiotic for the infection and needed to continue taking more. I was to follow up with the neurosurgeon within three weeks. I signed a bunch of release forms, and we were ready.

Part of my planning included figuring out her transportation home from the hospital—Alex would need to travel home lying on her stomach. The music minister at our church, Becky Weese, suggested I contact one of the members who was a fireman with the Coral Gables Fire Department. The department was pleased to do it and even agreed to play her favorite radio station, 99 Jamz. I was grateful for their help. I was also relieved to bring Alex home—but going home was not feeling right. How could it, I thought. She hadn't had the surgery for which we'd been preparing for nine months, and she'd still have to have it. None of the originally expected outcomes had been met.

The air was thick on that hot and humid fourth of July in Miami. We all made our way downstairs to the fire rescue truck, a hospital aide assisting us. Jaime pulled the car around, and we watched as they lifted Alex onto the stretcher and rolled her into the fire rescue truck. We couldn't climb in beside her due to regulations, but I was pleased that she was being given a ride by someone we knew. She was unusually quiet, even solemn. We all were. The heat of the day sucked the life out of us—not to mention the exhaustion that comes from facing death and surviving it.

Earlier that morning, a hospital equipment company had brought an adjustable hospital bed and situated it in her bedroom, directly across from the door. The four fire rescue workers carried Alex in on the stretcher and gently transferred her onto that bed. Alex's eyes sparkled when she saw her room. She couldn't have been more pleased. It was fitting for a beautiful little girl. Strange that I had chosen to have her room painted pink, a princess color, right at the age she would have been outgrowing this. I unpacked the bag of stuffed animals she had received while in the hospital and placed them on her newly arranged dresser and desk.

Jaime drove to the pharmacy to pick up the prescribed antibiotic. When I opened the bottle, I was in disbelief. The pill was hard, thick, and an inch long. How was I going to be able to administer this? I got out my wooden mallet from the Dominican Republic, once used to mash up cooked green plantains. I smashed the pill into the smallest pieces possible and added the bits to her applesauce. I coaxed and prodded until she swallowed most of the make-do concoction. Since she had been on a heavy dosage of IV antibiotics for seven days, I felt her system would be protected until morning.

Joanne was the perfect guest. Her lighthearted humor carried us into the evening. It was July 4; our son Jaime's birthday had been the prior day but had gone uncelebrated. His father took him out in front of the house to set off firecrackers for Jaime's celebration; he knew when to fill in the emotional gaps with Jaime. When they came in, we all hung out in Alex's room, chatting. She was subdued and even seemed uncomfortable at times. To help her feel more at ease, Joanne and I rearranged her electric bed. I was trying to match what they had done in the hospital, but the bed adjusted differently. Eventually, she said she felt better.

Around ten o'clock, we all went to bed. Joanne slept in Alex's room, another comforting reality as I fell into a heap of exhaustion. Of all things, the air conditioning unit was not cooling, and the house was miserably hot. Another task for the morning.

I didn't hear either my husband's alarm clock nor when he got dressed to leave for work. I arose around nine o'clock, tiptoed past Jaime's room glancing in, still asleep; then past where Alex was also still sleeping in her room to the telephone located in the kitchen.

At first, I mostly didn't remember the four times I had gotten up in the middle of the night, most of the details of which were recounted to me later that day by others, but I awoke knowing that Alex had passed a restless night. I called my friend Helen, who is a physical therapist, and left her a message to call me. I explained that Alex had felt uncomfortable during the night and it seemed to have to do with her positioning. Next, I spoke with her exercise therapist, who explained that she couldn't stop by until the end of the day. Then, I called the doctor's office to ask for a new prescription, as the large-sized tablets were impossible to swallow. My tone was calm and steady, but inside I was so exasperated with medical errors, both large and small. As they phoned the seven other different pharmacies necessary to locate the antibiotic in liquid form, I got dressed. As soon as I heard back, I headed out to the pharmacy, about three miles from the house. I returned home to a quiet house: every mother's wish—a quiet house.

The House Falls Down

I BROKE OPEN THE PRESCRIPTION BOTTLE of pink liquid and headed into Alex's room with a tablespoon. I immediately sensed something was terribly wrong. Her skin looked pasty, even bluish. I ran over to her bed and placed the medicine on her table stand. Alex stared at me with unmoving eyes. No! Somehow, I turned her over on her back and gave her mouth-to-mouth. Next to her bed was a house phone. Between breaths, I called 911 and then the pediatrician's office. When Alex didn't respond, I ran around the house screaming, "She's dead! She's dead!"

Jaime bolted out of his room and ran behind me, saying, "No mom, maybe Alex is still sleeping," over and over again. An endless loop of she's dead, no, maybe she is still sleeping—she's dead, no, maybe she is still sleeping. His words were just the buffer I needed to not completely implode.

Within minutes the Fire Rescue men—the same ones who had brought her home the day before—were back in Alex's room. Shortly after their arrival, her pediatrician arrived. She conferred with the fire rescue workers before they left the room. There was nothing for them to do. They left looking defeated. Death had won that day.

Her father took my call as he was getting out of the elevator at work. "Alex is dead. You need to come home." I hung up the phone to find my dear friend Carole Abbott standing in my living room.

"We are leaving on vacation tomorrow, and I wanted to bring Alex this." She handed me a stuffed animal.

"She's dead," I sobbed.

"I am so sorry," she said, giving me a hug. My friend Joanne, who knew Carole, shared what had happened as I went back into Alex's bedroom.

I was in such shock that I do not recall the moment my husband arrived home. Nor when he entered Alex's room, nor who told him what happened. I don't remember seeing him communicate with Jaime. I don't recall an embrace, nor his own look of shock. I do remember, however, standing next to him as the coroner arrived and when the pediatrician said, "There has to be an autopsy, Mr. and Mrs. Lalinde. It's required when a child dies at home." Photos were taken as if it were a crime scene. At around eleven o'clock, Alex's body was put on the coroner's stretcher and wheeled out of her room, down the hallway, and out our front door. We all stood motionless in disbelief.

A flood of people began to arrive. The department chair, the associate chair, Terri, her husband Rick, and the mother of the little boy who had passed away the month before; then later, the minister and other friends from church. At some point, I retreated into my room.

In late afternoon, the pediatrician came back to the house to check on us. She found me in my bedroom.

"How did this happen? I asked.

She stood at the end of my bed giving a medical explanation of what she believed might have occurred. I could not process the information. Everything I had learned about spina bifida—a lot—was inaccessible to me at that moment. My confused look only meant that she tried again, clearly deeply saddened and upset about what had happened. However responsible the pediatrician's office may or may not have been, it did not matter. My unconscious default pattern to blame myself overrode everything. I began flailing my arms, sobbing, and proclaiming what a terrible mother I was. I didn't say it once and calm down. I went on and on, thrashing myself onto the bed. She stood there looking very perplexed. I don't remember her leaving the room.

Over the coming days, people reached out to offer their sorrow and support. They called, visited, cooked, made phone calls, and brought us food. During the moments in between, we discussed what happened.

"She had a restless night. You got up three or four times to help her," my husband said to me.

"What?! I don't remember getting up. Oh, maybe I did. I can remember one time. I recall Alex telling me that her neck was sore. That she couldn't turn her head. She was on her tummy facing the window."

"You came in a few times, but very quietly, and you didn't turn on the light," Joanne, who had slept in Alex's room, said, I began to recall more details.

"I remember adjusting her pillow and the electric bed, like they did in the hospital. I said to Alex, 'Does that help?' She slightly nodded her head. I remember telling her that I would get someone to help us in the morning. She said, 'Okay, Mom.' "

We would revisit what happened that night again and again, each time remembering a few more details.

Becky, the choir director, and our minister Burt guided most of the funeral preparations. However, when we were asked our opinion on various choices, it was hard to answer. It all felt horribly wrong. Iliana and her husband took us to the cemetery where their daughter was buried. We chose the same cemetery, also a crypt. We couldn't decide what to put on the plaque, so we left that for later. Members of our church owned a funeral home, which seemed suitable for the wake.

Planning the funeral service was most difficult.

"I think you should play the Disabilities and Possibilities segment in the foyer, so people can watch it when they arrive. I can get you a high-quality VHS copy," suggested Chris, Ven's wife and the executive producer of the referenced show, which had aired on our local PBS station for months prior. Alex's twenty-minute segment represented a life well-lived and the triumph of spirit over matter. She was a role model for others. She could swim, dance, sing, and ride a bicycle, she had friends, and she was integrated into regular education. The segment ended with Alex swooping her right arm up into the air with utmost enthusiasm, all while answering the question, "What do you want to be when you grow up?" "I want to be a TEACHER," she proclaimed. Sam, her cat, was sitting on her lap. They had become inseparable. I replied, "Okay, thanks."

The day of the funeral arrived. Flowers overflowed the church, and so did friends and family.

"Paula, we should begin, it is ten past the hour and there are a lot of people waiting," said the minister.

"I want my son to do his reading, and he is not here yet. He left on time with his cousins, but they must have gotten lost."

The minister was concerned but waited while I fumed. Over the years, I had spent hours waiting for my husband, who had taken Jaime with him and their cousins. Why had I agreed that Jaime could go with them? I scolded myself. He arrived a few minutes later. Hundreds of people were seated when we entered the sanctuary. A flutist began exquisitely playing Ave Maria. On cue, our son went up to the podium, climbed up on the stool, and read the twenty-third psalm. He looked frail and strong at the same time, mature in his delivery, but almost like he wasn't totally present. I was thankful we had waited for him.

As we made plans for the memorial service, I had promised our son that if he got too uncomfortable, he could leave. Shortly after he finished his reading, he pointed to the close-by exit door. But I hadn't thought through my promise—where was he going to go? So, he stayed, twitching and wiggling beside me and pointing toward the exit. Roy and Barbara read a beautiful tribute to Alex, and the minister's eulogy was powerful as he told stories that represented Alex's triumph over self-pity. As we were leaving the church, he offered me his written words, saying "I had more to share, but there wasn't enough time. These are yours." I just couldn't receive them. I don't know if I didn't feel worthy enough or if, perhaps, the words were an admission of a reality that I could not yet accept. I so wish I had been able to receive his gift then.

Alex's body was buried in a mausoleum crypt, a few steps away from Iliana's daughter. I rode to the cemetery with out-of-town friends in the church van. Jaime rode with his father and his father's cousins. In the wretched July heat, we sat outside on folding chairs facing the crypt. I was a bit distracted as I was looking for my counselor, Dr. Morgan, who had confirmed earlier that she would be attending, but had gone to the wrong cemetery. The minister read passages from the Bible and talked about children having a special place in heaven. When he sat down, the man came with a ladder needed to reach the crypt's marble panel; his job was to seal it by tightening the four screws. The minister nodded in my direction, indicating it was time to depart. I didn't move. I had to watch her tomb sealed shut. Afterward, I thanked the gentleman on the ladder, feeling grateful that he, unlike those at the hospital, had correctly completed his task. Back in the van, someone said something funny, and we all laughed for a long time. My emotional releases came in many forms.

That afternoon, Dr. Morgan came to my house. We sat in my daughter's room as I began to recount what had happened. She was her perfectly proper self—beautifully dressed in black with a large brim hat. I admired her style. As she left, my mother turned and said, "Cold fish, if you ask me." My mother always felt compelled to tell me what she did not like about the people I befriended. I thought, "Look who is talking." Upon reflection, Dr. Morgan's 'coldness' represented firm boundaries. Something I did not have growing up.

The painful aftermath of the death of a child is incomprehensible. When everyone goes home, you are alone with your tormenting thoughts and feelings. I used my three weeks of vacation I had set aside for Alex's post-surgery recovery to spend time with my son. It was summer. Barbara suggested we all head to the beach. We went to the calm waters at Crandon Park on Key Biscayne, where we plunked down our beach chairs in the water and watched the kids play in the ocean, shouting and laughing. Barbara's daughter, Mary, played with the boys, but we knew she missed her best friend. We were both quiet most of those days at the beach.

As we mourned, our well-meaning friends and family tried to comfort us. Some were more equipped than others to share their condolences. As I listened, I knew which ones saw Alex as disabled and those who saw her as our child. A therapist told me, "She is no longer suffering, she had a lot of hard times ahead of her." My mother-in-law shared that Jaime and I would now have time for our marriage and our son. Alex's exercise therapist felt compelled to share her doctor friend's theory about the cause of Alex's death, "Perhaps they had clipped her bowels during her last surgery, and that invaded the bloodstream, and she died of sepsis." She was last in line at the four-hour wake. I was exhausted and already close to hyperventilating. I quite literally stumbled back to a nearby chair and sat down before I fell over. The idea that my daughter had been suffering and that I had been a neglectful wife and mother was shocking enough news, but oozing bowels into the bloodstream was too much. The most comforting words were spoken by the executive director of the United Cerebral Palsy organization. With a heartfelt steady look, she said the simple words, "You will so miss her." And the assistant chairman of the department of pediatrics stood in our living room shortly after Alex died with a smile on his face and told me, "You are strong and will make it through." He was a man with strong faith; I believe he saw what I was unable to see at that time.

Then there were those who felt compelled or were told to visit me at my home: alone, and in the evening. They were health administrators and practitioners. Their intention was clear by the time they left, i.e., they were there to tell me that I would be selfish and greedy to hold the hospital liable for its actions. Everyone had done the best they could. The hospital was grieving too. I rarely said much, but thought, "Remorse and wrongful death are two different things. Either the hospital did or didn't provide the required standard of care." That question would need to be answered.

For months, I felt a bit wispy and ghost-like, as if I wasn't at home in my body. I was rarely hungry, and when I ate, my stomach hurt. Our son was obviously affected as well. At one point, I was interrogated by a new pediatrician to rule out neglect. In a short period of time, Jaime had fallen off a trampoline, was hit in the eye by a baseball, had a skateboard accident, developed allergies, and had some rounds of colds and flu. On more than one occasion, I demanded x-rays, and once even a brain scan. We were a mess.

As a mother, I was overwrought with guilt. How did I not notice the signs of Alex's malfunctioning shunt? A stiff neck is the most recognizable sign of a malfunctioning shunt. It was the alarm bell I had been trained to recognize. Over the years, we had made many urgent phone calls to the pediatrician's office ruling in or out a malfunctioning shunt. Each time, the pediatrician determined it was the flu, an "off day," or a urinary tract infection that was causing the fever and lethargy. I had relaxed into a shunt that was steadily working. And more than anything, my exhausted mind and body could not compute a medical emergency less than twenty-four hours after discharge. No one else could either.

I wasn't the only one carrying guilt. A while after Alex died, Jaime, then nine years old, made a confession. We had just returned home from his weekly appointment with a counselor. Standing on our front doorstep, about to go in, he tugged at my hand.

"I want to tell you something, mom. You have to promise not to tell anyone else, not even dad."

"What is it, Jaime?"

"You promise not to tell?" he insisted.

"I promise. Unless you are being unsafe, then I have to tell your dad."

"Mom, when Alex was in the hospital and we were watching television, she told me that she was afraid that she was going to die."

"What did you say?"

"I told her that she was going to be okay. She told me not to tell anyone, so I didn't."

Realizing the significance of this for him, I squatted down, gently put my hands on his shoulders, and looked him in the eyes.

"Your sister loved you so much. You both were so close that she could tell you what she was afraid of. That was a big relief to her. You did what you were supposed to do, listen and be her brother."

In his hand was his drawing of our family. All four of us were together. Later the counselor told me that he had built a tall, well-constructed building out of the wooden blocks and then with a big sweep of his hand had knocked it all down. His sadness lay on top of mine. I worried that his life would be ruined by such an early and profound trauma. The little holes in his T-shirts were a measure of his anxiety, as he was sucking and chewing on his shirt collars. I thought summer school would be a healthy distraction for him, but he lasted one day— the day all the children were asked to talk about how their summer was going so far. Jaime couldn't speak. He fought back his tears. He begged me not to make him go back. I didn't.

As I was medicating myself to fall asleep, he was staying awake for hours fretting. Falling asleep had become increasingly difficult. After story time one night, I discovered why. "Mom, I won't go to sleep for a long time, but I am using my mind to help me," he said. He then proceeded to describe his remedy—which was not an ordinary remedy like a teddy bear, night light, prayers, or reading a book until his eyes got tired.

"I imagine I am in a big, long, thick glass tube that can open and close. When I get in, it closes up really, really, tight," he said.

"Well, how do you breathe in there?" I asked.

"There is an air hose that comes into the glass tube, from back here," he said, pointing behind his head. "I don't want anyone to get to my back in the middle of the night."

When I asked what he meant, I discovered that he thought someone had entered Alex's room through her window in the middle of the night and had killed her by stabbing her in the back. "Jaime, let me explain to you how your sister died," I said, realizing how confused he had become. All the images and partial conversations had gotten all jumbled up: Alex's death in the middle of the night, the open wound on her back, her side-hinged casket at the funeral, and our own confusion about the cause of her death.

Our conversation that night, I hoped, gave him clarity and comfort. Soon after, Jaime began to give his father and I body and foot massages, setting up shop in what had been his sister's bedroom. He posted his schedule and fees on the side of Alex's school desk. He also began telling jokes and performing magic tricks. We signed him up for a magic class, and a photo of him juggling appeared in the *Miami Herald* newspaper. Anything to help normalize his life.

If I could have afforded to resign my position at the medical school, I would have. My son needed me at home, and I yearned to be that stay-at-home mom, the one I had originally wanted to be, before Alex and disability. My son's life and mine were interlaced in a new way. My work had lost its luster. If our finances and marriage had been stable and my husband of a more generous nature, I believe I would have. Instead, the need to work was ever more pressing.

CHAPTER

10

Complicated Grief

WITH TREMENDOUS DREAD AND ANTICIPATION, we received the autopsy report. A part of me feared it would read in a large font, *Mother's Fault*. Instead, the word 'Draft' was written on its front cover along with the cause of death: Malformation of the Arnold-Chiari. This is a neurological condition in which the cerebellum (or more specifically the cerebellar tonsils) is descended out of the skull into the spinal area. This condition exists at birth for most children born with myelomeningocele, as it had with Alex. With increased cranial pressure, the risk of the cerebellum collapsing into the brain stem, thereby cutting off the oxygen to the brain, is high. By stating that the cause of death was an already existing condition, the coroner's office was absolving the hospital of neglect. Regardless, I silently carried the blame.

Because of that, who I was as a parent always came up in a negative light as I perseverated in dwelling on 'sleeping through her death,' as I referred to it. I also recalled every misguided interaction ever and replayed them all over and over in my head: the time I read a paragraph she had written and screamed, "You don't even know what you are talking about;" or the time on the way home from school when she'd said, "No mom, I didn't do well. I got an F." I screamed, "What? I am not helping you study any more if you can't do better." In my mind, her school successes were also mine, and we had both failed, even after hours of preparation.

Guilt is such a wretched emotion. It is debilitating, and when not reckoned with, it festers and contaminates everything. In addition, where there is guilt, there is someone who will want to feed it for their own needs and pleasure. The one consumed by guilt is unsuspecting, having placed everyone else on a pedestal. So it went with me.

Upon receipt of the draft coroner's report, I sat on my bed with a medical dictionary, deciphering its meaning. My brain could not make sense of anything in the report. Naively, I thought Alex's former neuro-surgeon, now retired, who had worked at the community hospital and had not been involved in her recent care, could give us an unbiased medical opinion. I called and asked for his fax number and faxed it to him. Soon after, at eight thirty that night, the neurosurgeon called our home. I answered the phone and my husband got on the other line.

"I am very sorry for your loss. This did not need to have resulted in her death," he said. With those words, Alex died all over again. He went on to explain, "The cause of her death was obviously a raging infection throughout her body."

"I only gave her half of her antibiotic that night. I had to grind it up and put it in apple sauce. She didn't swallow all of it," I blurted out.

"I am sorry," he said, "This did not have to have happened. I too lost a daughter. Good night."

While Jaime immediately saw through the deceit, I felt that I had just been given a death sentence. I had killed my own daughter by neglect. Sitting on my bed, I sobbed uncontrollably into my pillow. Alex was dead all over again. Jaime went into the other room. I even-tually fell asleep. Years later, I would come to realize that my misery's cause was not anyone outside of myself, but rather my own guilt. I kept attracting those who would collude with me, confirming my belief that it was indeed my fault. I was a sieve of guilt, as our marriage counselor had once described me. Growing up, it too often felt safer to hold myself responsible for what I witnessed in my household, rather than my siblings or parents, the actual perpetrators, which is how a young child's mind normally works.

Compelled to know the truth, I telephoned Terri in the morn-ing; she offered to come over that evening and review the coroner's report with me. As Jaime had known all along, and as the autopsy had indicated, there were absolutely no signs of an infection. The autopsy described the white and red blood cell counts as being within normal limits. I had just experienced the medical community's ability to lash out at anyone who dared challenge their authority. At that moment, I was too emotionally frail and broken to fully comprehend the neuro-surgeon's level of cruelty. That would take time.

That incident, coupled with the continued lack of a final autopsy report, contributed to Dr. Morgan's suggestion for me to see a psychiatrist. Dr. Rosen diagnosed me with complicated grief, a specific disorder defined by psychiatry. It applies to those who are significantly and functionally impaired by prolonged grief symptoms for at least one month after six months of bereavement. He prescribed Xanax and an antidepressant. "Yes, complicated grief all right," I thought as I left Dr. Rosen's office with my prescriptions.

Due to the nature of my prescriptions, I had monthly appointments with Dr. Rosen. I liked my sessions. He had a different role than Dr. Morgan and gave me good advice.

"How are you doing?" he began.

"I think I will feel better after we get the final autopsy report. It all feels unfinished," I said.

"I assumed that had been resolved," he said, looking concerned.

"We got the draft report shortly after her death but are still waiting for the final," I explained.

He offered to help. "A final report is important. Would you like for me to facilitate the communication with the coroner's office?"

The arranged conference call took place in his office the following week. He took the lead.

"This is Dr. Rosen, Mrs. Lalinde is a patient of mine. She is here with her husband. They are deeply grieving the loss of their daughter. Their daughter's final autopsy report is important to them."

"I am sorry for the delay. We have not completed all the analyses. We suspect that her death was due to her existing Arnold-Chiari malformation," the coroner replied.

"I have the draft report in front of me. That is what it now states. Is that conclusive?" Dr. Rosen asked.

"We haven't completed all the analyses. I can fax you the final report when available."

We hung up and stared at each other. I was thinking this hadn't gotten us anywhere, and I don't think I was alone in wondering if the coroner's office was in cahoots with the hospital. We thanked Dr. Rosen for his time and effort. When the fax arrived months later, the cover page still read 'Draft.'

In January that following year, 1997, five months after Alex's death, I made a decision that had been a long time coming. It was a

Sunday night, and I was out to dinner with Becky, the music minister. She was checking on me the way church leaders do, by simply listening and spending time together. Becky picked me up, and we went to a casual diner in Coral Gables. Our dinner conversation was pleasant and included lots of laughter, as Becky was known for her wit. I shared that I was feeling better and that I had a new project at the university that entailed helping adults with disabilities seek employment, something I had been hoping would happen for Alex. I also shared how my relationship with my husband was worsening. He was rarely home, and I suspected he was having another affair. He resented paying the bills, and I was always broke. Outside of the mortgage and medical insurance, he contributed little, it seemed.

After dinner, while driving back to my house, my criticisms escalated. Sitting in my driveway, I reached for the car door handle.

"Well, what are you going to do about it?" Becky asked. The question fell with a thud. I was so used to complaining that the thought of action was jolting. What was I going to do about it?

"That's a good question," I replied. On the way from her car to the front door, something sparked. Perhaps I was the one who needed to make the decision to call it quits. Could I give myself permission to do that? It felt like I just had.

Jaime was sitting at our dining room table as I walked through the front door. I walked over and leaned in and said, "I think we should divorce." He responded, "I do too."

I was surprised by his simple and quick response and his willingness to agree. He sounded forlorn yet resolved that this was needed. I felt the same. Seventeen years of marriage, many of them debating whether I should stay or leave, all came down to a brief conversation. We didn't discuss it again.

Our attempts to please each other after Alex's death had been short-lived. He was back spending his nights either working at the office or out with the woman he was later to marry. I was back writing grants for Parent to Parent of Miami on my off hours. My saddest moment was watching our son's small-framed body shrink and lean forward as we told him our decision to divorce. In a barely audible voice, he said, "Okay," and he got up and walked back to his room. Neither one of us followed him. We were too grief-stricken. We each found our sad space. Jaime slept in the master bedroom. I slept in my daughter's room.

Once my numbness from Alex's death wore off, it left me with a great urge to scream. I did yell, in my way. I compiled the research from a university course on death and dying I had taken and added my personal experiences in a lecture to a large audience at the medical school entitled, a bit morbidly, "Disability Follows You to the Grave." I wanted practitioners to become aware of how their prejudiced views of people with disabilities are reflected in their language and actions. I spoke about the negative impact of viewing the child as a burden on the family, rather than an integral part of the whole, giving examples of noncomforting words from people who should have known better. I spoke about the destructive power of pity, recounting my son's admission that he didn't like to tell people that he had a sister. Instead, he would say he was an only child just to avoid people's pity. I sensed that people were listening. They wanted to really know and understand how to be supportive to their patients. The next day, I received an email from one of the faculty, "I felt privileged to be there yesterday. I hope everyone else understood the importance of your words." Such kindness, I thought.

My healing was a long process, and it came in many forms. One was particularly mysterious and unexpected. It was in September of 1997. My church broke all customary traditions and invited two spiritual healers, a husband and wife, to hold an evening event at the church. The invited couple were members of the United Methodist Church in Melbourne, Florida. I attended the ceremony with my friend Helen and my mother, who was back in Miami for the winter.

"There are more people here than I thought would come," I said to Helen, leaning toward her.

"I know what you mean," she said. The couple spoke about their spiritual gifts and their ability to transmit light and truth to bring a spirit-guided healing. After their presentation, the wife stood near the altar on the right side of the church while the husband moved to the left side, where we were seated.

"We will now begin. As you feel called, come up to either one of us." Two lines readily formed, and we joined the one on our side of the altar. When it was my turn, I walked up and stood in front of him.

He leaned forward and whispered in my ear, speaking in tongues, an ancient healing practice referred to in the Bible.

"Did you feel anything?" he asked after a minute or so. I replied, "No." He paused as if listening to someone, and told me, "Within fourteen days you will receive a message." It felt ominous. I went home with combined dread and anticipation.

Thirteen days later, I was in the foyer of a church listening to Ven describe how our mutual friend's daughter, Lauren, had died. Lauren and Alex had become friends at the Genie's Workshop, a performing arts group that practiced weekly and then performed in a televised talent show. They both loved participating. Lauren had cerebral palsy, and like Alex's, her neurological condition brought with it the need for an intraventricular shunt. Her mother worked on the medical campus as a mental health counselor, and her father was a nurse practitioner.

Right there standing in the foyer, I learned that Lauren's parents had taken her to the pediatrician's office suspecting her shunt was malfunctioning. Lauren had been vomiting, had migraine headaches, was lethargic, and couldn't hold her head up. Instead of directing them to the emergency room, they were referred to neurology and sent home.

With no response yet from the neurologist, that night, the parents rearranged their three-sectional living room couch to form one big bed. They wanted to keep a watchful eye on their daughter. But despite their vigilance, Lauren died in the ambulance on the way to the hospital. It was around five in the morning, the same approximate time as Alex's death and for the same reason.

That day in the narthex of the church, I felt the ominous message had been delivered. I could only grasp part of its intent at the time, i.e., the understanding that physicians screwed up and that I was to forgive myself. These medically trained parents who I admired had reacted as we had. Obviously, medical advice had the ability to override our own ability to make coherent decisions. There was a subliminal power in the doctor's white coat that needed to be acknowledged. As much as I mourned their loss, I found an inner peace knowing that I was not alone.

Lauren's death, however, stirred questions about life after death. Were these medical signs meant to be missed? Had our children been "called home" in a spiritual sense? Was it their time, perhaps just as had been planned for them? After the funeral, Lauren's mother shared a perplexing story. At Lauren's birthday party earlier that year, her daughter kept insisting on watching the replay of the Genie's Workshop competition. She wasn't interested in watching the entire one-hour program, but rather just the segment where Alex was floor dancing. Watching the video was consuming so much of the birthday celebration that she had to put the video up out of reach, albeit after verbal protests from Lauren. Our lives continued to intersect for several years, with each of us finding comfort in the other's story.

We never did receive a final autopsy report from the coroner's office. However, seven years later, we agreed to an out-of-court medical malpractice lawsuit settlement, for which the neurosurgeon had to pay a portion out of his own pocket. I imagined that the words on the missing report's front cover read, *Mother Not Guilty*. It had become obvious, not only to me, but also to my husband, the malpractice attorney we hired, and the expert witnesses he had deposed that Alex's malfunctioning shunt was the cause of her death. The fluid's inability to drain through the shunt placed increased cranial pressure on her cerebellum. This pressure had collapsed the cerebellum into her brain stem in the middle of the night.

But knowing all that was not enough for me. "What were Alex's last minutes of life like?" I asked. We were in a hotel room in downtown Miami, and the individual being informally deposed was Salomon Hakim, the famous Colombian neurosurgeon who had invented one of the original shunts. Jaime knew his family and had suggested our lawyer contact him. He replied, "She would have been unable to breathe during the last few minutes of life." However painful it was to hear, knowing exactly how she died gave me peace.

CHAPTER

11

Gifts to Heal

THERE IS AN ADAGE THAT tragedy often comes in threes. I wish that had been true for me. After Alex's death, that next year I lost my marriage, my beautiful home in Coral Gables, which was no longer affordable, and our cat, Sam, who had been a constant companion for Alex. In addition, my leadership role in Parent to Parent of Miami waned, as my open wounds made it difficult to be with other families. Our dear neighbors the Helms moved to North Carolina, our minister was transferred to another city, and Terri Urbano became ill.

My initial grief over Alex's death, however, was so immense that at the time, the subsequent losses seemed almost inconsequential. I often described my divorce as being as painful as stubbing my toe. The devastating hurricane had already blown through.

Although it was not always obvious to me, life's gifts of family, creativity, purposefulness, and deep introspection arrived as others left. Knowing that my son Jaime would be there when I woke up made my day worth facing. He was a loving, smart, and sensitive child who needed me. I particularly enjoyed our early mornings. As it was difficult for him to fall asleep, waking up was challenging. When I was at my best, I pretended he was a prince and I was his valet. I invented a funny accent as I helped him dress, while he was still lying on the bed, which always got a big giggle. Many mornings we stopped to have breakfast together before school, and arriving on time became meaningless, as evidenced by the threatening official letter I received toward the school year's end stating that he had been tardy twenty-nine times. I couldn't say no to his skateboarding and rollerblading escapades, either. One night I watched as he skated off the top of a nearby low-lying building. I could tell that he was proud of himself; in the midst of the emotional chaos, he was gaining control over something—his body. I didn't want to take that away from him. Worried about how he was coping with so many losses, I insisted, as did his father, that he see a therapist. I didn't want to be the only overseer of other potential disasters. I no longer felt qualified.

My emotional refuge became our church. The donations from Alex's funeral contributed to the finishing of an elevator to its second floor. I touched the installed plaque with her name on it every time I rode it. At the Sunday service, our minister often referred to Alex as a heroine, an example of how someone can experience so much joy despite her limitations.

I also found comfort at the university. My idea of creating a family resource room was well received by the administration. I wanted families to have pleasant and informative environments during their long waits. Terri and I found just the right space, an oversized, junk-filled closet. Although the department couldn't dedicate the space to my daughter, her presence was felt at the well-attended ribbon cutting ceremony. Wearing one of Alex's headbands in her honor, I delivered a passionate plea for more information and education for families.

That beautiful room left the rest of the Center's 115,000 square feet looking grim. Its 1970s' construction and decor, which included twenty-foot-high dusty beige lobby curtains, had never been updated. The fact that we had a pediatric asthma clinic on that floor hadn't been enough to force change. But now it was time. My interest in the arts was shared by our department chair, Dr. Rodney Howell, who became an avid supporter of what became one of my most meaningful endeavors, a new program called ArtAbilities. I joined forces with the public school's art department to create an annual art competition and award ceremony for children living with a disability. The art teachers were overjoyed that their students were being recognized for the artistic endeavors in which they excelled. So were their parents. The department splurged with valet parking, food, rented equipment, and framing for the artworks. We turned the first and second floors into an art gallery, with the selected artwork placed on easels with a brochure describing the winners. Each student artist received a large Olympic-style medal that I enjoyed putting around their necks. The hundred parents and teachers in attendance enthusiastically clapped for each one. Slowly, the Center's cement walls came alive with colorful images of portraits, animals, and nature. A selection of the hundreds of ArtAbilities art pieces went on display at the Miami International Airport, and a special tactile exhibit was created for people with visual impairments.

My work at the university gave me the opportunity to find meaning in Alex's death. The summer Alex passed away, Jeff Brosco, a recently board-certified pediatrician, came to work at the Mailman Center. He had a doctoral degree in history and was interested in the history of children with developmental disabilities. I formed a bridge for him to be able to reach and understand families, and he integrated my work into the medical school through a ten-hour curriculum I developed and taught to pediatric residents. The 'Understanding A Family's Perspective' curriculum included disability public policy, grief and loss, and how to deliver diagnostic news. A collaborative, qualitative study on the curriculum's effect on pediatric residents was published in a peer-reviewed journal. By sharing myself with others, I slowly healed.

My work with Dr. Morgan transitioned from cognitive therapy into psychoanalysis. Gratefully, my brother paid for the first year. For forty-five minutes, four times a week for five years, I lay semi-reclined on Dr. Morgan's off-white linen couch in an office building in South Miami. The emotional upheavals of grief and my subsequent losses gave me the opportunity to radically change my perceptions of myself. As with my other endeavors, I put my full self into the effort. The process lent itself to deep inner exploration, allowing my unconscious thoughts to surface, shining the light of awareness upon forbidden memories and inner secrets. Reliving my childhood experiences now as an adult lessened their grip. It also made shifts in my thought and behavioral patterns as I became aware of my almost complete inability to sustain a positive thought. Even in my dreams, success met with heartbreaking failure. Ultimate disappointment in everything I did or said was hardwired into my brain. Now aware of the thought pattern, I began to intervene on my own behalf.

Dr. Morgan's brief comments would often create big aha moments that would give me a framework within which to understand clusters of behaviors, such as when she observed, "Your mother was more able to nurture you in infancy than able to support your independence, which begins around age three. She couldn't offer you something she was unable to do for herself." I recalled then and later the many uncontrollable sobs with my empathetic mother. When things went wrong, she was there; like when we went to see the movie *Born on the Fourth of July* starring Tom Cruise. As we walked out of the theater, I began to weep hysterically, saying, "That is exactly how I feel," referring to the heartbreaking betrayal the protagonist felt after being paralyzed on duty during the Vietnam War and coming home to a country of false promises. We circled The Falls shopping center several times before I felt calmer. Although my sobs were about the deplorable forms of discrimination against people with disabilities, under the surface laid the false promise of the happily ever after marriage, of beautiful and gifted children, and the shining Prince and his Castle. Even deeper was the false promise of a loving and supportive family, as portrayed in the *Leave it to Beaver* television show aired weekly during my childhood. We lived in a country that was ignorant of the hardships of most of its citizens, I thought. Instead, we were gripped by the illusions created through pomp and circumstance using symbols of freedom, justice, and fairness. Fairy tales, embedded deeply in our psyche, were creating unconscious expectations, leaving us unprepared or unwilling to see the realities of our own and each other's lives.

Dr. Morgan's observation, "Supporting your independence was more difficult," helped me understand my mother's difficulty in supporting my success and why our family conversations and humor focused on each other's blunders and disappointments. These were unconscious interplays used to create a dependency; not to wander too far from home—emotionally. It left me vulnerable to future bosses and group leaders who held their positions of power using the same ploys. Once the bubble of illusion burst, I withdrew, only to later find another bubble, until I finally could easily discern what was fake—when people were espousing one thing and doing another. I no longer entered those bubbles.

Through my work with Dr. Morgan, I also came to understand the roots of my "Pollyanna" personality and its significant impact on my life. When I was very young, I donned a protective blindfold, a way of distorting reality in order not to fully absorb the impact of the dysfunction surrounding me.

My mother was hot-tempered and moody. Her dislike for housework, and she was burdened with most of it, meant that you didn't want to get on her wrong side while she was doing it. My brother was mischievous and cunning, someone who enjoyed other people getting into trouble, including me. "Mom, Paula called her cousin fatty," referring to a blurted-out comment to my cousin when I didn't win the card game that we were all playing downstairs in our rec room. "Tell her to get up here right now," my mother said. Unfortunately, my mother was washing dishes, so she was in a foul mood. "Take down your pants. That was a mean thing to do." Scared and confused, I knew things would get worst if I didn't. I pulled down my pants, an extremely humiliating thing for a ten-year-old. After many hits, lying across her knee, with her wet hands on my bare bottom, "You go tell her you are sorry." When I got back downstairs. my brother had a mischievous gleeful look, a look I knew well. I said I was sorry to my cousin, who was confused by all the hubbub. How to avoid punishment and ridicule was unclear. What was safe to say when was a complex formula. I slowly withdrew from my own thoughts and feelings, burying them deep inside.

Rediscovering what I had buried was an arduous process. Although I would go on to learn more efficient and life-giving modalities, I deeply benefited from the process of psychoanalysis. Perhaps foremost was the ability to share my thoughts and feelings without suffering any repercussions. Years later, while going through an exhibit at Sequoia National Park with my son, I saw my healing process mirrored back to me through the exhibit about forest fires. I was surprised to learn they occur naturally and are a necessary part of a healthy ecosystem—a sort of sacrifice unto itself. A fire removes the low-growing underbrush and opens the forest to sunlight. The reduction in forest floor growth results in more moisture reaching the soil's surface. I learned that the organic material that is left behind feeds the soil and that the fire activates new growth in those plants that have smoke- or heat-activated seeds and buds, bursting them open to scatter and reseed the forest. Yes, I, too, benefited from the fires by consciously choosing to excavate those dark repressed levels, pulling my own inner weeds, and planting new seeds. By the year 2000, my inner work was bearing fruit, creating new stability in my life. The first was a new home.

On July 5, 2000, the four-year anniversary of my daughter's death, my landlord knocked on my door.

"I won't be renewing your lease. I am getting married, and my mother will be moving into this apartment. I own other properties, so you can just rent one of those."

"I will let you know," I said, "Two months is not much time. I actually have been thinking about buying a house." He scoffed, and his spit almost landed on my face.

"That's so unrealistic. I can show you the two apartments I have. They are more expensive, but that's the way it is." Now more determined than ever, I decided to ask my father to help me with the down payment, remembering the voice of my high school guidance counselor when I was feeling too poor to afford college, "You know that your father would really do anything for you, don't you?" she had said. Most of the time, I didn't feel that, but it rang true for me in my moment of need.

My father hemmed and hawed a bit, but in the end, he said yes. Other family members were as shocked as I was. He was notoriously tight with his money. His seemingly eternally long reaching to pull out a dollar from his billfold could be described by anyone who knew him well. Throughout our elementary school years, my brother and I witnessed his antics every week as we asked him for lunch money. "How much is it?" he would ask, and then with a look of hardship, he'd count out the difficult to grasp dimes, nickels, and pennies from his billfold.

With the hope of a real home of my own, I plotted out my desired geographic area in North Gables. Sunday after church, I took Jaime, who was now twelve, and drove by a cute yellow home with a For Sale by Owner sign in the front yard. Taking a chance, I knocked on the front door.

"I happened to see your For Sale sign. Any chance we could take a look?" I said, standing on the front step.

"Well, I guess you can. I was actually waiting for someone, but they didn't show up," she said with a slight laugh.

"I love these 1930s vintage homes. Your wooden floors are so shiny, and in good shape. We actually need only two bedrooms, so this works perfectly," I said. Jaime was quiet the whole time. Years later, he explained that he had felt the house was too good for us and it wasn't going to be possible. He didn't want to get his hopes up for anything nice. Losing his sister and his parents' divorce all in one year had a measurable effect on my little guy.

Now seated in her living room, I asked, "I am curious: Why you are selling your home?"

"I'm getting married, and we'll be living in his home."

"I am very interested. I will get back with you soon."

That night, I called her back with an offer, which she accepted. Two weeks before the closing, however, she called to ask if by chance I wanted to back out of the contract. I empathized with her predicament. She had broken off her engagement and thus did not need to sell her house after all. I did not hesitate in letting her know that I wanted to proceed with the purchase, which we did. Later, I discovered that my old landlord hadn't married, either. Were people's lives shuffled around to make owning this lovely home possible? This cute little house gave Jaime and I a new sense of safety and security.

The exchange of money between my father and I had a ripple effect beyond making it possible for me to purchase a home. I at last felt protected by my family—a welcoming back into the tribe that I had left when I married. Having equated money and attention with love, I felt worthy. Owning our own home was good for us. We were close to the church, Jaime's school, and my work. We returned to a predictable routine feeling like we had a real home.

With a real kitchen, I started to plan our meals better and enjoyed cooking more. I became known among Jaime's friends for my well-received home-cooked breakfast of French toast, pancakes, and scrambled eggs. He and his friends also made good use of our empty garage just as a place to hang out. Jaime got interested in graffiti, and several friends would join him in creating symbols and images on the inner walls of the garage with cans of spray paint. He read and talked about the different graffiti artists springing up in Miami. They were his heroes at the time, which gave me something else to worry about.

"Thanks, Mom!" he said, with an expression of shock and appreciation, as he came home to his already set-up new bedroom furniture. The double bed, dresser, side tables, and mirror were all in a beautifully rich brown stained heavy oak. It was what was needed for a fast-growing teenage boy. I was proud of myself for doing it and was amazed at how much it meant to him. So much attention had gone to Alex and still did through my grief that my love and attention for him I think often went unexpressed, to the point that several years later, Jaime's

psychologist said to me in a raised voice, "You have to stop this," referring to my tears about Alex's death.

My folks liked Jaime's new digs, too, when they came to visit that
year. "Yup, it is a nice house, Paula, it should be good for you here," my
dad said. I believe he thought my house was a good purchase, and as he
had been raised in the Methodist church, he liked that we lived close
to our church; he liked going to church with us. My personal qualities and achievements were appreciated by my father. Mostly, those
same qualities were irritants to my mother and brother. When I shared
that family contrast with Dr. Morgan, she theorized, "Perhaps they
were envious." Facing that reality as a child must have been scary. As
I peeled off my Pollyanna lens, I could more easily identify not only
their envy but also other people's—which made life easier, I stopped
owning other people's stuff.

CHAPTER

12

Something New

"YOU KNOW, JAIME, WITH MY faculty position, you can go to University of Miami tuition free," I tried to persuade my son.

"Mom, there is no way I am staying in Miami. I want to get as far away as possible," he said. It was hard not to take it personally, but I knew my hovering and worrying had worn thin. Mostly, though, it had to do with his aspirations; staying in Miami for college as most other Hispanic high school students did looked like a dead end to him. He began his freshman year at Florida State University. Ironically, at that time, I was the one attending the University of Miami, having been accepted into a doctoral degree program in special education.

Dr. Batya Elbaum was the perfect faculty advisor. She was focused, driven, intelligent, and no-nonsense. I had met her during a presentation I made to the advisory board of a US Department of Education Project of National Significance funded through Louisiana State University. The project entailed measuring parents' perceptions of their child's special education services. As that project expanded, there was a need for a content specialist in IDEA Part C family-centered care services. I was invited to join the team. The results of that project were the foundation of my doctoral thesis, and what grew from that would inform the rest of my life.

Dr. Elbaum became a colleague and friend. Her love for running was contagious, and I decided to try it. Between her inspiration, a holiday gift of an iPod, and the music of the Beatles, running became my most healing endeavor. The iPod was a Christmas gift that year from Jaime. It was the original: It was white, long, thin, and came with a matching carrying cord that went around my neck. When I asked Jaime to load some tunes on it, he included a number of songs by the Beatles. The rhythm of "She Loves You" slowed down my running pace significantly, which meant I could run beyond my usual limit of a couple of blocks. With a love of dance but no steady dance partner, I instead pounded out the beats of songs onto the pavement. My legs glided while my hips and arms swayed to the music, which were often love songs that I silently sang to Alex. This powerful alchemical combination became a daily essential for a long time—and eventually evolved into my Moved to Learn program for children and teens with disabilities.

On April 17, 2006, I lay on Dr. Morgan's off-white linen couch for the last time. I wish I could say that I had actively chosen to end my analysis; in actuality, however, Dr. Morgan was moving to Tennessee. I had mixed feelings. I enjoyed the fact that I was done, which implied the illusion of being healed and whole, but it was hard to imagine my life without her. Her stillness had become a mirror for me to receive my own answers. On that last day, my voice was halting as tears rolled down my cheeks.

"You have been like my mother, father, brother, daughter, son, husband—everyone to me. But mostly, you helped me to survive my daughter's death and find my way through my messy inner world," I said. As usual, she just listened.

"I feel like I am me, again," I continued.

"Yes, but without your shackles and self-restraints." So it was. I no longer felt my hands were tied behind my back, and layers of self-deception had been removed. I was also much freer to choose life-affirming thoughts and actions. We had never hugged or even shaken each other's hand over all those years. That day was no different. She leaned in as I said goodbye; she was perhaps ready to receive a hug, but I wasn't prepared for the moment. I felt a bit forlorn as I walked back into that long hallway for the last time.

By August of that year, I was depressed and physically unwell. I had joint pain, headaches, and chest pain, and on many days, I struggled to get out of bed. At the height of this misery and mental distractibility, I ended up literally driving my new BMW convertible into my house. One morning when I was already late for work, I realized that I had forgotten my briefcase after I'd left for work and driven one block. Pulling back into my driveway, I hurriedly opened the door and began to get out of my car without remembering to first turn it off. With my feet off the brake and clutch, the car leaped forward, half dragging me with it. I struggled to find the right pedal and, in a frenzy, unwittingly slammed my foot onto the gas pedal. The car lurched forward then suddenly stopped as it hit the front of the house—imploding the back-seat safety headrests and incurring great expense. But I retrieved my briefcase and drove to work as if nothing had happened. My son couldn't believe what I had done to my new car.

There I was, no longer on the couch releasing all my mental yuckiness every day. Nor was I on the couch preparing for a far distant future. My future had arrived, and now that it was here, my body was letting me know it wasn't happy. Feeling miserable, I scheduled an appointment with Dr. Hutson, my primary care physician. I was in so much pain and distress, I was convinced I had cancer. Was my path going to be the same as my Aunt Babe's, the one who'd had two children born with spina bifida? She had died of pancreatic cancer six months after her diagnosis. Dr. Hutson listened to my complaints about my aches and pains.

"We will rule out cancer and everything else today. You are not dying. Your health issues may be related to how you are feeling about yourself over there," she said, nodding in the direction of the medical school. She took her pen and on a prescription pad, jotted down a web address: thesecret.com. She also suggested I watch the new movie with the same name.

As I left her office, I muttered dark words under my breath. I was genuinely angry that I wasn't dying. I was pissed that I had more internal work to do—more yucky internal stuff to clear. Wasn't I finished by now? I had secretly hoped that psychoanalysis and my doctoral degree would help me feel better about myself and my work at the medical school. I had accomplished so much that I felt I "ought" to be happy, but I wasn't. I so wished things were different. A larger life was pulling me forward, and I was holding on to the shoreline.

During my years of analysis, I successfully removed layers of protective blinders, which meant I could see things more as they were rather than as I would like them to be. I had been deceiving myself and needed to admit that I was unhappy at work. The department had been restructured, in part due to the medical school's changing income streams. This had created a growing divide between our original mission to support children with disabilities and their families and our current efforts. I, too, felt further and further away from my original mission as a voice for a family perspective. I had acquired a lot of administrative responsibilities. My creative juices had dried up.

Although we had redecorated the Mailman Center's physical environment, transforming its inner workings proved a more difficult task. Everyone was doing exactly what they had been trained to do, and they did it exceptionally well. Diagnosing disease, illness, rare disorders, and complex learning disabilities requires years of training and experience. However, a treatment modality based primarily on what is perceived as broken had severe limitations. I felt that I had accomplished everything I had come there to do.

I gifted myself my resignation, and immediately my aches and pains went away. In order to be able to afford my new life, I put my house up for sale; it sold for the asking price, the night before my last day at the university. I gave away most of my belongings to a grateful Haitian immigrant father of a child with a disability. My brother Jeff made me an offer: He would buy me a condo in downtown Chicago next to his but keep it in his name. This helped me to more confidently take the financial risk of quitting my position. The condo never materialized, but his lovely home in Costa Rica was available. I came and went from there.

Buying me a condo was not my brother's first offer of financial assistance—of a sort. He had made me a proposal shortly after Alex died. "I just bought the largest dairy farm east of the Mississippi. I think you are the best person to help me manage it," he said in 1997. The farm was in Wisconsin, one hour from where my folks lived. I was honored to be considered, and leaving Miami seemed inviting. I talked to Jaime about it, and he loved the idea of living on a farm as I had when my brother and I were young. In the end, my mother helped me to realize that I could move up there only to have my brother pull the rug out from under me if things didn't go his way.

A few years later in 2001, he needed help buying, furnishing, and decorating a vacation home in Costa Rica. I was dating someone at the time who helped identify both a realtor and a promising location: Escazu, a suburb of San Jose, the capital city. Doing things with Jeff always brought some unexpected excitement. There was always something wonky, like the time at the airport before we boarded the airplane when he handed me $30,000 in cash and asked me to put it in my pocket. He had twice that in his. As I was barely managing able to pay my bills, the cash was a lure. Purchasing furniture, linens, china, and silver for a divine 15,000-square-foot home overlooking the city was an extremely fun creative endeavor. It included traveling to Guatemala City to purchase seventeenth century antiques. Whatever we liked, he bought. We kept spending and spending; a fantasy come true.

Along the way, I agreed to leave my position at the university and move to Costa Rica to manage the property, including the live-in staff, which was the best part. The house was my dream house, and having my brother as my manager felt familiar. With so much loss, I reverted, returning to childhood patterns and fantasies. Being in a sort of servitude to my brother in exchange for the illusion of being taken care of was one of those patterns. It was so compelling. But dissolving that pattern would soon become painfully necessary.

Jeff's first divorce happened shortly after Jaime and I had gotten married. My brother lost his beautiful home as part of the divorce agreement and moved into a small apartment in Rockford. It was there we visited him; he looked depressed and forlorn and was drinking to ease the pain. That night I cried, at times uncontrollably, with a strong sense that I wouldn't have gotten married if he hadn't. I felt trapped and unable to talk about it, perhaps in the same way my mother had. "You were a little upset last night," Jeff said acknowledging my swollen eyes and face. Unable to express my sadness, I simply said, "I had a bad night." Jaime just looked confused.

Here I was decades later with the opportunity to manage Jeff's home in Costa Rica. I found it hard to say no. What I did was I put off the decision. When it was time to sign the university contract renewing my job, I signed it. I managed Jeff's property from Miami and traveled there as often as possible. In exchange for my help, my brother paid for my first year of psychoanalysis, no small amount. I took several vacations there with my son that included zip-lining, scuba diving, and surfing. One of the trips included two of Jaime's best friends. I felt a tad like Mother Mary with Evita Peron's budget on those occasions. I was in my element.

In May of 2007, I went to a Mastermind gathering in Miami, a group event that was also attended by my longtime friend Helen. She loved everything spiritual and metaphysical. She had joined the group a few years back and was hosting that month's meeting at her house. Their meetings were grounded in the concept of manifestation, the ability to create what one desires through focused attention and faith. I had no clue what they were talking about most of the time. At the end of the evening, they huddled together and chanted, "Money, money, money," while jumping up and down. The money chants were off-putting, and I found that this Mastermind group was certainly not for me—but I did learn something valuable.

I was only half-listening to an announcement of a medium coming to South Florida until I heard the leader say that this medium would start seeing clients on July 5. My body came to full alert—a fire alarm went off, as it always did upon hearing that date.

"Who is this person?" I asked.

"His name is Bert Farr. He has a master's degree from West Georgia College in Humanistic and Transpersonal Psychology, where I got my doctoral degree. He has had psychic abilities since childhood. Now he helps people communicate with their deceased loved ones." Although the details were relevant, they weren't necessary. Once I heard the date, I knew I would see him. I asked her to save me the first appointment. A most precious gift had just landed at my feet. I was going to get to talk to Alex.

CHAPTER

13

Meeting the Wizard

LONG BEFORE ALEX, EVEN BEFORE my marriage, I lived for a time in Cuatla, Morelos, Mexico. It was 1973, and I wanted to observe a small-town celebration and ceremony for the Day of the Dead. On November 1, I boarded a public bus, one of those that only costs a few pennies and you pray to arrive at your destination before the bus gives way and breaks down. I sat next to a *mestizo* woman, a term used to describe a person of mixed European and indigenous ancestry. She had long black shiny braids and a black and white woven *rebozo* (shawl) wrapped around her head and shoulders. I had the window seat. We didn't speak. Two hours later, I arrived at Totolapan, a small mountainous village about two hours north of Cuatla. With my father's brown eight-millimeter camera slung over my shoulder, I walked from the bus station to the village cemetery. Along the way, I fell in step with villagers walking the same way. The women carried baskets full of marigold flowers and *la comida* (lunch) as they walked through the cemetery gate. No one seemed to take any notice of me. I felt invisible. As I came to the gate, I witnessed just beyond it a beautiful tradition of venerating one's ancestors.

The women sitting at various graves in the cemetery removed each marigold flower from their baskets and slowly and methodically pulled off the flowers' petals. Each petal was placed next to the last one on top of the family graves. After a short time, each grave was blanketed with the orange petals, majestic in their beauty and simplicity. The children ran and played with ease, returning to the family graveside for *la comida*. I learned that a special plate of food had been left in each home on the family's altar for the ancestors. An Indian woman explained that the food might still be there in the morning, but not its essence. I had no idea what that meant in those days, though it makes perfect sense to me now.

When I inquired about the returning ancestors, the Indian woman explained. "Sometimes we can see their spirits wandering in and out of the houses. The food is usually still there but something has gone."

A few hours later, I boarded the bus again and safely made my way back to Cuatla, where I was living. Although I wrote about the Day of the Dead as a folkloric tradition, the mystery behind wandering spirits and food essences remained with me. Our human need and desire to commune with our deceased loved ones, and perhaps their need to communicate with us, whether for emotional resolution or information and guidance, has led not only to ceremonies and traditions but also practices and tools.

Now, decades later, my curiosity about wandering spirits could not have been more personal. I wanted to know what happens when we die, and reading about life after death was not going to be enough. I would not find my daughter in the pages of a book. Instead, I had my upcoming July 5 appointment with a medium. I felt anxious but ready.

The Fourth of July that year was like most others, i.e., I did not feel very well, went to a party, and didn't stay long. On my way home, I got stuck in bumper-to-bumper traffic on the causeway. As I was inching along behind hundreds of people trying to get to South Beach to watch the fireworks, my car began jerking and shaking. The clutch suddenly had no resistance, and my car came to a halt. Two men jumped out of their cars to push mine over to the shoulder.

My insurance company ordered a tow truck, but the driver soon let me know that due to the holiday, he would be delayed. I put the top down on my convertible and watched the fireworks from the causeway. Two hours later, I climbed into the cab of the tow truck, where I sat next to the driver's girlfriend. The parallel between my car's breakdown and my daughter's life systems shutting down eleven years before was not lost on me.

Undeterred by the car problem, the next day I woke up early and finagled a ride to the car rental location two miles away. By nine o'clock, I was en route to see Bert Farr, the transpersonal psychologist and medium. I was nervous and smoked a cigarette on the way. I had taken up smoking again two years earlier, on the day after my son Jaime left for college. I had gone into his room to look for a pencil,

but instead I found an almost empty pack of extra-long Capri cigarettes, a girlfriend's, no doubt. The one remaining cigarette looked
so appealing. I hadn't smoked in twenty-five years, and I figured one
couldn't hurt. The first two puffs gave me a headache, and I felt nauseous immediately. I swore I wouldn't have another.

But there I was, two years later, fifty-four years old, blowing cigarette smoke out the window of the rental car as I was on my way to meet
with a medium. A tall, kind-looking man with wispy white hair greeted
me at the door. He invited me in and asked me if I would like to have a
cup of tea. We sat across from each other at a small kitchen table.

"I resigned my faculty position at the medical school and have
no job," I said. "I have no idea what I'm going to be doing. I am living
in a furnished three-hundred square foot apartment with a few things
in storage. I gave everything else away a while back. But I don't have
any questions about all that. I'm here to commune with my daughter."

I had never used the word commune before in my entire life. I
wasn't even sure what it meant.

"Oh, yes. I know that. She's been here waiting for you," Bert said.

The session could have ended right then, and I would still have
left satisfied with the knowledge that my daughter wanted to be with
me. The remnants of my hidden fears that Alex was upset and disappointed with me lifted. I realized the scathing voice I feared was my
own, not hers. It had always been my voice. My deep-rooted pattern of
directing blame to myself for whatever happened was still there, despite
all those years of therapy. Alex was not angry with me.

"I got confused when I saw you drive up because your daughter
has dark skin and you are so light."

I explained that her father was from Colombia. When Alex was
in the sun for very long, she would turn a stunning bronze color.

"Must be sunny wherever she is," Bert said with a smile; "She's
got a tan."

He was joking, but it stirred up a real question. Where is she? The
thought flew in and out of my mind as the medium continued.

"She's appearing like the Indian woman, Pocahontas."

My mind caught onto the word "Pocahontas." The last time I'd
heard that name uttered was from Alex's elementary school principal.
My daughter was the only child in her class of six hundred students
who gave the principal a Valentine's Day card. The image on her card

was of Pocahontas, and the principal did indeed look like her. At the memorial service at Alex's school, the principal had shared that story. Questions were popping up left and right in my mind, but I didn't want to interrupt his flow. My questions would have to wait.

"Your brother is also here," Bert said. I had a younger brother named Jim who had died in a motorcycle accident on Thanksgiving Day in 2001. Bert said my brother was laughing at me for smoking, which sounded like Jim. My grandmothers were also there to say hello. One grandmother loved me very much and said so. My paternal grandfather, who had died when I was three years old, was there too. He said he is always with me, especially when I run on the beach. He asked me to imagine him with me the next time I went running.

How could he run with me on the beach? How would I connect with him? I believed what Bert was saying, and yet I couldn't process it. I was so young when my grandfather died—why would he still care?

Then Bert said, "Alex is always near you, and you will be able to sense her presence yourself before too long." When I asked about her death, Bert said, "It was her time to go."

According to him, for most of the session, she stood behind me. How could he see her? I wanted to be able to see her, touch her, talk directly with her. In those days, her memory came mostly in the form of sadness, a sensation of something missing, an ache in my heart. As he ended the session, he told me that Alex blew me a kiss and handed me a white carnation, telling me how much she loved me. My hour was up.

I left and walked to the nearby beach. I smoked to temper my bubbling emotions. It was a cloudy, humid day. I thought it might rain and I almost turned back, but I needed some reflection time to integrate what had just happened. As I plodded along the ocean sands, I felt heavy. My mind whirled with questions and renewed curiosity about death, afterlife, and love connections that exist beyond this physical realm. The imagery of Pocahontas, carnations, and uninvited family members confused me. I realized that I had assumed it would only be verbal messages—I didn't expect him to be able to see her. So much mystery. Regardless of all the unknowns, the experience settled into my heart as a reality. I had found my daughter. I felt a great sense of relief.

My next appointment with Bert was a week later. It occurred to me to ask about Alex's cat, Sam. I now suspected that Alex was the reason for Sam's disappearance. On the night Jaime and I had moved into our apartment after my divorce, Sam had meowed loudly for hours, and in desperation, I had finally let her out the back door. I can still see her shocked look as she walked away. I was exhausted and just assumed she'd be there in the morning—she had always been an indoor-outdoor cat. But in the morning, she was gone.

When I asked Bert about Sam, he was silent. I started feeling uncertain and wondered if I hadn't given him enough information. I added, "Just to let you know, Sam was Alex's cat."

He said, "Oh yes, I know that. But I keep hearing 'Over the Rainbow,' and it's distracting."

He paused. "Oh, there's Sam. She's Toto, and she's in the basket. Alex is riding the bike. She's Dorothy. Your son is the Tin Man. His heart was broken."

He continued with each Oz character. The Scarecrow turned out to be a man I was dating, and the Lion was my friend Susan. After he described all the characters, I wondered where I was in the story. I felt a bit diminished and unimportant. But before I could ask about it, Bert said, "Alex wants you to know you are the Wizard."

I perked up. I wasn't sure what that meant but felt honored to be such an important character in the story, a fitting role for the mother.

"And remember, Mom, the Wizard is fake."

My moment of elation came crashing down. What did she mean? Was I fake? Was my love for her fake? I felt judged, as if my worst fears were coming true. My daughter was revealing my hidden frustrations and anger about the taxing role of motherhood—the internal "Why Me?" voice that had come into existence at her birth and had never completely left. I had wrestled with those feelings for years in my sessions with Dr. Morgan. I just could not accept them as a normal part of motherhood and being human. I believed that to be worthy—of love, of being seen as a good person and a good mother—meant having only pure and loving thoughts. The part of me that I couldn't accept, my shadow self, raised its head as I pretended to know what "the Wizard is fake" meant.

My quest for the meaning of those four words led me to this understanding. The true Wizard does not reside outside of self. He/she lives within—in our divine spark, our eternal connection with Spirit, the magical forces of our innate nature. The Wizard takes us back Home toward Self. Returning Home is an adventure into the unknown. My adventure was about to begin.

CHAPTER

14

Crossing New Thresholds

M Y SESSIONS WITH BERT WERE life altering. I had the unique opportunity to hear my daughter's side of the story—how she experienced our relationship. It fed my curiosity, and I dug into the research on life after death. I read about near-death experiences as documented by Dr. Raymond Moody. Dr. Brian Weiss's clinical reports of the past life experiences of his patients while under hypnosis were fascinating, so much so that I attended one of his retreats. Dr. Alan Botkin's discovery of an extended EMDR technique that facilitated communication with the departed also validated my experience with Bert. I learned unequivocally that communication with one's departed loved one results in less grief and sorrow, hopefulness, and feeling happier. I found myself in their research findings.

"Alex is on roller blades, moving gleefully with her arms swinging at her sides. She is a young woman with long flowing hair," Bert said at the beginning of a phone session. Alex always begged me to let her hair grow long. "She wants you to know that she is always with you and loves you very much."

I called Bert often with questions and for guidance. It was hard to get my head around the fact that Alex was still so much alive. I asked, "Is she always with Jaime too?"

"She loves to play tricks on him—move his stuff around a bit and then watch him try to find it."

"I lost another pair of earrings, maybe it was her," I said half-kiddingly. Bert and I laughed.

"Paula, Alex wants you to know that she chose to die when she did. In fact, she was going to die the year before but says that her brother was not prepared yet, so she decided to wait. Her life was difficult." Hearing that her life was difficult pierced my heart, but then, how couldn't it have been. Bert went on, "Alex wants you to re-remember that you both agreed to your lives being together in this way. She chose you as her parent. And you agreed." I felt honored to have been chosen and realized we were not victims, neither one of us.

Bert became a mentor to me. Our long conversations shaped my current views on life and death. I learned that each lifetime comes with a blueprint, one we ourselves create based on what we want to achieve in that lifetime. Some parts of the blueprint we can alter and some not. I now understood that having a child with a disability, along with a child's death, may at times be a fixed piece of the architecture. Alex's birth and death were planned occurrences that brought the deepest sorrow, as well as the opportunity to grow and expand in ways that would have been otherwise unattainable. With time, I saw how the very nature of Alex's death was in perfect alignment with my darkest self-torments. To fully live life, I would have to choose to resolve them.

The timing of my encounter with the mystic was no accident. I was uprooted, having sold my home and resigned my position at the medical school. My personal finances were flush for the first time in my life. Jaime was away at college, and Dr. Morgan had moved to Tennessee. Most importantly, I was soon to complete my doctoral degree in March of 2008. However, it was in special education, a field of study I was no longer interested in teaching.

I was now intrigued by a whole new set of questions and had the skills, time, and flexibility to investigate. Who am I? Where do we go when we die? What's the meaning of "the Wizard is fake"? Where do I fit in the world? On the left side of my Murphy bed were the books and professional articles for my doctoral program. On the right side were a growing pile of books on life after death and past lives, which I read eagerly. My quest for answers opened doors that I had never known existed. The river was carrying me forward to where I needed to go, and I went along with great enthusiasm. I wanted to feel worthwhile, find purpose and meaning in life again, and continue experiencing the connection with Alex.

It was my strong desire to have my own direct experience with Alex that led to an unanticipated moment. It took place in my small condo on South Beach. The condo was on the top floor of a five-story art deco building. My only window faced east, and with a stretch of my neck, I could see the Atlantic Ocean. I had gutted and redesigned it to my liking. I made a beautiful nest. My Murphy bed and built-in shelves were all of the same dark brown material, and a marble floor and the serpentine-granite elongated windowsill gave it a feeling of permanence that I needed. I had carefully chosen the ceiling light, a small square chandelier with petal-shaped crystals that became a multicolored spectrum in the morning light.

Jaime was visiting from college. He was not quite so enamored with my new living quarters and lifestyle as I was. My resignation from my longtime position at the medical school, my having sold our home, and my distribution of our material goods was unsettling and confusing for him. His most frequent question regarding all my changes was a simple but profound one: Why? It would have helped if I had been able to come up with a simple and logical response. But too often I began to ramble about my latest synchronistic experience and deliver recitations from my latest reads on past lives, near-death experiences, and Edgar Cayce's healings. I mostly ignored the questions he asked about the progress of my dissertation.

It was eleven o'clock, the hour when the morning is turning to mid-day. My sofa was reassembled, and the Murphy bed had been closed back into its frame, making room for a breakfast chat between Jaime and me. As we were talking, something caught my eye. I glanced up toward the ceiling and could see a white swirling substance surrounding the crystal chandelier. My eyes flashed from the milky white substance to Jaime and back. I was convinced that we both could see it, that we both felt how profound the moment was. My heartbeat quickened as I reached for a chair to climb on, to be a bit closer to what I felt was Alex.

As I was positioning the chair underneath the chandelier, I smelled something. I noticed that the white swirly substance was thickening and seemed a bit darker than seconds before. Simultaneously, Jaime and I noticed a trail of what appeared to be smoke emanating from the Murphy bed. In a flash, I lurched forward and yanked down the Murphy bed. Jaime was amused as I ran to the kitchen for a container of water. I had left the halogen reading lights that I had installed on the upper frame of the Murphy bed on, and my favorite green cotton sheets were on fire. My desire to see my daughter in the form of spirit quite literally went up in smoke that day. But my day would come. When I was ready.

One evening in summer, 2008, I was having dinner at a restaurant on Brickell Avenue in Miami with my old friend Olga, another banker's wife, who I hadn't seen in ten years.

"Getting divorced was hell, but I am glad I did and that it is behind me," she began. We knew each other as wives of bankers and had divorced at about the same time, for similar reasons. Much had changed since then.

"Mine felt more like stubbing my toe; when you are already broken, you can't feel much, I said.

"I healed a lot on my trip to India and by studying a spiritual system called the Akashic Records," she shared. It sounded mysterious, and my interest was immediately piqued. My appetite for all things spiritual was voracious.

"Is it similar to what mediums are able to do?" I inquired, telling her about Bert and reconnecting with Alex.

"The Akasha makes all that possible. I will put together a training and invite you, if you are interested," she said. I was definitely interested.

Over a few glasses of white wine, we shared our dating escapades and other woes and called it a night. Three short weeks later, I was sitting in her living room with a spiral-bound notebook with a cover that read, 'Level I Akashic Records.' Fortunately, the only other student was my friend Helen. Olga's class instruction began with an explanation of the Akasha, a Sanskrit word that means primordial substance, the primary substance from which all life is formed. The Akasha is an aspect of the nonphysical realm, the ethereal quantum field in which we dwell. We learned that its existence has been openly acknowledged by many religious and spiritual traditions, e.g., those of the Christians, Hebrews, Tibetans, Chinese, Greeks, Persians, Egyptians, and Mayans. I recalled biblical references to The Book of Life from my bible studies as an adult. I also recalled sitting in the pews of the Seventh-Day Adventist Church as a child, cringing as the pastor emphatically pronounced that we were always being watched, that God knew every thought and action. The Akasha is somehow related to the mystery of who God is, I thought as I sat on her porch, looking out over Brickell Avenue. God is said to know all our thoughts and actions. I connected it to something my mother would say, "What goes around comes around." Oh, okay, our thoughts and actions are stored somewhere and have an impact on our future. The Sanskrit term karma and the universal law of cause and effect were related concepts that I would learn about in time.

In class, we were given a sacred prayer from the Mayan tradition to call upon the Masters and Teachers for protection and to raise our vibration enough to be able to access the available information. Now, with a bit of background knowledge, we each practiced opening our own Akashic Record. The specific Sacred Prayer was in our class materials. After reading the prayer, I asked, "Are my Records open?" I saw in my mind's eye three monks in brown cloaks. I heard a voice say, "Yes, your records are open." With my records open, I asked the question that was provided by the instructor. I wrote down everything I heard. As I read my answer out loud, I realized that the vocabulary, tone, and rhythm were not mine. The style was distinct, more formal, yet airy and heartfelt. The distinct voice seemed to offer some level of proof that there had been a channeling of information that I was able to capture. Helen and I both took to the work easily and enjoyed the class.

The proof of our ability to access information from the Akasha came toward the end of class. We had practiced opening up our own Records and then each other's, and now it was time to test our ability. Were we able to retrieve the information accurately? The test was carried out by two people opening up the Akashic records of a third person. To begin, the instructor and I opened up Helen's records. We each read the prayer, first out loud, and then twice silently. Upon completion of the prayer, three Franciscan monks appeared to each of us in our mind's eye to let us know about her records. Helen then asked a question about her retirement. Questions, we'd learned, had to be clear and direct. For both the instructor and I, a brown vintage suitcase appeared in our mind's eye. Then we both heard, "You already have all the tools you will need. They are in the suitcase." Her guides gave examples of the tools; it was a long list since she had a doctoral degree and a wide range of interests. As we described what we heard and saw, Helen said it resonated with her, which was most important.

We reflected that perhaps the instructor and I had only read each other's thoughts, rather than having accessed information from a higher realm. Even if that was so, for me it begged the question of how reading another person's thoughts would even be possible. In our discussion, we kept coming back to the image.

"Images and symbols are the language of the soul. Our guides often speak to us in just that way. It is our job to interpret them," explained the instructor. I left in awe. The reality that there exists a higher realm and that I could tune into it was something I never had considered. This meant I wouldn't have to rely on anyone else to reach Alex. It gave me a sense of control over my own fate; I could ask the higher powers to guide me. I took her Level II class and went on to study with others.

By this time, I was no longer doubting that there was more to life than just this physical existence. I was confident in what I heard and saw intuitively. As I became more confident, I explored even more ancient spiritual traditions and practices. I wanted to learn it all. I wanted to know everything, and Alex was pulling me forward through it all.

In August that year, I traveled to New York City to celebrate my birthday. I had become friends with Bert, the grief psychologist and medium who'd connected me with Alex, and I invited him to attend. I enjoyed his company and secretly felt closer to Alex when I was with him. My niece Mia and her boyfriend, Alex, who knew all the trendy and outrageous bars and clubs, joined us. Helen and other friends came too. I was making up for all my years of restraint, hardship, and sorrow as we popped into one bar after another in the West Village. I was particularly struck by the gay bar with the male pole dancers and outrageous outfits. That night, we crashed in my friend's spare condo at 55th Street and Second Avenue. New York City was fun and fascinating. I didn't go home when everyone else did. I lingered in museums, ran in Central Park, and continued my volunteer work for the Obama campaign. When my friend needed her condo back, I wanted to stay, but finding an affordable short-term rental in New York City is daunting.

One Sunday, I selected the Neue Galerie art museum at 86th Street and Fifth Avenue as something new to do. As I gazed, gemstruck, into one of the glass cases, I noticed a very attractive and vibrant woman walking toward me. Before long, we were looking at the ruby and diamond-studded jewelry, oohing and aahing together, and discussing our favorites and where we would wear them if we had the chance. Each glass exhibit case was more inviting than the last, each bringing with it more sparkling illusions of fame and fortune. At the end of the exhibition, I said goodbye to her and walked up the flight of stairs to the second level. Just as I was bemoaning the fact that I hadn't shared my contact information with my new acquaintance, as I was virtually friendless in the city, I felt a tap on my right shoulder. She offered me a narrow piece of paper with her name and telephone number. We shared a smile, and I said I would be in touch.

The next week, we met for a drink at a midtown bar she'd suggested. Over drinks, I learned that she had not worked for two years due to a medical condition. I shared that I was looking for a place to stay. Generously, she offered to rent her second bedroom to me on a monthly basis. Three days later, she was offered an overseas position with the US State Department, a return to her work on human trafficking. She left for Germany the day before I moved into her apartment on the Upper West Side. From her balcony, I could easily see Central Park; I couldn't believe my good fortune.

As I settled in, I noticed two large blue leather-bound books on the dining room table. From afar, the gold engraving reminded me of the Bible. The gilt titles read *A Course in Miracles*, one of the most recognized and studied spiritual teachings of the twentieth century. My acquaintance's mother, Helen Felgun, who was recuperating from eye surgery and would be my new roommate for the next ten days, was the official translator of the *Course in Miracles* into Russian. I was wonderstruck. Of all possible apartments in Manhattan, how had I ended up here? I had read about synchronicities and doors opening when your actions are in sync with your soul's desires. I was coming to understand what that might look like.

Helen Felgun owned the apartment, which explained its floor-to-ceiling shelves stocked with books on psychology, philosophy, religion, and spirituality. I found the books' content daunting; in one glance at them, I realized how much I didn't know. Instead of delving into all that wisdom, I did what was more familiar—I spent time on the arts, politics, family, and of course, running. I ran miles every day, often on the path along the East River, and spent time at Riverside Park. The many nooks and corners of Central Park became familiar. I especially loved anticipating the invigorating run up and down the stairs in front of the Bethesda Fountain.

When I wasn't running, I visited with my niece Mia, who worked downtown. I also volunteered for the Obama campaign, making phone calls, and traveling to Pittsburgh to help Get Out the Vote, and I made it to Grant Park to hear Obama's acceptance speech. It was an invigorating and hope-filled time in my life. But however much I loved New York City, after three months, I felt the pull to return to Miami. I was ready for my next step on the spiritual path.

Having learned of Claudia Edwards, a psychologist and practicing shaman in Miami, I sought her out. Her office felt like any other psychologist's, i.e., it was furnished with a two-seat sofa, an end table with magazines, toys for children just in case, and a bell to communicate one's arrival. Claudia even looked and sounded like a psychologist—she was easygoing with a calm voice and wore relaxed-fit clothing. Our opening chat felt familiar. I described my life, and she nodded and listened. It was when she invited me to sit on the floor and opened her medicine bundle that everything changed.

The bundle was composed of thirteen stones wrapped in a Peruvian ceremonial cloth called a *mestana*.

"Choose one of the stones and blow your confusion and sadness into it," she began. I did. After I lay down on a mat, she placed the stone on my root chakra at the base of my spine, put on drumming music, and began to clear my luminous energy field, using her Peruvian rattle to draw out the heavy energy. At the session's end, I felt lethargic. Within the promised three days, though, I felt lighter. My next session with her included sitting across from each other two feet apart and staring into each other's left eye for ten minutes. We both experienced a shifting of the face opposite us. My face became that of an eagle to her, while to me, her face was transformed into that of an elderly Native American woman. I was intrigued, curious, and excited to learn more.

Underneath my sadness was my desire to find purpose and meaning in my life, as I had during my years with Parent to Parent. During my last session, Claudia handed me a book, *Courageous Dreaming: How Shamans Dream the World into Being* by Alberto Villoldo, PhD, her mentor and the founder of the Four Winds Society. I flipped to the back cover, looked at the author's photo, and read that he was a medical anthropologist. I said to myself, I need to meet this man. Inspired, I read the book in two days. I began to understand that how I experience the world is within my power to create or change. I wanted to live consciously, to be aware of my thoughts, words, feelings, and intentions, to inform and shape my future. I could either create my own life or unconsciously live by the dream others wanted for me. I immediately knew I wanted to learn more about shamanic energy medicine and set an intention to attend his shamanic energy medicine program.

CHAPTER
15

Destiny Unfolds

I ARRIVED AT THE PROGRAM, NOT to be healed, as that had already occurred in my years of intensive psychoanalysis, but rather to learn a new skill: an ability to help others and have an income, and hopefully to once again gain recognition for my accomplishments. The Four Winds Society referred to itself as the Harvard of shamanism. That should suffice, I thought. However, there was much more to learning those skills than I ever imagined. I soon found out that the first step had to do with shedding—letting go of my sorrows, grief, and limiting beliefs. My trip to Peru that summer gave me a jumpstart, so to speak.

It was seven o'clock one evening when fifteen of us boarded a motorized canoe to travel across the Rio Madre de Dios, a tributary of the Amazon River. It was a short ride. My appreciation of the beauty of the starlit night was tempered by my foreboding about this experience. Plant medicines, I'd heard, could be harsh, especially ayahuasca. The word itself translates into spirit or death vine, "*aya*" meaning spirit or death, and "*huasca*" meaning rope or vine. The scientific name of the vine is *Banisteriopsis caapi*. In making the medicine, the vine is pounded to remove the outer bark and to soften its ropelike fibers. It is then cooked with a large quantity of *Psychotria viridis* leaves. The vine and leaves are layered in a large pot. Water is added, and then the mixture is cooked over a fire for many hours, leaving a small quantity of liquid as the water evaporates.

Landing, we walked north along the beach and then up toward a tall pile of yoga mats. Following instructions, we placed our mats about fifteen feet apart in a circle. The shaman sat in the middle of the ring with his tobacco, a flute, and the ayahuasca. This shaman's plant medicine was known to be the strongest. Having heard about the purging effects of the plant medicine, I strategically dug out a "sink" in the sand a few inches from my mat. I even tested it, leaning up on my right elbow and making sure I could reach the sink with ease. Once everyone was settled, the shaman brought around the ayahuasca, and one at a time we drank from his tin cup. After he completed his rounds, he returned to the center of the circle and continued to commune with the plant spirits, protect our ceremonial space, and track our progress.

When needed, he enhanced our experience with sacred black tobacco, walking over to each one of us and blowing its smoke into our face. On a nauseous stomach, its odor is especially memorable. He continually whistled *icaros*—songs which carry the intention to evoke the plant spirits, enhance or subdue the effects of the plant med-icine, and to dispel dark spirits. His twenty years of experience as a shaman meant he had hundreds of *icaros* from which to choose. This was unfortunate. The *icaros* became a source of irritation for me as the night progressed, at least during the moments I was conscious. They magnified the effects of the ayahuasca, leaving me less and less in con-trol of my own thoughts and feelings. I wanted to scream, "Just shut up for a moment."

For the next four hours, I regularly vomited in my sink and then fell back to sleep. This meant that every thirty minutes or so, though it was very hard to estimate, I would suddenly wake up with a burn-ing, rumbling, nauseous stomach. My head felt too heavy to lift up, but there was no alternative. There was no choice, it was coming out regardless of any counter attempts to hold it in. My hole in the sand worked better than expected. I did not have to stand up as I witnessed others doing. I am not sure I could have. In addition, through the effects of the ayahuasca, the round twelve-inch-wide hole in the sand was transformed into a ceramic bowl, complete with a traditional geo-metric design.

The face that appeared on the bowl's upper edge was Mayan: The individual's lifted chin, high forehead, and forward-leaning plumage were markers. Each time I leaned over to purge, spirit was there in the form of these ancient motifs. Additionally, I would see animals carved out in the sand for several hundred feet. They were the bear, jaguar, eagle, and serpent. The scene never changed. I was being held and protected.

Around midnight, accompanying the last unheard *icaro*, my neighbor walked toward me and asked, "Can I help you up?" I reached my arm out for him to grab and hold; "That would be great, thanks."

"Lean on me, and we will move our legs at the same time," he advised as he began to slowly walk toward the canoe. "Did you have a good time?" he joked. I moaned, "Very funny," as I leaned into his body and matched his stride.

I could only surmise that the purging had to have helped in some way, but it was not at all clear how. The next day, I asked Alberto about the face on the bowl, and it was suggested I journal as to its meaning. That did not produce any results. In our daily debriefing, Alberto explained that with the ayahuasca medicine, one's inner maps, fears, beauty, and potential are projected, giving us the opportunity to witness what is inside of us. By walking through death and through the hungry ghosts, they no longer stalk us. I left the Amazon hoping that my hungry ghosts had ended up either in my Mayan sink or devoured by the power animals. I also left curious as to the meaning of the Mayan face on my beautiful ceramic bowl.

The answer came two years later. I was having a cup of tea in the home of Dr. David Grove in Gainesville, Florida. I was in Gainesville for an intensive summer program in arts in medicine. Dr. Grove was my former anthropology advisor as well as having been the director of the Chalcatzingo archeology project in Mexico that I had worked on forty years prior as an archeology student analyzing pottery shards. I was delighted to see him again and share a bit about my shamanic studies. After our apple pie and tea, he went into his office and returned with a book.

"This was given to me by the author, Barbara Tedlock, when I ran into her at the airport. I would like you to have it." He handed me a book entitled, *The Woman in the Shaman's Body: Reclaiming the Feminine in Religion and Medicine*. I took the book and thanked him, immediately noticing the image on the book's front cover. It was the face that had appeared on my ceramic bowl in the jungle. My arms were covered with goosebumps. The image is described as an ancient Mayan carved shell of a woman in an ecstatic trance. Wow, I thought; a female shaman and her power animals had held sacred space for me while I purged. Was the female shaman my past or future? Perhaps both, I hoped.

From the jungle, I went on to join the Four Winds group to climb Sallqantay, the glacier-capped sacred feminine mountain located directly south of Machu Picchu in the Cusco Region. Our goal was to reach 19,500 feet, which would take us five nights and six days. It felt challenging, rugged, and life changing. The path we walked on served as a footpath connecting Cusco with Machu Picchu during the time of the Quechua people, known as the Inca.

After a couple of days acclimating to the altitude, we all made our way to Mollepata, where we reached our first campsite; our group included our leader, Linda Fitch, two Q'ero shamans, seven horses, four cooks, numerous helpers, and thirty-three students. Although it was only labeled as an "expedition," journeys into sacred lands are often far more than adventure travels, they are transformative. As such, they can result in unexpected experiences—which are often emotionally, physically, and mentally disruptive and painful. So it was for others. So it was also for me.

My first night on the mountain, while I waited for dinner as the sun went down, I took out a bag of potato chips from my knapsack and start chomping away. The combination of 'sundowners' (disorientation when the sun goes down), the potato chip grease, and the high altitude was lethal. Altitude sickness is a wretched way to purge the unwanted and to open one's heart. Nauseous, I lay down in my tent as everyone headed into the large tent for dinner and ceremony. I was only half-covered as I leaned out to vomit.

The temperature falls rapidly in high altitudes, and I wasn't prepared. Hypothermia set in as the temperature dropped to twenty degrees Fahrenheit. After dinner ended, Judy, my tent buddy, arrived back to our tent and became concerned. She asked the medic and Don Francisco, one of the shamans, to assist. Judy climbed into my sleeping bag with me for a few minutes and used her body heat to warm me up, but something had already been set in motion. During that sleepless night, I had an experience like that of Ebenezer Scrooge in the movie *The Christmas Carol*, revisiting scene after scene of my adult life with a voice inside of me letting me know how I could have chosen a more loving action. Some of the scenes were about my recent time with my father in Marco Island, Florida. I wept silently for hours. My head felt like it was splitting open. In the wee hours of the morning, I heard Judy ask, "Are you okay? Can I get you anything?" I said, "My head is pounding, but it is too cold for you to have to move." She didn't hesitate. I heard the zipper of her sleeping bag and the rustling of her overnight bag. "Here, these aspirins should help," as she handed me her canteen and two pills. Finally, I was able to sleep, but the next morning, too exhausted and dazed to hike, I was hoisted into the saddle, where I remained for several hours. As we rode out, the morning fog and dew lifted.

The next days were filled with blue skies, the quiet hum of Mother Earth, cool air, and a radiant sun that felt kinder and gentler than the sun in Miami. We spent evenings together in a large tent, elbow to elbow; first, we would gather for a dinner of soup, quinoa, bread, and a simple main dish of meat or fish. Then each night after dinner, the shaman, or *paqo* as they are called, would hold an *ayni despacho* ceremony, a tradition hundreds of years old. It is a prayer bundle or offering of gratitude, and its purpose is to heal emotional and physical ailments and to restore balance and harmony. It held our prayers, which we blew into cocoa leaves, which were then placed into the bundle. Each night's prayer bundle was shaped differently, but the offerings were similar: sugar, corn, other grains, red and white carnations, beans, cotton, tiny doll figures to represent male and female, and a fake dollar bill for prosperity. The *paqo* blew his prayers into each offering. Every night, I included prayers for my son and prayers for my continued learning and growth. I so wanted to be useful again, but I had so much to learn.

On the fourth day, our switchback trail, which had started at an elevation of 13,500 feet, ended at the Sacred Lagoon at 19,500 feet. The snowcapped mountain rising above it against the day's majestic blue sky created the idyllic backdrop to our stacked pile of healing bundles, each wrapped with its uniquely designed Peruvian textile. During our moments of calm gazing into the lagoon, I heard an inner voice ask me to total the number of people in our group. I counted twice and then confirmed it with my tent buddy: forty-three people. I made a mental note of that number as it seemed significant. Back at the base of the mountain, Don Francisco gave each of us a white stone from the mountainside of Sallqantay. It became the thirteenth *kuya* in my healing bundle.

By this time in the program, I realized that healing is truly like peeling an onion. Each layer exposes the next one; I had many layers to go. However, I was hoping the plant medicine and the mountain climb would result in a detailed action plan for my life. Do this, then that.

I felt an inner plea, "Please, someone just tell me what to do. I don't want to make any big mistakes again." I also felt like I was running out of time—I needed a quick fix and specific directions on how to get wherever it was that I was supposed to go. But Spirit is not a life coach. She gives us the mythic map, the star, the destination, but we need to create our own blueprint. Clearly, I needed to stop asking the question and realize I was already living it in each moment. That lesson took a ghastly long time to learn.

Back in the States, I continued to take the seven required courses. For each of the first four courses, we were asked to bring three stones. During the first part of our week-long course, we converted our ordinary stones into healing stones, called *kuyas*. This conversion process entailed extracting our wounds with the stone. The latter part of the week was spent learning to use our *kuyas* in healing processes to benefit others. We began with practicing what was called a chakra illumination, clearing the chakras of dense energies and restoring the body's equilibrium. After watching an in-class demonstration, we broke up into pairs. The last words of advice were, "Believe whatever you see, hear, smell, or sense. Do not doubt yourself."

When it was my turn to be the client, I climbed onto the massage table, blew my anxiety over my uprooted life into my classmate's *kuya* and lay down on my back, closing my eyes and taking steady deep breaths in rhythm with his. He placed his *kuya* on my root chakra, located at the base of my spine. Moving his rattle in a counterclockwise direction over the *kuya*, he lifted and extracted the stuck, heavy energy. After several minutes of rhythmic breathing and listening to the sound of his rattle, I felt something move inside my lower abdomen. I wanted to bolt off the massage table or scream, but instead, I lay quiet to sense what it was. With my inner eye, I saw long black fur and suspected it was a monkey. However, its body was too elongated, and then I could see its large paws. It began to walk up toward my shoulders. As it reached my heart, I realized it was a black panther. It curled up around my neck and shoulders. I was in awe; I felt special and chosen. It was part of my initiation.

Later, the black panther would appear to many of my clients, those who resonated the most with shamanic energy medicine. I came to understand that the black panther is an archetype, a primal energy that lives in all of us. When asked, she helps track energies both backward and forward in time. She is a protector.

During one of my courses, she whispered something gently into my ear, which rippled into a nice friendship and delightful experiences: "Work with the person to your right. You will be able to help her with something." On cue, I turned to the woman next to me, Maryann, and asked if she would like to team up for the next experience, an unwinding of our ancestral family wounds from our energy body. As I learned about her family, I was moved to offer an Akashic Record reading. She thanked me for the offer, and we agreed to meet at the lake the next morning.

The fog was just lifting off the lake when we arrived. For the next forty-five minutes, she asked questions and I described what I was being shown in my mind's eye. After the reading, as we were walking back up the hill to breakfast, Maryann inquired about my plans. I explained that I was uprooted for the time being and not sure where I was going next.

"I have a second home on Martha's Vineyard, maybe you would like to go there," she said. I couldn't believe my ears.

"Wow, that would be wonderful. Are you sure you don't mind a house guest when you aren't there?" I said.

"We will be out to the Vineyard while you are still there. We can visit then."

"That sounds perfect. Class will be starting soon, we better head back," I said.

At the agreed upon time, I arrived at her lovely home in Edgartown, on the east side of the island. It was a modern home with a bedroom downstairs and a loft upstairs with two more bedrooms. I settled into the bedroom downstairs with its adjacent bathroom. The Morning Glory Farm, which featured scrumptious bakery goods and fresh fruits and vegetables, was five minutes away; even more importantly, the beach was only a few blocks from the house.

I loved to run to the soundtrack of my music along the beach's shoreline, and I'd pretend I was back in Miami when I felt lonesome. One day, about two miles into my run, I noticed something sticking out from the sand. I ran up to see what it was. Bending down, I saw that it was a stone. This beach is full of pebbles, not stones, I thought, as I dug my hand into the sand to retrieve the stone. While digging, my hand hit another stone, and then another and another. The stones were large, with each around four inches by three inches and every one unique: Some were perfectly round or egg-shaped, others oblong with colors varying from reddish to blackish, as well as to motley colors of white and gray. I dug and dug. When I had retrieved the last stone, I sat back, awed. I had uncovered forty-three stones! The hole I had dug was round, about one foot across and one and one-half feet deep, as if the stones had fallen from the sky with tremendous force, all at one time. I stood them up as if they were Stonehenge and built stone altars and concentric circles.

Forty-three stones, the same number of people I had counted on that mountaintop in Peru. I realized that I had just had an encounter with the Stone People, recognized by many Native American traditions as the record keepers on Mother Earth. Their mission as teachers is to hold the energy and give the seeker knowledge about the planet and its people. They are our allies, composed of mineral matter billions of years old, and are from the same Source energy that lives powerfully in everything; as such, they also live within us.

Dark clouds were forming, and with the threat of rain, I headed back. However, I had connected with the stones and promised that I would return the next day; I left, but not before placing the whitest stone into my sports bra.

On my return trip, I noticed up ahead an object lying on the sand—it looked like a towel in a pine tree green color. I had passed this same spot a short time ago, how had I not noticed the towel? I was apprehensive as I reached down and pulled up the soggy bath-size towel. When I saw what appeared to be embroidered letters on it, I gulped. There I was on the beach with dark clouds filling the sky, a white stone stuck in my bra, and a love song blaring through my iPod earbuds, holding a soggy green towel with the name Alexander sewn on it in four-inch embroidered red letters. Tears welled up in my eyes. I felt that Alex was part of this mysterious day of stones and now the soggy towel. The following day, I retraced my steps and collected my stones. Several years later, I attended a lecture at the Explorer's Club in New York City by Maria Cooper, actor Gary Cooper's daughter. I learned Maria is a member of the board of the American Society for

Psychical Research. Inspired, I purchased the autobiography she had coauthored with her husband, renowned concert pianist Byron Janis. In one of the scenes in the book, they are running in the forest while dodging a deluge of stones falling from the sky. Shocked, I reread that passage many times. The forty-three stones remain a part of me and my work to this day.

CHAPTER

16

The Ruse

In 2009, AFTER THE HOUSING market crash, my brother Jeff moved into a condo, a penthouse suite on Marco Island, a small island on Florida's Gulf coast, to supervise its remodeling and to scout out investment properties. My son and I were invited there for Christmas, along with Jeff's six children and my parents. I arrived after dark, which created a dazzling aura, with the subtle lighting of the condo silhouetted against the backdrop of the black ocean and sky. My nephew Josh came down with Jayda, my brother's four-year-old adopted daughter, to greet me and unload my car. "Your dad sure did it up right again," I said, gazing up at the beautiful twenty-seven story building. I felt close to Jayda, and I was thrilled that we could spend time together. I settled into the guest suite on the lobby floor, complete with a balcony from which I could observe pods of dolphins in the afternoons.

Over the holidays, my brother offered me the guest suite as my new home in exchange for help with Jayda. Driving back to Miami, I was shocked that I could actually contemplate moving in with my brother. Clearly an old family pattern was being reenacted. Growing up, Jeff was my overseer, the person I deferred to in times of trouble and doubt. Now, with no husband, boss, advisor, children, or concrete path forward to direct my course of action, I was out to sea without a paddle. In lieu of forging forward—I went sideways in the end, for a good reason.

I was also astonished that I would consider selling my condo. Albeit tiny, a total of only 310 square feet, I had spent four months redesigning it. I recalled Bert's having foretold that in a year's time, someone would walk off an elevator and offer to buy my condo. I scoffed at the idea. But true to his prediction, when I got home, as I was standing in the lobby of my condo, the owner of the condo unit next to mine stepped off the elevator and said, "I would like to buy your unit, if you are interested in selling." I agreed to meet with him the following day.

At this point, after I'd finished my dissertation, I had run along the beach north to 55th Street and south to First an endless number of times, had viewed hundreds of art exhibits, and had ended a relationship with a man who wasn't that into me. I decided to sell. By now a fanatic about running, I jogged to the closing. As I was quite sweaty upon arrival, we all had a hearty laugh. The owner of the title company predicted that I would return to Miami. "Oh, I don't think so," I said.

Give me a pair of running shoes, quiet space, sunshine, and the smiles of a child and I am content. For a while, Marco Island provided all of that. I joined a Buddhist meditation group in nearby Naples led by someone who had been given their authority to teach by the renowned Vietnamese Zen Buddhist master Thich Nhat Hanh. I rode to the group gatherings with two women from Marco Island; one became a dear friend. She had a son with autism, and her own life and then his had been transformed through meditation. The Sunday night sangha had one important component in common with Christian churches: There was a set rhythm and flow, born out of rituals and ceremonies that were thousands of years old. I flourished in those rhythms. Aside from that, everything else felt different: round cushions on the floor, the aroma of incense, and a gong and *tingshas* to mark the beginning and endings of meditation. We didn't wear shoes, talk much, nor look into each other's eyes. It was designed to be an inward experience—a time to renew oneself and be fed spiritually.

We began with a thirty-minute mindfulness meditation. To stop thinking, luckily, was not the goal, but rather to become mindful of the mind. I began to view my mind as separate from myself, more like a computer chip than a person. The profound realization that I am not my mind has had more impact on me than any other experience. I also realized how my mind was continually getting in my way of feeling good about myself and others. As I moved toward being better able to quiet my mind and be witness to it, I felt more in charge of my thoughts—and my life.

After the sitting meditation, there was a walking meditation; we would slowly place one foot down on the floor while methodically lifting up the other. I had to adjust my usual walking speed, which was notoriously fast-paced, or else I would run over the person directly in front of me. I was used to solitude by then and didn't find it challenging to be quiet, but walking slowly was a challenge. When my mind wandered, I brought it back to quiet by focusing on my breath and on simply observing my feet moving along the path. We listened to a charma talk on learning how to apply loving kindness in our everyday life. Invariably, we would discuss that day's teaching on our drive back to Marco (as locals referred to Marco Island). The rhythm of ceremony and ritual and friendship kept me balanced and centered while everything around me was swirling. I felt fortunate to have these two friends in my new surroundings.

While I was on Marco, I also ran on the beach, collected seashells, and spent time with Jayda. Aspects of Jayda's personality reminded me of Alex's. In conversation with Bert, he told me, "What I am being shown, Paula, is that Jayda is part of Alex's oversoul. Yes, our soul can split off into two people during certain lifetimes." I said, "I am not sure what that means, but I feel especially close to her." But my approach to raising children brought friction with that of my brother and sister-in-law. "Paula, we don't believe in that psychology stuff, so I'm not sure you should spend time with Jayda," said my sister-in-law, in reference to my children's art projects for Jayda and her friend and cousins. That was my chance to resign from my unpaid position. But instead I felt that I had done something wrong and found myself defending myself. I had a doctorate in education, yet there I was feeling intimidated. Unexpected and irrational attacks often left me speechless.

While I was living there, my brother asked me to do him a favor: to go check on the condition of his house in Costa Rica and to meet with his lawyer and his lawyer's wife, who were managing the property. I balked, remembering our previous Costa Rica dealings, which had begun with a phone call from my sister-in-law, Sylvia, telling me, "I'm calling to let you know I am going down to pack up the house. Jeff wants to bring all the furnishings up here to Rockford; he says he is done going down there. I will leave you some things in case you go back down." When I returned to the house, I found one silver spoon left on the kitchen counter. The Cinderella story flashed into my mind. "The clock struck midnight while I wasn't paying attention," I thought.

However, I had to let go of that, acknowledging the house was never mine anyway. I appreciated all the wonderful memories I'd made with Jeff's family, my son Jaime, and friends. I was also still easily convinced to do things for him; the three thousand dollars also made the trip desirable. Upon my arrival in Escazu, the lawyer began, "Paula, I don't think Jeff realizes that there is now little furniture left in the staff's house; they are sleeping on mattresses on the floor, and there is no kitchen table or sofa." My brother's instructions rang loudly in both my ears: "And don't buy any furniture for that cottage house." Now cornered but wanting to protect the family's image, I replied, "Oh, I am sure he doesn't realize that. Let's take a look at what they need while we are at the house." In the end, I handed the lawyer a personal check and asked his wife to choose the furnishings. After she emailed me the photos of what she wanted to buy, copying my brother, I received this text, "If you are so liberal, use your own money next time." My text reply was short; it said, "I did." The price for my defiance—what my brother would consider my brazenness—would be felt soon enough.

After six months in Marco, the real reason I was meant to move back there began to unfold. "Hello, Paula, this is Margaret, a friend of your folks up here in Shullsburg, Wisconsin. I know you or your brother would be here if you knew how bad off your parents were." I said, "Oh, I had no idea my dad was that unwell. I will fly up soon. Thanks for calling." My father's Parkinson's disease had worsened, and my mother was not sharing the whole truth with me. She no doubt thought we should care enough to come up and see him on our own initiative. The next day, I flew to Wisconsin, while my brother drove there. My father was thin and confused, and my mother was tired and overwhelmed. Even though our parents wanted to stay in their home, my brother and I saw that wouldn't work. Instead, after much discussion, we decided it would be best if they moved to Marco Island. One of the belly-up properties my brother had bought up was on the seventh floor of the condominium where we were living. As I flew down to Marco with our parents, my brother resettled back in Rockford, leaving me alone with the responsibility of looking after them; although it was an encumbrance, I will be forever glad I took it on.

Even though the flight to Miami went smoothly and without incident, the two-hour drive across the Everglades on the Tamiami Trail seemed to take forever. Midway, my father wanted to go home. I kept reminding him in a calm, steady voice that our goal was to all be together and that we needed to be on Marco Island. Despite the beautiful surroundings, my father was miserable. Sadly, if he hadn't been ill, he'd have found this setting ideal. He worshipped the sun and had spent a number of winters in Florida with my mother, playing golf. Now, however, their patio overlooking the Atlantic Ocean from the seventh floor felt more like being on a ship to him, and most days, he wouldn't even venture out. This sent my mother into despair.

As my father's ego-self dissolved, the quiet, stubborn, emotionally reserved man who had raised me evolved into a loving, expressive, and caring person. The words and actions that came tumbling forth surprised all of us. One night, after telling my mother how much he loved her and sharing his favorite memory of their first date and the yellow sweater she'd worn, he explained that he had always wished to be able to say "that kind of thing," but he just couldn't. My mother's pure goodness toward my father flowed as she rubbed his feet, combed his hair, and held his hand while they listened to their audiobooks together.

My father's final days gave him time to heal some past hurts with my brother. Their relationship had gotten off to a bad start. However, ultimately, when Jeff had followed in my father's footsteps as a home builder, it was with little financial support or guidance. Jeff had established his own business, buying home lots from my father in the beginning. Shortly, it was clear that their approaches to business and building could not have been more opposite. Building cautious, thorough, customized homes was my father's approach; high-risk, large volume, and mass-production building and development was my brother's. Jeff schemed, while my dad plodded. Mistrust and old hurts swam beneath the surface, emerging when there were new attempts to create joint ventures, with my brother wanting recognition and my father wanting to protect what he had. As with all conflicts and misunderstandings in my family, nobody spoke, and nothing was resolved.

But there they were, together on a small island on the Gulf coast of Florida in the final days of my father's life. Acknowledging each other's importance now felt safe. That night, my father, who rarely finished his meals and didn't enjoy small talk at the table anymore, did something unexpected. When he was ready to leave the dinner table that night, he asked my brother to accompany him back to his bedroom. My brother's face brightened with the unexpected request. With tears in my eyes, I watched layers of mistrust evaporate as my brother helped my father stand up, and with arms interlaced, walk down the hallway.

My father's words and actions also left an indelible mark on me. One day when my mother went out with my father's caregiver to run an errand, I had some welcome alone time with my father. Sitting next to him on his bed, I spoke to him about my mother, on perhaps the first and only occasion I ever shared my private thoughts about her with him. "Mom is sure difficult to be around. She stares hatred into me sometimes." Living in close proximity to my mother again was triggering childhood hurts and preoccupations, and I found that without realizing it, I was avoiding visiting them, due not to my father's dementia, but to my mother's harshness. My dad responded with a surprising insight, "Maybe she is jealous of you. Maybe she has always been like that with you." I replied, "I hadn't thought about it that way. I think you may be right." He continued, "She always did like getting your letters and loved it when you came to visit." I was surprised by his openness and ability to say something so reflective. I wondered at what age I had stopped sharing my thoughts and feelings with my father. I wished this intimate vulnerability had always existed. I would not have felt so alone, like I had no safe place or person to turn to. When my mother got home, my father shared, "Paula and I had a good visit, perhaps the best visit we have ever had." Smiling, I nodded in agreement. My mother looked perplexed and anxious at the same time. The relationship she most wanted me not to have had just deepened, and she seemed worried. But I was not aware of that even then.

One night, we had dinner on the lanai, and when my father was ready to go inside, he stood up, leaned across the table, and whispered to me, "Paula, don't stick around here after." Then once a few weeks before his passing, when we were standing in the kitchen, he leaned over and whispered, "You will do good in front of those hundreds of people you will be speaking to." His perception that I had significant work yet to do beyond Marco Island made it so in my mind. Rarely having heard pride-filled or encouraging words from him, these words profoundly impacted me. I cried the kind of tears that well up when you experience something in adulthood that you sorely missed in childhood.

On January 9, 2010, my father, with my mother by his side, was transported to a hospice center in nearby Naples. After calling my brother, who was back living in Illinois, I went to the hospice center.

As I entered the room, my mother asked, "Do you hear that music?"

"No, mom, what music?"

"It's big band music, but I can't find where it is coming from." I walked around the room and checked the air vents, the TV, and the radio. I didn't hear anything, but clearly my mother could. Their lifetime of dancing lessons and their love for big band music was being reflected back to them from the heavens.

I sat next to my father and held his hand. My mother sat across the room, forlorn and sunk down in her chair. I wanted my last loving words to be between just the two of us, and I knew enough to realize that my dad could hear them telepathically. We communicated that way for a while. Tears ran down both of our cheeks as our feelings of gratitude and love were silently exchanged. He died that evening. Family and friends drove long distances to honor his life. I gave my mother Brian Weiss's book *Only Love Is Real*. Her heart was now open to the possibility that life after death exists. She told me that Weiss's message of eternal love had given her great comfort.

CHAPTER

17

Things Go Wonky—Back in Oz

OUR FAMILY TIME TOGETHER ON Marco Island was soon to dissolve into a new situation. Once when my mother, brother, and sister-in-law were on vacation for a long weekend, my brother's son and his girlfriend, who just showed up for a visit, stayed in my mother's condo. When I entered the condo in the morning to prepare for an upcoming visit by my cousin Denise, it was in disarray. I froze until I heard the bedroom door open, the door to the bedroom that had been my father's. My nephew stumbled out with his girlfriend walking behind him. He seemed to be in an altered state as he began yelling at me. I unfroze and let loose, "What the hell are you doing? You can't be here like this." He didn't agree, "I can do whatever I want. You don't own this place." He kept yelling as I walked out the front door.

My brother rarely answers his phone, and I felt alone in solving this problem. My nephew needed to move up into his father's condo, and I did not feel equipped to deal with him. I called the police.

When the police arrived, my nephew exploded. Pounding his chest and addressing his plea to the policeman, he declared, "She and my grandma are just here leeching off my dad. My dad is the real owner of this property. She can't kick me out," pointing at me. Since neither myself nor my nephew owned the condo, the police were in a bit of a quandary. Skillfully they convinced my nephew to move upstairs. They all left. With my heart racing, sweaty palms, and swirling thoughts, I busied myself cleaning up their mess. Then I called my brother. When he answered his phone, I found that my sharing of what had happened sounded more like a confession, like a small child telling on herself. In that confession was a habitual promise of self-defeat. Holding other people responsible for their actions was difficult for me. He didn't say much and hung up. He had already spoken to his son.

Children do not become dysfunctional because they have been consistently and lovingly held accountable for their actions. It is often just the opposite. In my brother's case, he had no difficulty in defining a culprit and punishing them. However, who the culprit—or scapegoat—was had little to do with any real facts. Life was like a game of chess. In lieu of taking responsibility for having agreed to let his son's girlfriend visit, who he knew would bring him drugs, and in lieu of holding his son responsible for his behavior, my brother sent me a scathing text throwing me out of his house.

"I want your ass out of my house now. Third time you have done this to me." His raging text included purchasing the staff's furniture. Clearly, my brother had new fish to fry. He was done remodeling the penthouse, had returned to Rockford, Illinois, and my father had been well cared for in his final days. I was no longer needed. My nephew got a free pass that day.

For myself, what left me curious was the fact that I had called my brother to basically turn myself in. But with no Dr. Morgan to help sort through the quagmire, it was left unresolved. Much later, I learned about a psycho-social construct called the Drama Triangle. The drama occurs when the Victim, Bully, and Rescuer roles suddenly shift. With the nephew situation, I had shifted from being the victim to the bully and then had quickly put myself back into the victim role, my default position within my family. It is so difficult to break free from family imprints. The ever-loving universe keeps sending us opportunities to transcend these self-limiting patterns. It was going to take a lot of effort to transcend mine.

After cleaning up the condo, I drove to the Fort Myers airport to pick up my cousin Denise, Mia's mother. I told her the saga and then added, "I should have listened to my dad's advice." She asked, "What was that?" I replied, "Not to stay around here after he was gone." "Maybe so," she said. My mother returned from vacation and displayed upset and surprise that I had been evicted. I believed her.

It took many years to realize that of course she had known about and acquiesced to my brother's decision to evict me. My mother was skilled at hiding her preference for my brother. I was equally skilled at pretending that it did not exist. She also was adept at saying whatever was necessary to not take action on anyone else's behalf. In fact, I hardly ever remember seeing my mother consciously extending herself to help anyone outside of family.

Additionally, my departure from Marco meant she now had a good reason to move back to her home in Wisconsin. That she would return to the Midwest also should have been obvious to me. I now understand that with my father gone, I had nurtured secret hopes of having mother-daughter time. I had long believed that my father was the barrier to that happening. However, my father being the guilty party who prevented that was a ruse. My mother found it difficult to be around me— or most anyone else really—for any extended time. It must have felt safer for her to blame my father than to struggle with her own feelings and fears. I remembered the time she'd jumped up and down screaming, "I so hate myself," when she found me studying for my doctoral exams and I didn't have time to spend with her.

But what was next for me? The speed at which I could turn lemons into lemonade was only surpassed by my inability to fully absorb the situation and be in touch with my feelings. In lieu of feeling, I planned. I would only have to make a slight adjustment to my original idea, I thought. Instead of coming and going to my shaman classes from Marco Island, I'd put my few belongings back in storage, drive to my class, and then just wing it. Surely I had already experienced the worst life could offer. I felt the risk was low, and the thought of an adventure felt exciting. "Mom, would you like to drive with me to New York City? We can visit Jaime for a couple days and then you can fly home from there." She said, "Sure."

It was the first time we had traveled alone together, and we were both a bit apprehensive. However, it went remarkably smoothly. For the morning drive, I would put the convertible top down and let the sunshine in to warm our faces. My mother often napped. Grief is exhausting. By afternoon, I'd close the convertible top and we would chat and listen to the radio.

It was on our second day driving through North Carolina that my mom shared an untold story about my younger brother's death. I already knew quite a bit about Jim's death. It had begun with a phone call on Thanksgiving Day, 2001. "Hey Paula, it's Jeff. Yeah, I am here with mom and dad in Costa Rica. Pat just called, and Jim's in the hospital. He is not expected to live." It was six o'clock, and I had just arrived home. Jaime was with his father. "What happened?" Jeff continued,

"He was riding his motorcycle. A young kid driving a van turned into him. The doctor is trying to stop the internal bleeding. They amputated his leg, but that hasn't helped. Pat and a bunch of them are at the hospital. They've all been drinking." I moaned, "Keep me informed." Soon after, my phone rang again. "It was hopeless. I had to give the physician permission to take him off life support. Jim's dead. We leave here the day after tomorrow. Go hold down the fort."

That part of Jim's death I knew about. I also knew about the funeral arrangements that I helped Pat make when I arrived. And there was the eulogy I wrote by asking his three young daughters to tell me funny stories: "Remember the time he was chasing us, and his leg went through the end table." "I loved the ice skating pond and the snow sledding hill he built for us." "Oh, the best was that stink bomb that he'd put next to someone and then walk away when it went off." I added mine, "Your dad wanted me to look inside the satchel mounted on the back of his bicycle. He was around twelve years old. As I was leaning close in, he pulled out a snake. Your dad laughed so hard that day." The girls loved hearing and repeating those stories about their father, how he loved to play tricks, tell jokes, ride motorcycles, go on long road trips, and play with his children. He loved his children. When my folks arrived, we went to the morgue to handle the funeral arrangements. His handsome face and lean well-shaped body were not the same. As my dad's gaze moved to his amputated right leg, his sorrow left him pale and weak. I felt his sadness much more than my own. I was numb most of the time. In lieu of feeling, I became the funeral organizer. Alex's funeral had happened just five years earlier, and feeling strong emotions for anything or anyone was not possible. I never cried, nor did Jaime. If Jeff or my folks cried, it was in private.

Yes, I knew a lot about Jim's drinking and his death. What I didn't know about was what had happened the year before. My mom began, "They were up to our house that year for Thanksgiving the year before Jim died. Jim had gone to the tavern to have a beer, and he ran into someone he knew and stayed longer than he planned. On his way home, the young man was killed on his motorcycle. Jim got the call about it at our house. When he hung up, he began to sob uncontrollably and said, 'I know that is how I am going to die.' I tried to console him and convince him otherwise, but nothing worked. I guess he knew all along."

"Mom, I am surprised you never shared that before now." Silence. All the emotions that went with that story were left pent up inside. In fact, my mother rarely talked about my brother. It stirred up too much sadness. Both my mom and dad had begged him not to marry the wife he chose. In their eyes, she was the miscreant, yet they never fully recognized how the family dynamic may have contributed to Jim's marriage decision and eventual struggles with alcohol. Pat was an easy target. She was one of six children who all had had their own battles with alcohol. Pat, fragile and saddened by my brother's death, died young of liver failure.

As my mother talked about Jim's premonition, I remembered my own sobbing the year prior to Alex's death, the time I was talking to my mother from the house phone at the Ronald McDonald House. That now felt like it had been a premonition. My mother was a good listener when there was bad news. She knew how to do that well. I benefited from that skill of hers and appreciated it on many occasions.

On the third night of our road trip to New York, we splurged and stayed in a fancy B & B. We were given the Yellow Room, a descriptor inscribed on the door's nameplate. "That was the color of dad's favorite sweater of yours, Mom." She appreciated the memory. She poured us each a gin and tonic as we sat by the fireplace and soaked up the elegance.

On the fourth day, we arrived at a friend's apartment in the Village where we stayed. My son was living in a small apartment in East Harlem, owned by an artist I had met during one of my trips. Unemployed and pursuing a career in writing, he was living off the proceeds from the sale of his car. In what was perhaps no coincidence, his car funds ran out the same month he got his first real job. He was hired as the assistant to the executive producer of Vanity Fair magazine. My mother and I spent time sightseeing with Jaime. After a few days, I took her to LaGuardia Airport for her flight back to Wisconsin. As I left, I put down my convertible top, turned on the radio, and drove two hours north to the Omega Institute. My new career as a shamanic energy medicine practitioner was waiting for me. I had no idea what I was really getting myself into. Of course, do we really ever?

CHAPTER
18

Sharing

Aᴌᴇх's ᴌɪꜰᴇ ᴋᴇᴘᴛ ᴏɴ ɢɪᴠɪɴɢ, inspiring me to create offerings that reflected what I had learned from her. One was the development of two early childhood education courses for Miami Dade Community College, part of their new undergraduate degree program in early childhood education. The courses were to help future preschool teachers effectively integrate children with disabilities. Susan worked on that project with me; we poured our hearts into developing the syllabus, classroom exercises, reading and video lists, and exam questions. In between working on it, we took beach breaks and consumed a hearty quota of white wine, resulting in roars of laughter.

Another endeavor began with a dream and a phone call. "Dr. del Moral, I woke up this morning with a great project idea and have already pounded out a grant proposal. I think the Department of Cultural Affairs may fund it," I began my call to the neonatologist I had worked with at the medical school.

"Great, send it to me, and then let's meet," she readily replied. Dr. del Moral and I synced from the first day she walked into my office in 2002. "Are you Paula Lalinde? People keep telling me that you are the one who can help me." I smiled at the acknowledgement. "I want to start a parent support group for the parents in the NICU (Neonatal Intensive Care Unit, the ICU for newborn babies) and am not sure how to begin." I looked at the manual she'd brought with her and offered to develop the training program for her. In subsequent years, she would apply for more grant funding and we would brainstorm training programs and special events to support both the families and the nurses.

This new idea, however, was based on my work with archetypes and reading Joseph Campbell's book *The Hero's Journey*, which was the name I gave the project. The heroes were the NICU parents; their personal transformation on their path was born out of the emotional suffering that came with having a premature infant, as many of the babies were born weighing just over two pounds. I contracted with an expressive arts organization in Sarasota and chose the lead artist based on her last name, Horne. Her mother, Alice Horne, had come to me in a dream while I was trying to find the right artist.

Kathleen Horne was perfect. Her team designed an area right outside the NICU that we filled with families' messages of change, growth, miracles, faith, and hope. Those messages appeared on mosaic-tiled columns, with each piece of clay handcrafted by a parent or NICU staff member. Their children's photos, poems, inspirational messages, bracelets, and other sacred objects were part of a family quilt that Kathleen stitched together and then framed in a shadow box hung on the surrounding walls. Benches were handcrafted with inspiring messages. The unveiling a year later was attended by over one hundred family members, hospital physicians, and other staff. A young man with autism played "Somewhere Over the Rainbow" on his flute as the now-grown children pulled open the curtains, revealing the mosaic columns and benches. A father came over to me with tears in his eyes and told me, "This has brought us closer as a family. I can now better appreciate what we all went through." Having a mirror for self-reflection can be life changing.

Since I still felt motivated to help the nonprofit I had founded years prior, I joined forces with two women I had met during my Four Winds shamanic training, and with available grant funds, we created a program for the staff and board members of Parent to Parent of Miami called the Path of Joyful Living program. It expanded upon my earlier leadership with a weekend intensive that included personal exploration using both the arts and the universal laws of oneness and mind action. In addition, each staff person and participating board member received five individual shamanic energy sessions scheduled over a three-month period.

It was in these individual sessions that I became aware of the deep emotional wounds that accompany broken family ties due to the loss of one's country, as many of their families had migrated to Miami from the Caribbean and other parts of the Americas. I worked with a colleague to evaluate the impact of the program. We found the group's stress levels and medical symptoms significantly reduced while their levels of mindfulness and joyfulness increased. After he finished analyzing the data, he called and asked, "What did you do to those people?" We chuckled. I knew that I was meant to circle back to Parent to Parent. I also hoped that what they couldn't yet fully understand about the universal law of oneness would reveal itself in due time.

The work with Parent to Parent laid a foundation that would lead to my most beautiful encounter with my daughter. It took place at Lily's home. She wanted another session with me because she felt stuck, as if something was blocking her from moving forward with her next big endeavor. We chose the deck off the master suite, looking out over the pool and inter-coastal waterway, as the best place. She lay down in a relaxed position on a large wicker lounge sofa on the deck. I called upon the four archetypal energies to create sacred space. Lily blew her emotions into one of the healing stones, and I placed it on the appropriate chakra. I began to sense and extract the stuck energies from her luminous energy field. A few minutes into the session, I felt a presence across from me, above and to the right of Lily's feet. I then heard these four words in perfect clarity: "The girls are here." There in front of me was a beautiful little girl about two years old with black curls, stout legs, and a round face. An inner knowing told me that it was Lily's daughter, Gabriela, who was born with no signs of life and died at birth. Lily still missed the daughter she'd never had.

Before I could complete my thought about what the word "girls," meant, I sensed the presence of my own daughter, hovering above my right shoulder. As I turned in that direction, I felt a light touch on my shoulder. Tears streamed down my cheeks. I wanted to stop, scream, and savor that moment, all at the same time. Instead, I started where I had left off, standing over Lily's body, rattling and pulling the heavy energy from her field. Sharing with her what had just occurred would have to wait.

Upon completion, we sat and talked.

"This is all pretty weird, but I feel lighter, calmer. It's a bit hard to put in words," she began.

"Well, we had important visitors," I related and started to explain what I had felt and seen.

"How do you know it was them?" she asked.

"People's energy field carries an imprint of who they are—their personality, you could say. When I am in that altered consciousness, I am able to read those imprints and see into the other dimension. The information often comes to me as an image or a sense or feeling, while at other times, it is auditory."

"So, you really think it was Gabriela?" she asked.

"Yes," I said. "Also, Lily, I suspect that somewhere in that heavy stuck energy were your feelings associated with her death. Know that by freeing yourself from any culpability, you are also releasing her from that same karma of loss. I also believe that same part of me no doubt was healed today, too."

I left Lily's house that day feeling thankful for the life I had chosen. I had gone through all my suffering for the gift of seeing. "All great religious teachers have recognized that we human beings do not naturally see; we have to be taught how to see. Jesus said, 'If your eye is healthy, your whole body is full of light'" (Luke 11:34).[2] That biblical passage had a whole new meaning for me now. The teaching that everyone potentially has the gift of seeing now included me.

Alex kept weaving herself back into my life, helping me to help mothers who were dealing with their life struggles. Seeking a good Netflix film one night, I stumbled upon a 2008 National Geographic documentary, *Stress: Portrait of a Killer*. The research with the baboons in Africa held my attention. Midway through the film, the scene changed to that of a researcher entering a support group meeting for parents with children with disabilities. My body sat more erect. The researcher's name was Dr. Blackburn, and she was about to have a major scientific breakthrough.[3] Stress, telomeres, the ends of your DNA, and lifespan are correlated. These mothers had shortened telomeres along with a shortened lifespan, by an average of ten whole years. Stress *is* a silent killer, and parents should know about this, I thought.

A short time later I received a call from my friend Susan.

"For some reason, I went onto the Developmental Disability Council's website today. They are looking for proposals to develop a booklet about coping with stress for caregivers."

2   Adapted from *Richard Rohr: Essential Teachings on Love*, ed. Joelle Chase and Judy Traeger (Orbis Books: 2018), 12, 25.

3   Blackburn, E., Epel, E. (2017) *The Telomere Effect*. New York: Hachette Book Group, Inc.

"You have to be kidding. I just watched a documentary about that. Let's do it," I said. The Federally funded Council offers a wide range of information and support as well as grants. Our proposal was selected, and I was awarded the grant funds. It was like old times being back at work with Susan. Our creative juices flowed easily. I hired an artist with a disability to do the booklet's illustrations. Iliana translated it into Spanish, and Ven's company did the printing. My extensive review of the literature informed the content. We included vignettes of parents using meditation, singing, journaling, music, exercise, and simple expressions of gratitude to reduce their stress. The booklet became one of the council's most frequently requested print resources, with over sixty thousand copies distributed as of this writing.

The project opened new doors. The next year, I submitted a proposal to provide a workshop on caregiver stress at the annual conference put on by the Family Café, Inc. The organization had grown tremendously over the years, and the conference now had over ten thousand people with disabilities in attendance. Lori Fahey, its founder and president, is someone I knew well when our children were young. When I began to explain the medium, Alex's message, and energy medicine, she didn't flinch. She had had her own unexplained experiences and easily understood.

She also understood my grief. For that reason, when one of the core members of the Café's youth council passed away suddenly, she asked me to create a Celebration of Life ceremony for the following year's conference. I was given a budget and permission to go create. I teamed up with an expressive artist, Dana Pezoldt, who had worked with children in hospice for many years. She was a creative genius who was at times in need of restraint.

"Paula, I couldn't sleep last night so I watched YouTube videos about how to make a bowl by turning it on a lathe, which could be the base of our Tree of Life for the ceremony."

"Oh, wow, great idea," I said.

"I think I could figure it out in time," she continued.

"Have you ever used a lathe before?" I asked. She hesitated.

"It didn't look too difficult," she said.

"Absolutely not," I said, and then we both roared with laughter. However, we kept turning the idea over in our minds, so to speak, and then lo and behold, the minister of her church had a lathe. Dana was dying to know what he was up to with that lathe, so we went to his house.

That was the beginning of a memorable six-month project. After being shown his lathe and learning that he had the largest lathe in South Florida, one that could turn a twenty-six-inch bowl, which no one else in Florida could do, we dug into the real details.

"I have eight hundred dollars, which is not much, but would love a large lathed bowl to hold our tree of life. Would you be able to do it?" I asked.

"Oh, I could do it all right," he said, "but you would never find a root ball large enough in South Florida. The trees here are not big enough, nor is the wood hard enough. And even if by some unlikely chance we found the wood, bowls that large often split during the process." I looked over at Dana and I could read her mind, thinking he has no idea who he is talking to. In the end, he agreed to the project if we could find him a big enough tree.

The next day, I began to receive texts and photos from Dana as she found abandoned tree trunks and downed trees along the Ingram Highway on her way home from work.

"Look at this monster. It may be big enough."

Then another text, "Ryan is going to help me get this one into my trunk." Although Ryan, her son, was only six years old, I knew Dana could finish any task she set her mind to.

Later came the celebratory text: "We got her in!" I roared with laughter and texted back smiley faces. We clearly were on a mission.

That Saturday, during meditation, I heard a voice tell me to go on a run today in the park. I began to argue.

"I am planning to swim instead, isn't that okay?

"Remember the new trail you like, go down that one," they urged. They seemed insistent that I go to Bill Baggs State Park, so off I went. As I turned onto the trail, I heard the motor of an electric saw and then saw a young handsome park ranger clearing heavy brush. Within seconds, I had walked up and was asking him if there would be any way we could possibly cut down one of his trees for a very important ceremony. His response left me incredulous.

"I don't see why not."

"We need one at least twenty-six inches in diameter, is that possible?"

"We have so much overgrowth and so many nonindigenous trees and plants. I would be glad to help you remove one." He handed me his business card, the last one he had. It had another person's name and the words 'art project' written on the back. He apologized for the used card as I internally rolled my eyes. I promised to be in touch soon.

Two weeks later, the minister, the park ranger, Dana, and I met at the park. Within a short time, we identified a buttonwood tree that was willing to be sacrificed. A week later, its five-ton root ball was loaded into the back of the minister's pickup truck. The root ball had the shape of a heart. Its natural cracks and textures were part of the human story we wove into the Celebration of Life ceremony.

We shared our spirit-filled recounting of how the bowl had come to be with more than three hundred grieving family members that day. I believe the story in and of itself was healing; not only for them, but also for me. I was back with my tribe. People with disabilities matter, and so does their loved ones' grief. My story of reuniting with Alex gave them hope and comfort. Now, every year during the Ceremony, individuals come and leave messages to their loved ones on the tree. Singing bowls are played as I take them on a journey into their Sacred Garden, a process described in the book *The Journey to the Sacred Garden: A Guide to Traveling in the Spiritual Realm* by Hank Wesselman, PhD. I had studied with Wesselman and taken my own journey to my Sacred Garden, so I knew this meditation helps those grieving find inner peace and possibly commune with their loved ones. I would always share Alex's photo and what I know about life after life along with the meditation.

The fact that I was now able to enjoy my time at Family Café was a sign of my own healing. I didn't suffer emotionally when I saw a child in a wheelchair, but rather felt at home with a community of people with which I had grown up and was now aging.

One effort with Family Café led to the next. A few years later, Lori asked me to create an annual Women's Summit for mothers to promote self-care. She wanted me to incorporate the stress-reducing modalities I had researched.

"Only if it can be mind, body, and spirit," I said. She said yes. Each year the team of experts I pull together shows large-screen images of chakras, meridians, the unified field, and the vagal nerve. The vagal nerve extends from the brain stem into the lower intestines. You activate your parasympathetic system by stimulating this nerve, allowing your body to relax and heal. Together we chant, do vocal toning, meditate, activate the chakras, go on shamanic journeys, and use expressive arts. The door prizes are salt lamps, baskets of essential oils, jade infrared mattresses, slow cookers, gemstones, and books on healthy eating. I ask the over two hundred women attending to consider their life as a soul's journey and to focus on what lessons they are here to learn, while helping them connect with their inner truth. In his book *Immortal Diamond: The Search for Our True Self*, Richard Rohr describes this process as love itself becoming love in this unique form called "me."

Living on the beach the small island of Key Biscayne was quite wonderful. Most days, I would stick my earbuds in and jog down the beach listening to my favorite tunes. I often headed to Crandon Park, about one mile north. At the park, I would make my way to an isolated and nature-filled area referred to as the old zoo. Now, the only animals in the cages were painted on the walls. I loved this small park. There, I meditated, walked barefoot, laid on the grass, fed the ibis, looked for the one known alligator in the small pond, got spooked by the huge iguanas that would suddenly run by, and climbed the banyan tree. I brought paints and sketch pad to capture the beauty of the wood cranes and watched the male peacocks try to lure a mate, apparently with a very low probability of success, a fact I discovered after much enjoyable observation.

Most fun was seeing Bubba, the tall white male goose who knew how to untie my shoes while saying hello. He let me stroke his long white neck and seemed to chatter away and listen attentively. I felt most at home here with all the wildlife. I swear, on several occasions the peacocks greeted me by fanning their tail feathers for a long period of time. It was here that I began to understand what oneness with nature could mean, represented in a quote by Albert Einstein. "One experiences oneself as something separated from the rest—a kind of optical delusion… Our task must be to free ourselves from this prison by widening our circle of compassion to embrace all living creatures and the whole of nature in its beauty."[4]

---

[4]   Albert Einstein, condolence letter to Norman Salit (March 4, 1950). Reprinted in *The New York Times*, March 29, 1972, https://www. nytimes.com/1972/03/29/archives/the-einstein-papers-a-man-of-many-parts-the-einstein-papers-man-of.html.

However, by 2014, real estate prices were on the rise again, and living on Key Biscayne became less affordable. Its upscale Hispanic community felt less like me than the birds at Crandon Park did. And although the peacocks were great company, I thought there had to be more to life. With my love of the arts, I decided to move downtown to be close to the new Perez Art Museum and the Arsht Performing Arts Center. I rented a condo overlooking the ocean on the fifty-fifth floor, across from the American Airlines Arena.

Everyone who knew me was a bit shocked with my decision. "Nouveau riche and sky rise don't seem to fit you, Paula," said a friend. It didn't. It was the year my clients began doing better than I was. My clients' physical pains were disappearing, relationships with their partners were improving, deceased loved ones were coming to visit, and careers were being transformed. However, *my* life was not going so well. I had once again chosen an expensive living environment, under the illusion that great success and steady income were just around the next corner. In addition, not being surrounded by nature had a bigger impact on me than I could have ever imagined. I found it hard to do my daily meditation, and there was no good place to run. I was not replenishing myself and felt drained. However, with fewer distractions from the scenic outdoors and the animals, I did begin to write my book and took a memoir writing class at the nearby college campus.

It was that year that my friend Kathy Feldman invited me to an opera preview, an opera event held in a member's home, hosted by the organization The Young Patronesses of the Opera (YPO). The YPO is dedicated to cultivating a love of opera in the community. After the live opera performance, all eighty of us dined together on the outdoor patio. After dinner, two women asked me if I would be interested in joining the organization. I hesitated, but my long-frustrated inner philanthropist was eager to say, "Yes." That yes was fueled by the fact that a few years before, my brother and I had received equal gifts of money from our mother. I could now present the *appearance* of an abundant woman but lacked the tools to inhabit this new reality. Inside, I was not ready to give up my struggle with money and continued to recreate my relationship with it.

"Kathy, what do you think? I asked.

"I never thought you would join, but you know I would love you to," she said. I left this most enjoyable event considering it. What drew me toward saying "Yes," in addition to being able to spend more time with Kathy, whose son continued to feel a deep connection with Alex, the music, and the opulence which I so loved, was the involvement of the children. Their in-school opera program went to over thirty-five schools, many of them in low-income neighborhoods. However, opting out of a sorority experience in college had left me unprepared for this experience of sisterhood. I decided to stay focused on the group's positive attributes and have fun!

It began with a skit.

"Ladies, write and practice your skits. They need to be short, lively, and tell a story about who you are. We will see you back here next week. And start thinking about your speakeasy costume," Rebecca announced to the seventeen of us who were joining that year.

"A skit, something I've always wanted to do," I thought excitedly to myself. The next day, the words for my skit fell onto the paper in a flash. "I will sing the first line, and then transition into a poem rhythm," I told myself. After twelve weeks, twelve practices, and many more bottles of prosecco, we felt comfortable with each other and ready for our rite of passage.

It took place in the home of the president of the organization. Her living room became the theater, with décor creating the appearance of a speakeasy. We arrived and went upstairs to get ready.

"Marianne, do you have an extra pair of stockings? I can't find mine," wailed one.

"Why did I ever agree to do this?" lamented another.

"Do you think this looks okay?"

"Can I use some of your makeup?"

"Where's Jae, she's not here yet?"

Then, "Come on, ladies, everyone is ready for you," reported Rebecca, who was dressed up as one of the speakeasy bouncers. We all put down our glasses of prosecco; perhaps ten o'clock was too early to drink anyway. We filed down the stairs in our 1920s costumes, complete with plumage, low necklines, pearls, and black stockings. One by one we crossed the threshold into the living room and walked to the door of the speakeasy.

"What's the password," bellowed Rebecca.

My first blaring line went like this: "I have always wanted to sing, but I can't carry a tune, so this poem is what I have for you."

Kathy thought mine was the best performance, being the good friend that she is. I realized that I'd never had that kind of girly experience. It felt good. In many ways, I had spent much of my life alone. Four of us gravitated to each other and became friends; unsurprisingly, psychic phenomena were a common thread between us. We were provisional members that year, which meant we each had new-member volunteer assignments, e.g., cooking and/or serving the luncheons, introducing the school operas to the children, attending all the monthly meetings, and so on. It was in these ways we were brought into the fold. We became a support to each other.

My love for running continued to result in unexpected synchronicities. One Saturday, I wanted to check out a small vintage tour yacht that was docked in the bay in front of my building. Jaime was visiting, and I had hopes of getting out on the water together. As I was walking up the boat's ramp, I noticed young adults wearing Best Buddies® T-shirts. Best Buddies International is an organization that matches young people with disabilities with peers who are developing typically. Its founder is Anthony Shriver, and when I arrived, I happened to end up standing next to him.

"I met you and your parents years ago while I was giving a presentation to your Best Buddies International board of directors." I said as I introduced myself to him. His eyes revealed the pain of his loss as he heard his parents' names, Eunice and Sargent Shriver.

"I would like to thank you for everything you and your family have done for people with disabilities," I told him, adding a bit about Alex. I went on, "I used to teach pediatric residents about how your mother was the one who drafted the disability legislation and then would ask President Kennedy and Senator Bobby Kennedy to get it enacted." He smiled.

We all took a tour of the yacht and then walked back down the ramp back into the park. I heard my inner voice telling me to talk to Anthony about my "Moved to Learn" program—my program for children with disabilities to learn movement to music. I began with that, then went on to talk more about Alex, the medium, and the importance of young people understanding the power of their thoughts and intentions. He listened. He asked me to follow up via email as he saw a possible role for me at his upcoming International Best Buddies conference. The emails resulted in an invite to present a keynote presentation and two workshops. I practiced my twenty-minute presentation with a small group of friends so it would be just perfect.

There at the University of Indiana in Bloomington, I stood on stage in front of 1,600 youth, showing them images of the human form's luminous energy body and the unified field. I invited two volunteers to come onto the stage to demonstrate the reality that our consciousness extends beyond self. As my volunteers faced away from the audience, I instructed the audience, with a thumbs-down visual, to silently send negative thought forms toward the two volunteers. I used energy testing, also known as muscle testing, an outgrowth of the field of kinesiology, asking each volunteer to extend their arm straight out in front of them and hold it strongly in place. The audience witnessed the impact of their negative thoughts; each volunteer's arm easily fell when I put pressure on it. One volunteer even said he felt weak-kneed and nauseous. The audience then sent positive, kind, loving thoughts toward the volunteers, which had the opposite effect. I shared with them about Dr. Masaru Emoto, the author of *The Message from Water*, his study of water and how the power of prayer transformed disfigured water molecules into crystalline shapes. I ended with the message that we can manifest our desired future by aligning our intentions and thoughts with our heart's desires. I loved the sound of 1,600 people clapping. My father's vision of me speaking in front of a large audience had been fulfilled. A conference attendee later said, "I didn't know there was so much to positive thinking, thank you." There was genuine caring between the Best Buddies volunteers and their peers with a disability everywhere I looked. I was excited to be a part of the effort.

That year, I also shared my new way of seeing the world with someone who was very dear to me. It began with a telephone call from Rick Urbano. He and Terri now lived in Nashville and were both teaching at Vanderbilt University.

"Terri's cancer is back," he began. His voice cracked as he described the diagnosis, "She has triple negative breast cancer, which usually grows and spreads quicker than most other types." We both agreed that Terri had already endured so much, including colon and liver cancer during the years we'd worked together at the medical school, which had forced her to take a seven-month leave of absence to fully recover. For cancer to return fifteen years later felt unfair.

I spoke with Terri, and surprisingly, she knew exactly what I was talking about. She shared how she had always had a strong faith and an inner knowing ever since early childhood. Possibly this was related to her mother's early death and the hardships Terri had undergone living with her widowed father. That summer and fall, Terri and I had regular phone sessions. I was hoping to be her lifeline, as she had been mine after Alex's death. According to Terri, she succeeded in resolving issues that had been haunting her since she was a young girl. What still weighed on Terri's heart, though, was Rick's skepticism, which we couldn't do anything about. She so wanted him to believe in life after life. It would give her peace of mind if she knew that he would be comforted after her death in that way.

CHAPTER

19

A New Era of Medicine

IT WAS NOVEMBER OF 2010 when I arrived back in Miami and rented an apartment on the small island of Key Biscayne, envisioning myself living there for six months while I wrote this book. I felt fully alive and wanted everyone to come to understand life as I now saw it, and a book seemed to be the perfect vehicle to share how I'd arrived at my new perspective. It also felt like an answer of sorts to my quest for a future career. Always propelled forward by my search for a sense of worthiness coupled with my drive for success, I saw myself lecturing around the country within a short period of time, sharing my new revelation that indeed, we never do die with everyone who would listen.

However, I spent little time writing my book or even taking writing classes. In my enthusiasm, I had the illusion that the book would somehow write itself—in an immediate download of information, perhaps. As writing endeavors go, the book's purpose and content were clear in my mind, but how to get it on paper was elusive. Instead of pushing through that quagmire of the unknown, I did many other things.

One was to offer my shamanic energy medicine sessions, letting people know by word of mouth that I was available. Another step was to once again attend the Department of Cultural Affairs' All Kids Included (AKI) meetings. I was one of the original members; individually and collectively, they are a highly creative and productive group of women. Their mission is to ensure that the arts are accessible to children with disabilities. But at my first meeting back, I found the woman who would illuminate for me the mysteriousness of the world into which I had flung myself.

As the task force meeting ended, Yani approached me.

"I know what you do, and I want to come see you. I will call you to set up an appointment," she whispered. My calendar was bare in those days, and I wondered if she would really call. Six months later, I saw her again at the AKI meeting.

"I now really need to see you," she said. I opened my calendar.

"How's next Tuesday after work, around six o'clock?" I gave her my address, and she said she would be there. Yani was in her mid-thirties, had been raised a devout Catholic, and desperately wanted to have a child. That much I knew.

She arrived on time, bringing with her an ice chest with her fertility medicines, which she placed inside my front door. I had made a cushioned area on the floor for us to sit on and motioned for her to make herself comfortable.

"Paula, for some reason I just know you can help me. I have had two miscarriages in the past two years, both late in the pregnancy. I so want to have a child before it is too late."

She seemed frantic. I began to explain what we would be doing, but she didn't seem interested. She wanted action, results.

"Which one of these stones would you like to work with?" I asked as I opened my *mesa*—my healing bundle.

"I can choose any one I want?" she asked.

"Sure, you choose. The stone is your ally, it will help draw out the heavy energy that is making it difficult for you to have a child," I explained. She blew and blew into that stone. I then asked her to lie down on her back and make herself comfortable.

First, I directed my attention to her chakras; a chakra is a spinning energy center or vortex that is part of each person's luminous energy field. I determined which chakra was best for our purpose of healing and placed her stone on top of it. With the vibrating sounds of my rattle, I began to enter an altered state, one that gave me the ability to see into the invisible world and into her luminous energy field. I sensed dense energy in her lower chakras, seeing them as cone-shaped swirling vortexes of energy; I began drawing out the dense energy by reaching down with the tip of my rattle into the cone-shaped wells. Then, I laid my rattle down to observe her auric field in silence.

Oh my, I thought.

Unexpectedly, I was gazing into the inside of her womb. It was full of frenetically moving black flecks of energy. Their sharp, rapid movements reminded me of her personality. I then sensed a presence in the room. I looked over my right shoulder, and in the corner three feet away was a monk clothed in a brown hooded robe. He nodded to me, as if to say, "Proceed." I returned my gaze to her abdomen, placing my hands directly above it. I could not believe what I saw then in my inner vision. Two magnificently large white glowing hands entered her womb, reminding me of a Christian song I used to belt out in church when I was young, "He's Got the Whole World in His Hands." Time stood still. Her womb turned into a bright white light. Then, a thick black ring, similar to a rubber ring inside a mason jar, circled the inside of her womb. The black flecks of energy disappeared, as well as the glowing hands and the monk. As I was finishing, for just a millisecond, an image of a male and then a female infant appeared in my mind's eye.

I was astonished but stayed low-key while I explained to Yani what had transpired during the healing; I told her about everything except for seeing the infants.

"I know I am going to get pregnant," Yani said, standing at the door, fertility ice chest in her hand. She was almost right. That night, Yani was already pregnant. She had come for a different reason, to soothe, calm, and strengthen her womb. The twins, Max and Liam, were born on their due date: Christmas Day. Later, in reflection, I asked myself, "Were the hands mine, the monk's, those of one of the many saints to whom she had prayed, or perhaps a reflection of her own divinity?" I concluded that the answer is part of the mystery, and that to assert anything else would only be pretending to know.

Sundays felt empty without going to church. Pondering where to go, I discover that I had serendipitously moved across the street from the former and beloved minister of Unity on the Bay, Bill Cameron, and his wife Dori. They both had their own emotional pains related to their daughters' and offered empathy and friendship. Dori and I took to going on early morning walks on the beach together, as well as sharing many brunches after church services.

My longtime friend Helen sang in Unity's choir and knew them both well. In our time together, I learned about Unity on the Bay's history and came to understand why Bill was credited with saving the church. One night over dinner, Bill told us about the nights he had slept in the sanctuary armed with a baseball bat with his young daughter, and the time he was robbed on the way to a nearby bank to deposit Sunday's offerings. During the 1980s, Edgewater, an area just north of downtown. had high rates of prostitution and drug use. Bill described the pressure he felt from the scant church membership to sell this bayfront property and move to a safer location. He did not waver and instead rebuilt the membership. The books and the hundreds of articles he has written reflect his deep understanding of the evolution and importance of our search for life's meaning.

It was at Unity that I came to understand the power of affirmative prayer. I attended their prayer chaplain training and served in the church in that capacity for a year. Instead of asking God for something, I entered into communion with the spirit of God within and saw the desire already accomplished. This form of prayer is based on a metaphysical understanding of life, i.e., things are first manifested in the ethereal realm and then brought into the physical. Faith is the bridge that brings one's hopes into physical form. For myself and so many others, disappointment settles in before the universe ever has a chance to respond. Our timelines always create problems for us. Letting go of not only the when, but the how, where, and what is also part of the prayer formula. The realization that Source or God has a better grip on what is in the self's best interest is an aspect of affirmative prayer. There is an intelligence that is both "out there" and "in here" and is always working on my behalf. With time, I learned to trust that truth. Weekly reminders from the pulpit were essential to helping erode my old thought patterns.

At Unity, I also learned more about the universal law of mind action. If I want to be in a different movie, I can: The choice is mine. However, to create a new script, I had to first identify and relinquish my sacred cows—those beliefs and attitudes that I held immune from questioning or criticism. These lie hidden in the subconscious mind, where everything we have ever learned is stored. The subconscious mind is like a tape player or digital recorder that records everything and keeps playing it back. These programs or patterns become fixed and run our lives as we go about living, and if our mind is not in the present moment, our subconscious is in charge. The weekly meditations, conscious reminders of this co-creative power, and sense of community at Unity were a stabilizing force in my sea of change.

Unity also offered metaphysical courses and a bookstore complete with authors from many different spiritual and religious traditions. When I saw the Course in Miracles listed in the bulletin as a class offering, I smiled remembering New York City and my roommate, who had translated the Course in Miracles into Russian. Unity's doctrine is grounded in Christian belief yet inclusive at the same time, acknowledging the diversity of our hearts and the many paths that we can take, all ending up in the same place. As a friend used to say, there are many different telephone poles, just choose one and begin. That's how I could buy books on shamanism as well as Tibetan prayer flags. Also, it was in that spirit that Dori Cameron and I gave a workshop about the divine feminine, introducing women to the archetypal energies of Goddess Isis, Goddess Sophia, Mother Mary, and Mary Magdalene. And I was able to offer my monthly shamanic energy cleanse workshop.

It was in that sanctuary that I did my deepest work. I attribute it to Unity's belief in the power of prayer. Wanting to learn, I delved into the writings of Dr. Larry Dossey, e.g., *Be Careful What You Pray For*, *Reinventing Medicine*, and *One Mind*. His thorough reporting of research demonstrates that our thoughts, in the form of desires, prayers, fears, and doubts, have an impact on ourselves and others. In fact, as he describes, there are over 150 studies that support the ability of thoughts, wishes, and prayers to affect distant biological systems. The fact that some of these studies involve microbes and cells provides strong evidence that the power of suggestion is not in play. The reality that our consciousness exists outside of ourselves is possible because of the divine design of the Universe. We are all One, interwoven together in a connective web of energy. Western medicine's disregard for this truth has limited our knowledge and access to healing modalities that are inherently ours.

I began to see myself as part of the new era of medicine that he described: an era where dreams matter, acceptance of an illness is a strategy for recovery, love and intimate connections are sources of healing, and prayer for life is as predictive as a prognosis of early death. It will be an era when our body's ethereal field is seen as real and alternative healing methods become mainstream, an era where energy is medicine, and an era when you heal the body by activating its natural healing energies and by restoring energies that have become blocked, weak, or out of balance. A time will come when the physician's third eye is expanded and he or she can access information available not through technology, but rather through a merging with the patient's energy field. I saw myself contributing to the remaking of medicine and helping people realize that the Wizard lies within all of us.

This time would not come for my daughter, as regrettably, it was too late, but such a change is still possible for the countless other families who have a child with special needs. If medical doctors experienced the universal truth of oneness, they would create heart-centered practices—trumping even the family-centered practices I strove to implement. In contemplating returning the art of healing to medicine, I imagined stimulating acupuncture points to promote a healthy immune system for the chronically ill; clearing trauma and stress from the ethereal field with energy medicine, which is helpful for young children and others unable to communicate their feelings; and using telepathy with children who are nonverbal, as well as meditation to reset the anxious child's parasympathetic or "rest and restore" system, increasing the child's ability to focus and learn.

I was not the only one wanting to offer this new energy medicine. There was already an existing underground network of experienced practitioners doing just those things. But like the disability movement decades earlier, it was time to bring this new paradigm above ground into people's consciousness. I was excited to be a part of it. The idea of being a spiritual warrior was invigorating.

CHAPTER

20

Dark Entities

MY REGULAR LIFE WASN'T FEELING so good by fall of 2015. I was living in my high-rise condo, finding it difficult to maintain my spiritual practices; my book was unwritten, and I was having intrusive negative thoughts. I had moved four times, sometimes due to landlords, but mostly it was my own doing. I once again had chosen an expensive living environment, which contributed to my focus on producing income and conflicted with carving out ample time to write my book. I had a strong desire to move away from Miami, which made it difficult to scale up my projects and my individual work with clients. I was restless and couldn't find long-lasting satisfaction with what I was doing. I felt I was vulnerable to what in the shamanic tradition are called dark entities. I knew enough about them through my clients to know I did not want that misfortune to befall me.

My first intense exposure to entities was through my friendship with Michelle. We met at a memorial service, thirty miles south of where we lived in Miami. After the eulogy, while everyone gathered in the back of the room, a longtime friend introduced us.

"Paula, you should meet Michelle, she also lives on Key Biscayne." There across from me was a petite, middle-aged woman with an intense expression. We shook hands and began to share personal facts.

"I just moved into a condominium at The Towers and I like it," I said.

"That is where I live," she replied. We laughed at the coincidence. When I shared that I was a shamanic energy medicine practitioner, her face lit up. She immediately asked for my contact information.

Later that week, Michelle and I met on the beach. There was a cool breeze, and the stars lit up the sky. I came with the hopes of a new friend and Michelle with hopes on behalf of her daughter. She brought a bottle of white wine. She frantically chewed her fingernails as she spoke about her sixteen-year-old daughter's severe and chronic depression and her own feelings of helplessness.

"Andrea is assuredly failing tenth grade. Complicating matters is the fact that I am a single mother and I work full-time, which means Andrea is home alone during the day," she confided, holding back tears.

"What's been done thus far?" I asked.

"She has had so many psychological and psychiatric workups. They all have the same opinion: Her type of depression can be managed with therapy and medication, but not cured, if in fact she makes it at all. What we are doing is not working. Andrea just sits angrily silent during her cognitive therapy. Where is the real compassion and connection with her?"

The reason for Michelle's inviting me to the beach was becoming clear. I wasn't sure how my newly acquired skills could help, but I offered my help and then suggested that she contact Parent to Parent to inquire about Florida's medical homebound program. She seemed comforted by our time on the beach. But her ability to get things done became clear to me when, within a few weeks, Andrea was enrolled in that program. Much more challenging, however, would be motivating Andrea to study, or even to get out of bed. Michelle and I devised a plan. The plan was to introduce Andrea to shamanic energy medicine through the project I was working on, with the hope that she would be interested in this medicine for herself. The project included some photography, which was of interest to Andrea. She was to arrive at my condo at eleven o'clock three days a week and would be paid eleven dollars per hour. Given the fact that her mother was in debt due to all the unforeseen medical bills for her daughter's care, she couldn't pay me. It felt like a lose-lose arrangement for me, except for the unique privilege of helping a teenage girl in deep despair.

I enjoyed Andrea's company. She was quiet, unassuming, helpful, and incredibly smart. Petite in stature with long brown hair and matching eyes, she rarely spoke as we worked. Trust between us built over time through our shared experiences. She became the daughter I no longer had. In between tasks, I would give her an energy medicine session. Andrea connected with the work immediately, sometimes seeing and sensing the same things I did as I melded into the invisible realm to help shift her old thought patterns, which appeared to me in the form of images and spoken messages.

"Your soul is hungry to be in nature, Andrea. I saw the large white elephant again today, along with about every other animal in existence," I said, exaggerating for emphasis.

"I saw the white elephant too!" she replied. Those moments of mutual seeing, when we both saw the white elephant, a rabbit, or a dark shadowy figure, were of greatest value. This built trust in herself, created curiosity, and developed her confidence to delve into the work herself. The genuine challenge that there was a lot of hidden darkness and early childhood wounds within her was balanced by the fact that her energy field was always alive with animal helping spirits.

During their mother-and-daughter overseas vacation, they communicated amicably for the first time in years. They went to an elephant rescue center in Cambodia; they had previously identified a potential private residential high school, a B'nai B'rith school near Prague, for Andrea. Now in London, things shifted, and she had a serious downturn. It was nine thirty one night that I received their call. Michelle explained a bit of the situation and then handed her phone to Andrea.

"They are back. They say they are going to kill me," she said, repeatedly. I knew what she was referring to, dark shadowy forms of energy that were up to no good.

I began to energetically send her light and called upon my guides and spirit helpers, and hers, for protection. I reminded Andrea to do the same. She was panicked, almost sobbing.

"They are scoffing at me and my spirit animals. They are saying that they are going to get you too." I was by now really pissed and ready for battle. I became fearless.

"Imagine I am standing right in front of you. Look me straight in the eyes, now match my breathing. Andrea. Remember, you are safe, loved, and protected. Nothing can harm you."

The repetition of these words, my steady voice and tone of conviction, and the trust she had in me brought her to a calm state. Her mother and I spoke about a retreat center in Sedona and the plant medicine ayahuasca. Shortly after, we hung up.

I left my office building in a torrential rainstorm. It was a Friday night. I had parked on Giralda Avenue, a street lined with popular restaurants in the upscale community of Coral Gables. When I parked, I had consciously avoided the parking spots with a Valet Only bag over the meter. Regardless, my car was nowhere to be found—it had been towed. Completely drenched, I flagged down a taxi driver who knew well how to find the city lot for towed cars, which was in a deserted area of Miami, and drove me there. The woman working the desk at the tow lot not only looked but acted like a prison guard, with a gruff voice, tall hefty body, and few words. After shelling out more money than I'd made that day, I was given my car keys. I was relieved when I arrived home safely until the moment when I looked down at my phone and saw small white worms crawling on it. Ugh, I thought and went to bed. The next day's text from Michelle was a synchronistic shocker: "We got back to our hotel, and Andrea flipped out when a worm fell down from the ceiling onto her computer." I replied, "They are not going to win."

From London, Michelle and Andrea made their way to a holistic healing sanctuary in Sedona and then went on to Peru. It was there, five hours north of Lima, near Huaraz, that the dark energy was successfully extracted from Andrea's energy field in a series of ayahuasca ceremonies, giving her the chance to create a different future for herself. Although there is no overnight victory, as with any form of healing, her life immediately began to flow better. Andrea recently graduated from Bard College with honors.

Our work together introduced me to dark entities and their desire to attack humans as we move toward the Light. It is the struggle between the dark and the light forces, one that is as old as time. From a shamanic perspective, this darkness exists both within us and outside of us. Actual dark entities do exist and may invade one's human energy field when we are vulnerable, whether due to trauma, addictions, and/or intergenerational family patterns. Andrea had the worst of the worst—the dark entity whose sole purpose is annihilation. They don't let go easily. This is the same type of entity, I presume, that is extracted during an exorcism, a ritual still practiced by priests in the Catholic church. Yes, working with Andrea was eye-opening, and it prepared me for what lay ahead.

A friend called one night.

"There is a Lakota Yuwipi Ceremony in the Redlands, would you like to go?" he asked.

"What is that?"

"A friend forwarded me the invite, she said it is considered one of the most potent indigenous ceremonies for physical and emotional healing."

"Perfect timing," I said, "I want to go."

Forty-five of us entered a large converted garage space, its inside walls meticulously covered with black plastic. There were three basic rules: the room had to be totally dark, with no visible shiny metal objects, and women on their menstrual cycle could not attend. In the center was the medicine man's altar and a space large enough for him to lie down. Red prayer ties filled with tobacco wound around the altar space. There were four large flags that marked the corners of the rug, signifying the four sacred directions and the four aspects of self: soul or spirit, mind, emotions, and body. A large buffalo skull was placed at one end of the altar, and there were several groupings of large rattles. A small battery-operated lantern gave us light during the medicine man's introduction. He talked about his Choctaw ancestry and how ceremony is an essential component of everyday life. A cluster of sage was passed around, and we each put a twig behind our left ear for protection from bad spirits.

When it was time to begin, one of his five helpers stepped to the middle of the room and stood behind him holding a long, thick string. She laced his hands together behind his back, weaving the thick twine between each one of his fingers. She then draped a blanket over his body. Starting at the top of his body, she tied him up. Altogether there were seven knots along his backside, with a long stem of sage placed in each one. He was laid face down on the long, thin rug, with his hands tied together inside the blanket behind him. It looked like a very uncomfortable position.

The battery-powered lantern was turned off, and the room fell into complete darkness and silence. The five helpers broke into Lakota ceremonial songs, calling in the help of woodland spirits, stone spirits, and animal spirits. Meanwhile, we were sending forth our prayers. As the singing shifted to ceremonial healing songs, amazing things started to happen. The rattles began to move. We heard them above us, around us, and next to us. Wherever the rattles went, there were bursts of light, created by the energy expended by spirit to lift and shake the rattle. A strand of sage at the base of the altar space suddenly was on fire. The left corner of my shirt was lifted, and later I felt gusts of air on my face. At one point, two rattles were banging on the floor in front of our feet. There was a screeching sound above us to one side. Each sound, touch, and sighting happened very quickly and randomly. It felt more playful than scary, but there was a sense of urgency.

Spirit eventually untied the medicine man; the ceremony had been successful, as the communication between him and spirit had transpired. The lights were turned on. He lit his *chanupa* (medicine pipe) which contained kinnikinnick, a smoking mixture made from shavings from the sacred red willow tree, and passed it around, followed by small bowls of water, corn kernels, meat, and blueberries. As we ate and gave thanks, we talked about our experiences. Everyone had heard the rattles; some people had been touched, usually on their heart or head, while others were banged with the rattles. Some others heard healing messages, and still others had seen someone straddling the medicine man, no doubt untying him. The ceremony came to an end, and we filed out through the hanging black plastic and enjoyed a potluck dinner together.

Back home, I sensed that I was not alone. Perhaps a spirit had followed me. I took a hot bath in case he or she was not of the benevolent sort and slept deeply. When I woke up, I felt worse than ever. My gloominess deepened, and by mid-morning, I felt like I had been tied up. I heard a negative voice rattling around inside of me. I wanted my money back.

At the time, I reflected upon my prayer at the Yuwipi ceremony: "Align me with my true nature and abilities," and I remembered a biblical truth and energy truism: "And all things, whatsoever ye shall ask in prayer, believing, ye shall receive" (Matthew 21:22). I had a tinge of regret that I had made such a bold request. But the gloominess lingered, and at times, felt even worse. I had nights when I woke up to the voice yelling at me, not from within but from outside of myself. This had nothing to do with biblical promises, I told myself. This felt dark. The worst of the torment lasted for about a month. I stopped working with clients and mostly stayed home as my digestive system needed me to stay near a bathroom, where I daily swept up the globs of hair that fell out each time I brushed. In my downward-spiral state, I finally collapsed onto my couch. I was exhausted. The perfect storm had arrived. There was nothing left to do but to write my book. I started to make real progress. The voices went back into hiding.

CHAPTER

21

Endings Bring New Life

I N WRITING MY BOOK, MY greatest foreboding was reliving Alex's death; I wasn't sure what I would experience. Although the writing process was gut-wrenching for me, nothing unexpected occurred during the writing the book, but rather came with its completion. In the middle of the night, I awoke with a song from *The Wizard of Oz* echoing in my head:

'Ding Dong! The Witch is dead. Which old Witch? The Wicked Witch!

Ding Dong! The Wicked Witch is dead.

Wake up—sleepy head, rub your eyes, get out of bed.

Wake up, the Wicked Witch is dead.'

I became disoriented. Who was the witch? Me? Alex? Who killed whom? I watched the Wizard of Oz trailer for clues. The Munchkins sang that song after Dorothy's house landed and killed the Wicked Witch of the East. With the Witch's death, the Munchkins were once again independent, free of her torment as the song goes on to say. I, too, would become free of torment—the torment of guilt I had inflicted upon myself for most of my life.

During that spring of 2016, I sensed that my days in Miami were limited. Could I leave Alex behind? One afternoon, with a little downtime in between appointments, I drove to AD Barnes Park, a nearby green space, just to breathe in a little scent of nature. Many years had passed since I had been there. It is a park gracious to people with a disability, with its wooden ramps, extensive nature paths, and handicapped accessible pool. Images of long-ago picnics with the spina bifida association and Parent to Parent floated up from my memory bank. These had been our opportunities to be together without the typical ramifications of being out in public, e.g., unsolicited suggestions, pity-filled stares, looks of disgust, backdoor entrances through restaurant kitchens, heavy sighs, the need to explain the disability, and all the ways in which people let you know that you are not them.

Yes, the park that day was filled with unsolicited memories, and there was no stopping them. One particular incident came to mind, and I decided to drive over to that section of the park, where the nature center is located. Alex had attended a summer camp program there when she was six years old. She loved those programs—the arts, other children, being in nature—and people loved her. My memory was sketchy: for some reason, I had asked Alex to roll herself through the woods along the paved trail and to meet Jaime and me at the end where I would bring the car around to pick her up. Alex was fine with the plan. She arrived five minutes later at the end of the trail as discussed. Alongside her was a park ranger who was visibly upset. She approached with scorn and proceeded to rattle off all the potential perils that hadn't manifested, such as Alex falling off the edge of the sidewalk, a stranger doing her harm, or Alex being scared being out alone. Jaime shot a look at me, wondering if it all could have been true. Alex and I looked at each other, perplexed. We kept trying to live a normal life, and everyone was always getting in the way.

I walked along that same paved trail that day years later, feeling a bit melancholic. I realized how long it had been since I'd touched something that she had touched or walked where she had walked. Our life together was so many cities, homes, and cars ago. I'd been running from my sadness, perhaps, but at the same time running toward wholeness. I had to be uprooted and become unstuck and free-floating in order to heal. Sitting in the parking lot of the nature center that day, I felt closure: as if I had been pulled around the city in unexpected ways to heal, with memories triggered by settings, people, music, situations, all to release the residual toxic energies that were dormant in my energy field. As I left the park for my next appointment, I drove past the street that led to the cemetery. I thought, Oh no, not today.

When we buried Alex, a part of me wanted to have her cremated and to take her ashes home with me so she would be with me wherever I went. No one else thought that was a good idea, but it was. It is so hard to let go. My grief had become my reminder of her. But I knew that much of grief is a result of the illusion of loss. Alex was never mine to lose, and we never do die. Sorrow had become my connection with her. Letting go of sorrow felt like another loss.

As I was reliving Alex's death, Terri was dying. I flew to Nashville to be with her and her family. We did a last healing together and spoke of matters of the heart. More than anything, she wanted Rick to believe in the loving power of spirit. I shared that some people decide the form of afterlife communication ahead of time. Terri loved that idea; she chose a bird. I didn't tell Rick about the bird communication symbol as he was too distraught. He was losing his life partner and couldn't do anything to stop her from slipping away. Terri transitioned the following week.

Six months later, I was shocked to hear Rick's voice on the other end of the phone saying that he was going to attend my upcoming workshop. I panicked a bit, wondering how he was going to fit in with Peruvian rattles, votive candles, tarot cards, and eye gazing. This didn't match the Rick I knew. But there he was. He thought it would help him release his unrelenting emotional pain. Rick shared that Terri had appeared to him twice since her transition. Once was as he awoke from a dream; he saw her standing in the bedroom they had shared together. Another time she appeared to him in their den. That was the Terri I knew, stubbornly persistent to the point of being pertinacious. I smiled to myself. I could now share the bird communication. At the end of the workshop, everyone wrote a letter to themselves. I mailed their letters three months later. All of the desires Rick expressed in his letter were already unfolding by then, including meeting his future wife. When I saw her picture, Rick and I laughed, knowing that Terri had picked her out. They could not have looked more alike. He later sent me a picture while on vacation in San Diego—a photo of two birds in the middle of a meadow.

It was the summer of 2016. A friend and I traveled to attend Jonathan Goldman's Sound Intensive program in Colorado. I loved music, dance, and singing. Upon discovering that they could be natural forms of medicine, I wanted to learn more. Jonathan is a world-renowned teacher and sound healer; notably, he *looks* like a wizard with his long curly grey hair, flowy black velvety mid-length cape, hat, wide-legged pants, and mostly bare feet. Our ten-hour days of toning, chanting, and energy clearings were invigorating. Toning, making vocalized vowel sounds for an extended time for the purpose of healing, met my longtime need to use my voice. From Loveland, Colorado, we traveled south to Crestone to visit Singing Stone, a place of worship and spiritual healing dedicated to preserving indigenous spiritual ceremonies and culture founded by Christopher Long, the Lakota medicine man who had led the Yuwepi Ceremony in Miami. He performed a ceremonial blessing for the both of us. Looking into his quartz crystal, he shared, "I see you becoming quite a competent medicine woman." I beamed. We made plans for my spring Vision Quest there in Crestone.

From Denver, I flew to Albany, rented a car, and made my way to Cherry Valley, a small town in upstate New York, a plan that had its origins in a text message from Susan.

"A neighbor of ours needs someone to dog sit at their upstate home in August, interested?"

"Probably, can you send me the details?" I replied.

Soon I received an email with an attached photo from the dog owner, June Barwick, "This is our home, however, the man you see on the ladder is not included. Not shown is our pool." I immediately liked her sense of humor. Their large and historic home sat on twelve acres of groomed property, surrounded by rapeseed fields and trails. This is a no-brainer, I thought, and said, "Yes."

The time had arrived to meet the Barwicks and their dog Jesse. "Bring your suitcase, I will show you the upstairs," said June. At the top of the stairs, I heard a loud high-pitched screeching sound coming from the bedroom to the right. June didn't hear it.

"Would you like the bedroom to the right or the middle bedroom?" she asked.

"Ermmm, I'll go with the middle bedroom, thanks," I said, walking past the other room. It feels like I was just greeted, I thought to myself. During our visit together before the Barwicks left for France, I learned the original home on this property had been the site of the famous Cherry Valley massacre. Historically described as one of the most horrific massacres, the Cherry Valley massacre was an attack by combined British and Iroquois forces on a fort and the village of Cherry Valley during the Revolutionary War. The spirits of people who die suddenly are most likely to get stuck here in the middle world, which explained the books about the ghosts in Cherry Valley.

The routine of a five o'clock dog walk and swim, coupled with my newfound skill of vocal toning, eased my writing process. The words came pouring onto the page once again. An extended visit from my niece Mia and her now growing family, including her daughter, her husband,

and their unborn twins, due in five months, reconnected me with New York. By the end of August, I knew my days in Miami were over.

I returned to Miami, put my things back in storage, and drove to Cherry Valley with whatever I could fit in my car. I rented a studio apartment located above a local artist's art studio. Their property shared a property border with the Barwick's parcel. My expenses were cut by 500 percent, aligning with my goal to save money, as well as giving me ample stress-free time to complete the book. My hair stopped falling out as I settled into writing and taking long walks in the woods with Jesse.

I organized a shamanic energy medicine workshop. My fifteen posters went up around the five surrounding small towns. The workshop was well attended, and I felt that I could build a tribe of like-hearted people here. After noticing my poster, Trista Haggerty, the founder of a nonprofit that helps children and youth develop skills and confidence, called to introduce herself. She lived two miles down the road, so we met in town for coffee. We had much in common; her husband is Hispanic, one of her sons was born with spina bifida, her other son had worked for a magazine in New York City a few blocks from Jaime, and her daughter lived thirty miles from Jaime's current home in California. In a town of eight hundred people—uncanny! Our coffee visit lasted three hours. Toward the end, we talked about her upcoming trip to Egypt; she was taking a tour group to visit the ancient temples along the Nile River.

Egypt was an enticing new adventure, but at the same time, the tour was expensive, and I was challenged on my goal of saving more than I spent. I had become accustomed to travels to Latin America, where I knew the language and culture, so it was a bit unnerving. Also, my impulsive decision-making had waned over time due to its negative impact on my savings account. Furthermore, I wanted to remain focused on my book and didn't feel a need for adventure. I suspected, however, that possibly there was something in Egypt that was important for me to experience.

I asked that question a number of times in meditation; in response, the guidance I kept hearing was, "Go, you will benefit. You had many lifetimes there." Both my personal healing work and my shamanic work with clients had convinced me that we do indeed evolve over many lifetimes. In each lifetime, we come into physical form for specific reasons, always evolving toward greater wholeness. Part of my belief in such a preposterous notion came from reading up on the work of Dr. Brian Weiss. Under hypnosis, his patients spoke ancient languages and described details unknown to them when fully conscious. He was a psychiatrist who ultimately helped thousands of people free themselves from phobias and both mental and physical pain by regressing them back to the source of the trauma. My comfort with the concept of reincarnation also stemmed from my client work. As I asked each client to track their current emotion back in time, they would often begin to describe scenes that were from a different time. They were often a different gender and had a different station in life than in their current existence. Regardless, what did not change was the energetic thread of emotion that presented itself upon arrival to my office. I had learned to track the energy upstream and remove it from the source by working with the specific lifetime in which the blockage had originated. My teacher, Alberto Villoldo, would often say, "We pull weeds instead of mowing the grass." I knew what he meant.

Motivated by the hope of freeing myself from those dark voices and uniting with lost aspects of myself, I signed up for the trip to Egypt. I was not disappointed. I experienced two very powerful transmissions of energy during the trip. The first was at the archeological site Karnak, in Luxor, Egypt. Our twelve-person tour group had the opportunity to enter a small temple one by one, a shrine to Sekhmet, the Egyptian Goddess who is often depicted with a head of a lion. She is both a warrior and a goddess of healing. It is said that her very breath formed the desert. Each of us had four to five minutes inside her temple. When it was my turn, I stood in front of her five-foot statue and listened intently; "Remember humility and gratitude," I heard, then silence. As I bent down to touch her feet, she spoke again, "You are no longer in servitude to anyone or anything. You are only in servitude to your higher Self." My body felt tingly, and a sense of relief washed over me. The Wizard within wanted me to stop pleasing and relying on others and listen to my own drumbeat. I felt thankful for the message.

The second was in King Khufu's chambers inside the Great Pyramid of Giza in Cairo. By six o'clock that morning, we were on the historic grounds of the Great Pyramid. Our tour guide began with a few facts. "This pyramid was built during Egypt's fourth dynasty around

2575 to 2465 BCE. It remains close to its original height of 481 feet. We are going to enter on the pyramid's south wall," he said, as he pointed in that direction. A security guard stood at the entrance and granted us permission to enter. We walked up the steep and narrow staircase in single file, then bent over until we reached the expansive doorway leading into the King's chamber, located about one-third of the way to the top. Inside, we formed a circle and sang together. "Everyone, go ahead and find a spot in the room to sit. You will each have the opportunity to lie down in the King's sarcophagus," said Trista, as she pointed to the large bathtub like structure on the other side of the room.

The room was impressive. It was made entirely of pink granite, measuring thirty-five feet by seventeen feet wide and seventeen feet high. The King's empty red granite sarcophagus, which weighs an estimated 3.75 tons, was located to my right. Although historians describe this as a sarcophagus, Trista, and others in the group sensed something quite different. We felt the room and sarcophagus were used not as a burial chamber but rather for astral travel, an ancient Egyptian occult practice involving one's astral body and mind leaving the body and traveling to obtain information. I thought that perhaps like the shamans, the ancient Egyptians had orchestrated experiences evoking the feeling of dying here as one of their rites of initiation. "The shamans of old established higher order neural activity by choreographing an experience where they thought they were going to die," explained Alberto Villoldo in class one night.

"Your turn, Paula," whispered Trista. I walked over, climbed into the sarcophagus, and lay down. I was unable to astral travel that day and did not have a death experience while I was there. However, for a few fleeting seconds, I felt the warm presence of Mother Mary. I thought, "What is Mother Mary doing here? Perhaps as the later incarnation of Isis," I thought. Soon I felt a tap on my shoulder and knew my time was up. I slowly climbed out of the sarcophagus and went over to lie back down on the floor.

Suddenly, I felt movement inside, within my womb, like the feeling of a tiny baby moving around. I coughed several times, suddenly feeling full of clay dust. Then, in my mind's eye, I saw numerous small clay pieces being brought together and reworked into one whole piece, not perfectly formed but rather mushed together. I was being shown in these images what was occurring in the ethereal realm, an integration of aspects of myself that had been left in Egypt during my many lifetimes there. Then I heard, "Remember who you are." Was Spirit reminding me of our cosmic nature, or something more? An inner joy brought a soft smile to my face.

Then Trista reminded us, "It is time to go back down, everyone." Groggily, I stood up. A fellow traveler and I slowly gathered our belongings. As I was almost ready to follow the others down the staircase, we shared a look that said, "Do you hear that?" We both stood perfectly still, listening—to celestial voices singing to us. Goosebumps, often a sign of inner truth, covered our arms. We jumped up and down and screamed in pure delight. Our prayers, chants, and songs had elevated our vibration such that our inner spiritual ears could hear the melodic cosmic sounds of the universe.

Later, in talking with Trista, she had insights I had not considered.

"Maybe you are supposed to remember that you are of Isis. Remember, Isis is the mother who gathered up all the scattered and strewn pieces of Osiris's body to bring him back to life."

"That's interesting," I said. "I set the intention to retrieve lost soul parts on this trip, so perhaps I did."

"In addition, the God Khnum was a potter and is the symbol of all the Gods as one—a symbol of wholeness. In the Egyptian creation myth, Khnum reaches down into the Nile and pulls out the muddy clay, from which he creates a primitive form of a body," she said, "similar to yours, all mushed together, not perfect. The Goddess Nut then swallows the clay, and as it passes through her into her womb to be baked, it is transformed into an infant. For the Egyptians, it was Nut who gave birth to the divine child, also believed to represent a new consciousness."

"And for Christians, God shapes us out of clay, and Jesus certainly represents a higher consciousness. Has Christianity ever been accused of plagiarism?" I asked. We laughed together.

My trip felt complete. I received what I had asked for, a more integrated self, and I was proud of myself for having ventured out beyond Latin America.

22

Another Test

B Y JUNE 2017, I WAS settling into my new life in upstate New York. Doors with interesting people and opportunities behind them were opening. In one week, three people told me that the person I should meet was Nettie Jean Scarzafava. "That's Jeanie over there, Paula—the woman in the red shoes," said a friend at a full moon ceremony. I introduced myself. Jeanie was from Arkansas and had proudly kept her Southern accent, which meant that she stood out each time she spoke, which it was loud and often. At seventy-two, she had blossomed into her role as a sage and an elder. She had earned it. She had become the only female so far elected to serve as a county court judge in this area and had walked a path of indigenous wisdom for more than thirty years. Over tea at her house the next day, I imagined that we might become friends. What I did not suspect was that we would soon become business partners, I would buy a home from her, and she would connect me back to Miami in a most unexpected way.

On July 20, 2017, I received a text message from an acquaintance and the owner of a local spa. Cheryl's message read, "Call me, I have an exciting business opportunity to share." Indeed, it was an opportunity to purchase a small church built in 1853 and create a spiritually focused community center.

"Cheryl, that sounds interesting, for sure. I'm with family downstate. Could we meet at the church on my way back home?" I replied.

"Perfect. Nettie Jean is interested in partnering; she suggested I call you." Cheryl explained.

I hung up, realizing that purchasing a church was not a novel idea to me. In fact, it was the third time I'd contemplated such an endeavor. Could this be the right mix of people, circumstances, and location? However excited I was to see the church, I was not about to disrupt my time with my family. I, along with Jaime, Mia, her husband Alex, and their three children, Lilly and the now nine-month-old twins, Hahr and Severein, were renting a lovely home outside of Woodstock with others. Barbecues, sightseeing, long hikes, sing-alongs, and card games were all part of the fun at our house.

Ten days later, as we'd planned, I pulled into the church's parking lot, located behind the building. There were not one, but two handicapped access ramps into the building, I noticed. Disability was never far away from my mind, which was both a blessing and a burden. I could hear the other women talking as I entered the fellowship hall. When I crossed the threshold into the sanctuary, my eyes teared up. My whole body sensed the sweetness in the room. 150 years of singing and praying had had an amazing impact. At that moment, I knew I would say yes.

Building community was the most inspiring aspect of the venture. I knew I thrived better in community. As a young child, I enjoyed the benefits of a large extended family. Dr. Morgan had said on several occasions, "Your extended family probably saved you." I found times of reprieve with my thirty-one first cousins; we had sleepovers and family gatherings, and we went to church together. My parents didn't attend, so I went with those who did. Some cousins were Baptist, others were Methodist, but most were Seventh Day Adventists. I enjoyed participating in worship with all denominations. One Sunday, I was 'saved' in the Baptist church, which got me in trouble with my mother, but it felt good to me. I also liked singing the hymns, albeit terribly out of tune.

Following Alex's birth, I began to build community for myself and for other families experiencing the emotional pain that comes with being different through Parent to Parent of Miami. I then raised my children within a church community while I chaired numerous committees at the university: all forms of group membership.

A long time had passed. I felt ready to build community again. Going it alone had become exhausting; collaboration was essential. Reinvigorating a church, bringing it back to life with a new form of energy, felt just right. With the chaos of crumbling institutions, erratic gun violence, and newly destructive weather patterns arising, people felt vulnerable and frightened. It was time to create a safety net that was outside of government—a safety net that connected people to each other, to Mother Earth, and to their Self and Spirit, not through words, but through direct experience.

Shortly after we made our purchase offer on the church, my son Jaime came for a visit. Although he didn't resonate with my spiritual path, he was supportive of my initiatives, and even proud of me, it seemed. His stay was short as his school semester was starting. He was in his third year of a master's in fine arts program in fiction at the University of California at Irvine. He had a full scholarship, and I was proud of him. We were both writing books; our lives were once again running in parallel, a fact I relished.

As summer turned to fall, I made plans to attend the Four Winds Society's annual Great Gathering, a three-day retreat where our community would network, attend seminars, and meet with Q'ero traditional people from Peru. It was being held at the Menla Retreat Center in Phoenicia, New York. But as the event date got closer, I started to have stomach problems and became concerned that I would not be able to attend. This was followed by an increase in negative thoughts and an overall feeling of gloom. A week before the event, I was experiencing screaming voices inside my head. It felt familiar. I then realized that the same sequence of events had occurred two years prior when I had canceled my trip to the Great Gathering at the last minute for the same exact reasons.

My heart sank as I realized that the entity was still with me and that a pattern had emerged. Its attacks occurred before and after powerful ceremonial events. First, it would attempt to deter me from attending. If that didn't work, it would try to bring me crashing down afterwards. I reflected upon my difficulty with maintaining a daily practice, my many starts and stops with writing my book, and my inability to scale up programs as I was at times expected to do; not to mention the time I'd felt I had been pushed backwards into the ocean, resulting in a concussion. Plus, there were all my moves. Exasperated, I concocted a remedy.

I thought, 'Let it say its piece.' Maybe if I just heard it out, it would leave. Sitting down on my sofa with the entity next to me, I wrote down all the insulting and cruel thoughts I was hearing on paper. Four pages later, I was still writing. I buried the horrific list of insults in the woods next to my house. This produced some relief. When the voice returned, I was aggressive, "Shut up! Get the hell out of here." It was not going to disrupt my trip to Menla. And it didn't.

Lo and behold, at the Great Gathering, there was a Four Winds instructor presenting a workshop about how to work with dark entities, based on his ten years of experience identifying and extracting a specific type of entity. Over lunch, I described the voices and symptoms as Peter listened and nodded. He thought I might have the kind of entity that he had just described in his workshop. I agreed.

He explained that the entity invades its host with negative thought forms to such a degree that the person becomes immobilized and unable to function. To accomplish this, it shapeshifts, appearing in any guise necessary to dismantle the individual's physical, mental, emotional, and spiritual well-being. If the person's vulnerability, for example, is around self-worth, then it works through that portal. If there was an early wounding around sexuality, then its venomous negative thought forms would play to that already vulnerable area in the person's life. Impacting thought forms meant it could manipulate emotions, feelings, decisions, and actions—everything!

When I described how many times I had moved to different places, Peter said, "Staying in motion was a positive, adaptive response. You did not let fear grip you, paralyzing you, as I have seen with so many other clients." But the worst news came when he explained that this entity's form of self-preservation is annihilating its host, "This is not easy, Paula. A recent client had fifty sessions with me before she was cleared. And even then, the entity still continued to return."

My first session was on November 9, 2017. I felt relieved and grateful to have found someone who knew what he was doing. Plus, we had a lot in common. He had worked in construction, then in special education as the director of one of the first integrated elementary schools. He also had a doctorate in special education, and we were both trained in shamanic healing through the Four Winds Society.

Over the years, he had developed his own methods of identifying the presence of the entity, a low-life evil trickster spirit with some rudimentary form of intelligence. "It's there, but not as severe with you as in other cases, and not intractable," he said.

"What does it look like to you?" I asked.

"I see it as a wispy grey form. It lies underneath your chakras, blocking the healthy prana [energy] from entering your body. It has hooked itself into the back of your neck. I am extracting it using a special crystal," he explained. I felt subtle pressure on the back of my neck.

Still working, he said, "I see a five-year-old little girl who wants to come out of hiding." I saw her in my mind's eye at the same time. It was me as a child. "Fear had sent her into seclusion. Your brother felt as if he owned you—an old soul contract that I changed," he said. I was thankful. "She is bringing back an erecter set. I haven't seen that before," he said. We laughed. Now I am able to reconstruct my own life, I thought.

The entity was successfully removed. The next day, I was literally seeing through a clearer lens: Everything looked brighter, similar to the effect of a windshield wiper. I was amazed. The feeling of dullness that I had gotten accustomed to never returned.

When I asked where I may have picked up this entity, Peter explained, "Most people can track the source of the entity back to a specific person. For healers like yourself, Paula, it is often a client." That gave me chills. I explained, "I did have a male client with whom I got enmeshed. He was of the most devious sort, with lots of charisma. I met him at church, of all places." "You are on the right track. These forces envelop you in situations that result in guilt and shame, the two lowest vibrating forms of energy," he responded.

All the shamanic energy medicine sessions with Peter followed the same steps I used in my own work with clients. We discussed how I was feeling, the voices, if any, localized pain, re-removal of the entity, and then he would guide us in an illumination process to strengthen the Light within. I was hopeful. The entity was smaller in size each time, gradually retracting from twelve inches to four or five inches in diameter. Our work with the Lower World extractions, newly written contracts, and retrieved soul parts was helping to heal old wounds. I had more vigor and self-direction. In between sessions, I journaled and worked with my black spirit panther to help protect me. I often slept with my medicine bundle for the same reason.

To deepen my understanding, I read Paul Levy's work on what he calls "malignant egophrenia" (ME), described as a "cannibalistic spirit that consumes and takes without giving anything back. A parasite of the mind." It operates through our subconscious blind spots, those aspects of our self that we are unable to see. It is in those blind spots that the entity hooks into us. Levy explains that the ME virus plays into our existing illusion that what we are perceiving outside of ourselves is separate from us. As I was interested in discovering solutions, this most resonated with me, "[T]he best way to deal with the evil of *wetiko* is to be in touch with our inherent wholeness, what Jung calls the Self, which acts as a sacred amulet or talisman, shielding and protecting us from evil's pernicious effects."[5]

The Self, as defined by psychologist Carl Jung, represents an integration of the inner male and female aspects and an awareness of the existence of the shadow, both our own individual shadow and that of the collective unconscious.[6] Similarly, Alberto Villoldo explained in class, "In the shamanic tradition, evil does not exist as an independent principle, but rather only in the hearts of men and women." Thus, to live awake to the darkness that resides in our own heart is the best protection from the evil *wetiko*.

It also made sense to me that on one's journey toward wholeness, the Light within would ultimately reveal the dark, the shadow. Once we realize that shadows are just the absence of light, we can take the necessary steps to augment our Light, as well as steps to identify our own dark spots, which requires contemplation—an active inner gaze that lasts long enough to discover one's projections. As Alberto explained in class, "We need to look directly into the eyes of pain, of fear. That is the way your shadow becomes smaller and smaller. Shadow is that place that you do not recognize as yours." So, with an inner gaze, we can find our own self-pity, victimhood, greed, deceit, jealousy, envy, aggressiveness, vindictiveness, and so on. However, in lieu of contemplation, our culture promotes verbosity and outward expression. In the Asian culture, there is a wonderful expression, "Still waters run deep." We need to become still and deepen the river that flows through us.

During this time of turmoil, I received a text message from Joseph Emeka, my friend from college whose deceased brother had appeared during his Akashic Record reading. His text message read: "Dearest Paula, I had a dream last night that I thought I should share with you as usual. You were taking an exam that would make it or break it for

---

5   Levy, Paul. *Dispelling Wetiko: Breaking the Curse of Evil* (p. 39). North
        Atlantic Books. Kindle edition.

6   Hopcke, R.H. (1999). *A Guided Tour of the Collected Works of C.J. Jung.*
        Boston: Shambhala Publications, Inc.

you. I found you hiding in a classroom on the seventh floor of a very tall building. I noticed that there was too much noise for you to pass such an important exam. After a little pep talk, you agreed to move to a different room. When I returned, I found you in room seven on the seventh floor. You were all dressed in white and were bubbly with joy. I knew you must have passed." He ended his text with, "What do you think it means?" I replied, "I am experiencing a very tough test in my life now. I am glad to know I am going to pass."

23

The Cause Becomes the Cure

D ARKNESS AND ITS LESSONS RETURN in many forms. I received a phone call from my cousin Lynn strongly suggesting I come home right away; I did. My mother had fallen twice in two weeks. One of her shoulders was dislocated and the other in a sling. Her recent blood labs indicated she was not taking her medications properly due to her declining memory. Her thyroid-stimulating hormone level was forty-six points above normal. Her bottle of gin emptied too quickly. She was gaining weight but not eating; now, none of her clothes fit. Unable to shower without assistance, she looked disheveled. Due to theft, she had no personal identification. My mother lived in Roscoe, Illinois in her own home, across the driveway from my brother's home. However physically proximate they were, there was an emotional distance, and they rarely saw each other. She rarely saw anyone. That's what happens when you don't like people very much.

My mother's falls had created a family crisis, and the bedlam from my childhood was again playing out upon my arrival. My brother was pointing fingers of blame; he fired Lynn, who had been responsible for watching over my mother. What was next for my mother seemed up in the air. I steered clear.

In the midst of the family chaos was my next scheduled shamanic energy session with Peter. There I was at the hearthstone of where I'd grown up, with all the forces I'd dealt with in my life present as well. I knew that this convergence of circumstances was significant. I was again being poisoned with the same venom that had created my fears and my early alienation from myself. As Paul Levy describes, "Just like in the use of immunization and allergy treatments, a small amount of the pathogen or allergen is given to stimulate the immune response. As if giving ourselves a psychic vaccination, we inoculate ourselves from the disease by taking it into ourselves, for as the healing art of homeopathy has realized, that which causes a symptom can also cure it."[7] It worked; the entity was not seen again for a good long while.

Now, two weeks into my stay, I felt torn. I felt the right thing would be to bring my mother home to live with me. The decision weighed heavily upon me, in large part because I knew my mother would be difficult to live with and I wasn't even fully settled into my new environs yet myself.

I didn't see my brother during those two weeks. Due to his belligerence the year before, I decided it was best to protect myself and stay away. So I made the decision to bring my mother back with me to New York without him. I went to see him the day before we departed for New York. My brother's usual ploy, attempting to extract information to use to insult and intimidate me, did not work. Instead, I listened to his diatribe about my mother. He shared that at the end of her five months staying with him in his multimillion-dollar home in Costa Rica, she had only one thing to say, "You never took me anywhere." The beautiful house, the personal assistant, her dog, which was transported to Costa Rica to keep her company, home-cooked meals, the pool, the view of the city—it all still ended in her disappointment. He felt that she was impossible to please. In a loud voice, he declared, "I am done. I am done with her;" then added, "And she is dying in that house," he said, adamantly pointing to where my mother was living. "We will see about that," I said to myself. However, I was soon to better understand his frustration.

Back in Cooperstown, my two-bedroom, cabin-like rental home began to shrink. My mother's smothering and hot-tempered nature surfaced. The people I found to assist with her chronic shoulder pain were criticized. The acupuncturist, the massage therapist, friends of mine she met, the woman hired to help her on occasion, and even her morning coffee…all got a wrinkle of her nose and a 'blah' response. In addition, she showed no interest in my shamanic energy work; this, however, was not new. She never mentioned the booklets, professional papers, or newspaper articles I brought or mailed to her; later, I would find them buried in a drawer. She hid them both from her own view

---

[7]   Levy, Paul. *Dispelling Wetiko: Breaking the Curse of Evil* (pp. 6–7). North Atlantic Books. Kindle Edition.

and from my brother, whom she had a habit of protecting. I came to realize that the intersection between my mother's and brother's jealousy and my need to seek family approval by highlighting my successes was contraindicated for me as it was toxic, an explosive concoction that left me wounded each time.

Now, in upstate New York, all the unhealed parts of myself were screaming, 'Get me the hell out of here!' But this time, I was not eighteen years old and able to run away to college. Instead, I was in my own home, unable to leave and quite literally with nowhere to run. Six feet of snow walled in the back door of my house, and inside was my nearly immobile mother, who needed continual care and supervision. Unlike the teenage protagonist of the 2017 movie *Lady Bird*, played by Saoirse Ronan, up until now, I had been unable to share my truth with my mother. Regrettably, I never found the courage, which left this dreadful family imprint active until I finally tackled it in a different relationship.

I was caught in a whirlwind of emotion. I needed some insight. Per a colleague's recommendation, I read Maureen Murdock's book *The Heroine's Journey*. Her ingenious map of the feminine healing process and the unification of the masculine and feminine forces within us gave me an additional framework with which to understand my own journey and my current inner turmoil. She writes, "The daughter flees the devouring mother, who through her jealousy and envy of her daughter's talents and potential freedom tries to imprison her. She distances herself from the mother who is overly judgmental, rigid, and unsupportive..... The mother's bitterness about her own shattered dreams may erupt into rages or passive-aggressive behavior toward the daughter, who has had more opportunities."[8]

I realized that my periodic home visits hadn't been long enough to truly expose the shadowy underbellies of our emotional interactions. But there we were, both in the same room again, playing out the same old story. I tried to please, and she wrinkled her nose. When one of my clients positively complimented me on my gifts, my mother scoffed. When I would leave the house on business or for social reasons, she was angry and would pout upon my return. Most hurtful were my failed attempts to do something that I perceived as meaningful to the both

---

[8]   Murdock, Maureen. (1990). *The Heroine's Journey*. Boston: Shambhala Publications, Inc.

of us. One of these was a private ceramic hand-building class, as we had done ceramics together when I was in high school. The other was a private sound healing experience, an effort at introducing her to my new world. In advance of both occasions, she had eagerly said yes. But both times, on the day of the event, when pressed about our plans, my mother screamed, "I never said I would go, I don't want to go, and this was all *your* idea." I went to the ceramics class and the healing alone, unable to discuss my real feelings.

Had I unknowingly brought back the vaccination that I most needed with me?—what causes the symptoms can also be the cure. But what exactly needed to be healed?

It was not much of a surprise when the entity made its way back into my psyche. It arrived with a taunting female voice, "Nyah-na-na-nyah-nah, I am back, and you can't do anything about it." Its versatility was remarkable, yet at the same time, it was consistently vicious, cruel, sneaky, and relentless. What was it going to take? I started getting up earlier so I could fit in my morning meditative practice before my mother awakened. It became a required part of my day, as much as to get rid of the entity as help me to cope with my mother's impatience and passive-aggressive maneuvers.

My next shamanic session revealed the family imprint that I was reliving with my mother. It involved expending a great deal of effort on accomplishments that would end in dissatisfaction and disappointment. The feeling of incompletion left me seeking more: trying to learn more, do more, achieve more, move more, and please more, all the while living in doubt and fear of the looming disappointment. I felt exhausted recalling it all.

Disappointment was my mother's way of manipulating my brothers and me. Her averted eyes and barely audible voice let you know your achievement was not very important. Her disapproval communicated that somehow in your achievement was an abandonment of your real duty—tending to her. My achievements, even more than those of my brothers, stirred her own inadequacies, her own longing to do, to create, to be free. My accomplishments needed to remain hidden out of sight at all costs.

My mother was a smart and creative woman who never fully climbed out from under her mother's and then my father's repressive style of control. Her two months of employment as a young adult, which she thoroughly enjoyed, met with so much resistance from my father that she quit her job. With my father's death, she had the opportunity to begin to live life differently, but she chose to move next to my brother and live under his influence. In her book, Murdock urges women to find compassion and understanding for their mothers by considering the cultural context of their generation, "Women who were mothers in the 1940s and 1950s did not have many opportunities to pursue their own goals. They were manipulated, contained, and suppressed with the assistance of advertising, girdles, and valium." Her words reflected a historical truth but at the time did not stir my compassion. My mother had had so many opportunities and did not seize them. But then perhaps, had I not done the same thing?

It became clear that I hadn't just moved away to college as I had thought; instead, I had run away. I ran all the way to Mexico, Colombia, the Dominican Republic, Miami, and how many other cities since then. To take down the Wicked Witch meant I had to find her. Where had she taken up residence? My own impatience, frustration, and disappointment with myself was part of the answer. My excessive striving for perfection and fear of rejection and ridicule made it difficult to take greater risks, i.e., to dare to be that public speaker, hold spiritual destination retreats, take part in a healing arts singing group, or bring arts and medicine to children living in harsh conditions. I had many plans. But at age sixty-four, my dreams were still in three-ring binders, waiting.

Family imprints are powerful and tricky beasts. What I saw in my mother was in me. It was only packaged differently. Reading books was my mother's escape; she spent most of her free time in her bedroom with her steamy romance novels. Was mine writing this book? Was I avoiding taking new risks? I was gripped by fear that time was passing me by as well. Others' successes felt painful to hear sometimes. But I had all the wisdom and skills necessary to push through. Down deep, I knew I would do it; I knew that I had chosen this family and all that it would bring in order to discover my own truth about parenting, loving relationships, and ways to heal, and then to ultimately transcend it all. Time was running out, I felt.

It was now the winter of 2018. There had been six feet of snow piled up outside my door for weeks, and the ice-filled driveway made leaving the house a challenge. My mother and I were cooped up together most days. I worked on my computer, and she rested on the couch watching the Netflix show *Longmire* on my iPad. My physical health began to decline. I felt a significant tightness in my upper chest and my upper back ached constantly. I took ibuprofen for the pain, though my mother's prescription hydrocodone was tempting. Walking up hills left me breathless. By eight o'clock, I was in bed, exhausted. Concerned, I went to my doctor. She ordered a pulmonary function test, x-rays of my upper spine, and an echocardiogram. I was worried about my physical health for the first time in over a decade. Recounting my physical woes to a friend, she suggested I contact a colleague of hers, an energy healer who was helpful in identifying the emotional factors linked to clients' physical symptoms. I explained to my friend that during a recent Akashic Record reading, my guides had suggested an ancestral clearing, the removal of blocks and patterns that have been in families for generations. She was now even more convinced that her colleague could help.

Dawn lived in Central Bridge, a small town forty-five minutes east of Cooperstown. I chose to do a phone session with her. Remarkably, she began our session by stating, "Paula, what you need is an ancestral clearing. Your chest cavity is full of grief." It was generational grief. Her session lasted an hour; I felt light, airy, and a bit tingly during the process. Her process was like mine: She worked through spirit, focused on one's luminous energy field, used the power of thought and intention to remove heavy energies, and used crystals to help realign one's auric field. The following day, I felt better, and on the next, better still. Within a week's time, my symptoms had vanished. I could easily walk up steep inclines and was not exhausted by nightfall. The tests at the hospital all came back negative. At my follow-up appointment with my physician, I told her about the energy medicine session. She asked questions and was genuinely curious. Perhaps Western medicine was changing.

The emotional mother/daughter turmoil brought other new insights. I became aware that my years of intense longing for Alex were also a longing for what never was—for the mothering that I never had as a child and the wholehearted nurturing I was unable to give my own daughter. With Alex's many physical needs, I became the caregiver, the one who did for her. And too often, that was in lieu of just *being* with her, a role I was repeating with my aging mother. I not only missed Alex, I missed what I didn't get enough of at the time—a level of intimacy, nurturance, and satisfaction with motherhood. I had perhaps hoped that I could recreate that with my mother. But she was not Alex. This would be my last attempt at resurrecting a life that was no more.

After four months, my mother wanted to return to Rockford, Illinois, to live once again across the driveway from my brother. She missed everyone. I had to admit even to myself that I was not too fun to live with. And now, her thyroid levels were normal, her shoulder was healed, and she had more energy and was less depressed. She looked elegant in her new wardrobe. Though I knew she would need home health care, convincing her of it was not easy. I said, "I am not buying you an airline ticket home unless you agree to home health care."

"That is expensive. I can take my pills by myself." But I didn't budge, and eventually, she acquiesced. We talked about her coming back to New York in the late summer, when there would be warm weather and more things to do. It seemed improbable.

The owner of the home health agency I contacted happened to personally know my parents and my brother, which gave me some assurance that things would go well. I tried calling my brother about it, but there was no answer. He sent me a text: "I can't take care of her like you do, why are you sending her back?"

"I'm not, she wants to go home; she misses everyone." No response text. Cousins picked her up from the airport in Chicago. Her return to her home across the driveway from my brother's meant that the natural order had been restored.

In those trials and tribulations with my mother and brother, I became more aware of how, at the age of eighteen, I had stumbled out of a home that felt smothering and harsh. As I recalled more about my earlier self, I remembered an intimate moment with my former husband, Jaime, when we were in the horrendous throes of our divorce, living together in a steamy tension. As I walked into the kitchen one morning, I found him reading the note I had left for him; a set of instructions, perhaps, about something he needed to do. For some reason, in that moment, his silence and anger melted, and he began to sob. Leaning forward and putting his hands on the countertop for support, he blurted out, "Thank you for saving me. I loved you so much." I was shocked and speechless. His deep grief over his father's death at the time when we met had left him vulnerable.

Now, decades later, compassion for him washed through me as I realized that in fact, we had saved each other. However, our fragile love was unable to withstand the hardships that come with raising a child with a disability. It was not designed to endure. We were meant to part ways, each of us to pursue other dreams. Jaime returned to Bogota, remarried, had two more beautiful children, and became politically active. My hidden dreams awoke with my first visit to the medium.

With my mother's visit, I also realized that it was my inner longing for intimacy—to find a landing pad where I could feel safe and nurtured—that had led to my inward journey. The dark aspects of my childhood ultimately propelled me to seek the Light. My family dynamics and Alex's disability and death served as launch pads toward a greater self.

The devotion I poured into my shamanic studies flowed from that longing. There, in ceremony, I experienced the loving nonjudgmental force of our original Earth Mother, Pachamama or Gaia. She became my mirror—the love for Pachamama became the love for myself. Murdock shares, "We have separated from our feelings and our spiritual natures. We are lonely for deep connection. We yearn for affiliation and community, for the positive, strong nurturing qualities of the feminine that have been missing from this culture." Yes, our inner spirit, our creative intuitive intellect, has been extracted from our lives so slowly that its disappearance has gone unnoticed—both individually and collectively.

CHAPTER
24

True Wizardry

So, there I was in rural upstate New York, surrounded by mountains, rivers, streams, and grassy meadows, taking pottery classes, and turning my Young Patronesses of the Opera monographed apron into a clay-filled mess. I was meeting women who had spent decades in ceremonial circles, honoring the cycles of nature that live within them. There were full moon ceremonies, rituals, and other practices to heighten their connection to these forces: the moon, the sun, the stars, earth, fire, water, and sky. I met them everywhere I turned because I was ready, ready to join the circle that honored the buried parts of myself.

Through a friend, I learned about a Native American sweat lodge being held downstate. The term "sweat lodge" refers to a Native American purification ceremony that typically takes place in a dome structure that symbolically represents the womb. Song, prayers, and teachings are incorporated into the ceremony. I wanted to learn more about the traditions and knew it would be helpful to me in ways that were not yet clear. After I crossed the threshold, touched the earth with my forehead, and asked permission to enter the Lodge, with time, the sacredness of the experience spoke to me. I particularly loved the drumming and singing and being part of the community. The next year, I had the opportunity to do a vision quest. A vision quest takes place in nature and in solitude for the purpose of receiving direct guidance from Spirit. It is a rite of passage for youth in many Native American traditions.

I prepared with vigor: cold showers, vegetarian diet, daily prayers, practicing the appropriate songs, a Thursday fast, and adjusting my sleep rhythm to the sun's schedule. In addition, I had a quilt made that would serve as both comfort and protection up on the mountain. I asked the quilter to scan my favorite photo of Alex and an image of a black panther and stitch them onto the quilt. The quilt was beautiful, perfect.

After nine months of preparation, a few weeks before the Quest, I had a dream in which a voice came to me in the middle of the night, "A trickster will come to you the first night, do not pay attention to him." In the upper right-hand corner of the room, there was a spider web and spider. I was grateful for the warning. September 2018, arrived, and I went up on the mountain, just me and my blanket, with supporters singing and drumming on my behalf. Resting there, I prayed, breathed, chanted, toned, and sang. I asked to be shown what I most needed in my life in order to take care of myself and others. The seven saplings holding my prayer ties and forming my sacred space became the illumined beings I had come to know, i.e., Ganesh, Tara, Mother Mary, Isis, and others. I lay down, looking up and breathing into the earth most of the time. Time was kept by the movements of the sun changing the colors of the leaves on the tree branches above, moment by moment.

The instant that darkness fell on the first night, I heard a loud male voice to my left. I knew that voice with its gruffness and insulting tone, ready to intimidate and threaten. But before its first words were fully formed, I belted out loud, "Shut the f*** up." There was absolutely no value in anything that trickster could have to say. He was not going to scare me anymore. I then immediately sensed a male energy behind me. He seemed happily surprised by my reaction to the trickster entity. His next move was unexpected. With one big whoosh, Ganesh and everyone else were thrown out like false idols. In their stead came seven Grandmothers, which I later identified as representing the Spider Woman archetype. Spider Grandmother is an important figure, a wise elder there to help people, in the mythology, oral traditions, and folklore of many Native American cultures. The Grandmothers felt more powerful, authentic, and earthier. With them came an intensification of energy that gave me the gift of enhanced seeing and hearing.

The communication was intense over those three days. The Grandmothers shared during the day and Spirit at night. It was honest, nurturing, and full of wisdom. Spirit's primary message came the first night, "Stop seeking what you are perceiving that you don't already have. You have everything you need. Be grateful."

Um? Stop seeking? I knew what Spirit meant. I had become addicted to seeking in lieu of being present with what is. The future had always held promise, fame, fortune, success. The present moment never seemed like enough, i.e., *I* was never enough. All my ruminations about the past and future just created suffering. Living gratefully in the moment was my takeaway message that night. I thanked him.

The Seven Grandmothers were available during the day. As I was contemplating one of the saplings, I asked the Grandmothers who they were. I heard, "We are the weavers of life, the creators, the givers of life. We are here reweaving your life for you." I saw a spider web made of yarn material and the women with knitting needles working quickly; at times, I actually heard the clicking together of their needles. They gave me permission to call upon them in my retreats and individual sessions with people.

During those moments, I had a flash of a regret that had haunted me for years. With my brother's political clout, I had had the opportunity to interview for available positions during Obama's 2008 administration. I had volunteered on his campaign and had personally met him and Michelle on several occasions; I savor the photos I have with each of them. In one of the photos, I am in a downtown Miami law firm handing Michelle a brown envelope with my dissertation inside it. When I asked her a question that night, declaring that since I was fifty-five years old and had just finished my dissertation, thus nothing trumps hope, she quipped, "Man, do you look good." Everyone laughed. Their leadership had me tempted to try out living and working in Washington. I went so far as to call the White House staff to set up an initial interview. The only position that excited me was with the Bureau of Indian Affairs. There was an early intervention initiative to help young Indian children and their mothers, some of whom had become addicted to drugs. The Mexican drug cartel was wreaking havoc on the reservations. After intense consideration, I decided that I would probably drown again in bureaucratic paperwork and half-truths. Plus, who was I to represent the voice of the Native Americans, I thought. I pursued my shamanic studies instead. But there I was, with the same heartfelt connection to Native American culture.

At midday while gazing at one of the Grandmother saplings, I heard, "We are out looking for a man for you. A man who needs a hearth. Out West. A woman becomes clever and strong when she is next to a man." As my mind was beginning to run wild with possibilities, I brought my gaze down to ground level, and surprisingly, directly into the soulful eyes of a chipmunk who had made its way onto my blanket. He did not flinch. However, the intimacy in that moment was real, and with a jolt, I flinched. He, like so many others, scampered off. A man would be great, I thought, but how do I overcome my fear of intimacy?

Sudden and deep-seated loss has long tentacles that invade the psyche and seep into every aspect of one's life, particularly when the loss concerns relationships. Truly suitable men had not been in my field of vision since my divorce. I needed a back door, an exit strategy when things became too intimate; the men I chose were fervent bachelors, too old, intellectually boring, or were going to get divorced. These were all effective back doors. But all that was ten years back at that point, which I felt was enough time to have hit the reset button. Regardless, if the Grandmothers kept their promise, I was going to be in a heap of trouble, I thought to myself with a slight chuckle.

Later that day, I had the idea to carry out my own soul retrieval, a Shamanic ritual I had done for many others and one that others had done for me. "I certainly have enough time," I chuckled to myself, as I watched the sun change the color of the leaves in the tree branches above. Time was distorted, while my thoughts were laser-like and had immediate impact. In a flash, I was in the familiar meadow, then at the base of the tree, down its roots and deep into the belly of Mother Earth. At the gates of the Lower World, I asked for permission to enter. As I crossed that threshold, I opened my eyes to see a figure off to the right side of my blanket, beyond my prayer ties, on the path that led into the woods; a woman, my pure core-essence, walking toward me. She was beautiful, with shoulder-length blonde hair, a strong, naturally curved body, and an inner fortitude that was apparent in her steady stride. Adventurous! She was neither rushed, nor seeking, nor worried, with a posture and methodical movement that held my attention. I knew at that moment that my years ahead would entail more travel and adventurous outdoor experiences. Then I noticed her wardrobe. She was covered with the most gorgeous fur pelts. I heard one of the Grandmothers say, "We acquire the power of the animal by wearing its skin."

On the second night of my Vision Quest, Alex visited. I was hoping she would. She began, "The frequencies have been so busy, I couldn't get a channel through to you." We laughed. It was true. I was inundated with beautiful communications from the trees, plants, and spirits. "I will be with you more now, mom. I have been in classes and busy preparing the crystalline cities of the future." She was so vibrant and alive. She did not appear in a physical form, as with my soul's visit.

I didn't see what she was wearing, her expressions, or hairdo. I sensed it all. Her imprint of who she was now was available to me in this sacred, high-vibration space.

Our exchange had a certain quality to it. It was as if we had both been through many sacred initiations and we could finally understand each other. Her Light interpenetrated through me and surrounded me in an experience like no other. Her visit was short and to the point. By now, it was the middle of the night; I was tired and fell asleep.

On the third day of the Vison Quest, I felt complete. Spirit and the Grandmothers had left in the morning. My heightened and altered state had subsided. When my supporters came, I said I was ready to return. I went back down that afternoon, energized, nurtured, and grateful to be part of such a beautiful tradition.

Remembering Joseph's dream of finding me in room seven dressed in white, and of me having taken a bath or sauna, I texted him, "Remember that test I was trying to pass. I just passed it. I am on the other side of darkness now." I realized that there is a tipping point; there would be no more back-sliding. That had been the moment when I firmly told the entity to shut up. Then I called my son Jaime to let him know I was home safe. He grimaced at the fact that I'd had twenty-one ticks removed when I came down. Mostly, I listened to his progress on his book of short stories. His themes reflected his own life, i.e., identity, racism, the impact of the Colombian Cartel in both Colombia and Miami, and disability. He had recently graduated from UC Irvine, already had a literary agent, and was living on the cheap in Tijuana, Mexico, to finish his short story volume. His stories were taped all over his walls so he could organize his thoughts. I appreciated our parallel lives.

As promised, the next week, my daughter appeared to me in my sleep. I had embarrassingly overslept, leaving Susan and her husband Larry, who were visiting me, to fend for themselves. It was a beautiful encounter with Alex. I saw her face, much as it was when she was twelve years old, and for a flash of a second, her eyes and gaze felt just like her brother's. She was enveloped in a white thick creamy light, and I was smiling ear to ear. Perhaps she moved closer, because I woke up startled as she hovered just above my face. She continues to come to me during dream time, giving me advice.

The animal skin poncho began to manifest as well, "My brother used to work for the tanning industry, I am going to ask to see what animal skins he may have," said Eileen, my talented ceramic instructor. In a shamanic journey during one of my retreats, her sister, who had been killed in a car accident, appeared to Eileen, creating positive shifts in her life. Eileen wanted to reciprocate; the two coyote skins she gifted me would be central to my poncho.

In addition to the Grandmothers' actively seeking a man for me, they began to appear during my shamanic sessions. At first, their energy seemed a bit diffuse, but the more I invited them in, the more potent it became. I associated them with the Spider Grandmother who appears in several Native American mythologies as a leader, a wise individual who represents good things. I began to equate the spider web with our brain's neural network, meaning the work of the Grandmothers and other spirits had the ability to turn negative brain patterns into positive ones.

It was during Raquel's session that the Grandmothers' presence began to feel stronger than ever before. Raquel was fifteen years old and had come to me through a colleague who'd told me, "Paula, there is another young girl who needs your help. She reminds us of Andrea." "Of course," I said with a shivering remembrance of those dark days of worms falling from my ceiling, my car being towed, and feeling the threat of attack by entities.

Later that day, I spoke with Raquel's mother. "Raquel has been institutionalized four times in the past six months. She has meltdowns when things don't go her way, and her meltdowns can be very scary. She is severely depressed and now she can hardly get out of bed. Her grades are falling fast. I am so worried because she wants to go to college, and she has been unable to focus and study." Tears came to my eyes as I sensed the mother's fear and pain. "We were told you could help. Nothing else has worked," she entreated. I told her about Andrea, and we both felt hopeful.

I liked Raquel immediately, and although she was a bit sullen, I felt she liked me too. On a scale of one to ten, she said her anxiety was at one thousand. During that first session, as I began to rattle, I saw Delerus, the Grandmother who had been most prominent during my retreat on the mountain, standing across from me. I asked her to help, and the six other Grandmothers immediately appeared. I opened up sacred space, rattling over Raquel's body to break up the first layer of heavy energy, chanting softly to create a higher vibration conducive to healing. Raquel resonated with the sound of the rattle and enjoyed the shamanic journeys, using her vivid imagination to connect with her spirit animal and clear trauma from her own field.

Part of the problem became clear immediately. Raquel's electromagnetic field was contracted; she was not grounded in the earth. Interesting, she explained that when she'd get really upset, she frequently would not be able to feel her legs. Together we visualized solid roots extending down into the ground as I directed the Light energy toward her lower body.

During her second session, Raquel told me about the time she had tried to kill herself, stabbing herself repeatedly in the head with a dull knife. Her father had said mean things to her just before. She'd believed him then in much the same way as she was believing her hostile classmates now. Mean comments would result in emotional meltdowns that could last for days or even result in a trip to the hospital. I offered a reframe. "Perhaps you were only trying to stop your negative thoughts, not trying to kill yourself." That felt right to her. Seeing her own experiences through this new frame also helped redefine the problem and informed our solution. We talked about the fact that we are not our thoughts. Our mind is only one aspect of our self, and we can't let it rule us. I began to teach her about the Medicine Wheel, the four directions, and our divine design.

Raquel was smart and motivated. When we came up with strategies for her healing, she followed through and did the work. To help ground her and release negative stored energies, she began dancing throughout the day as needed. She kept a diary and used her art abilities to draw her shamanic journeys and reflect on them. Each energy session resulted in her auric field vibrating at a higher level—resulting in her newfound ability to attract a new set of friends. Birds of a feather flock together—she got to join a new flock. Life became more pleasant.

Two months and four sessions later, "Paula, Raquel got all A's and B's on her report card," her mother gleefully shared with me; "She started having so many nice things she wanted to go do, but I insisted she had to complete her homework first. And she did. It worked!" "Meltdowns?" I inquired. "None," she responded. In fact, Raquel has not had a major meltdown since we began our work together.

God is great.

CHAPTER

25

Coming Home

M Y NEW TWO-STORY HOME OVERLOOKED the beautiful Otsego Lake. The interconnecting staircase between the house's levels could be closed off, giving me the option to rent out one of the two floors. My favorite space, which became my healing studio, was above the garage: It had natural pine paneling and flooring, a pitched ceiling, stained glass windows, and railroad tie crossbeams. In the center of the wooden floor was an inlaid symbol of the four cardinal directions in wood. It came equipped with a small bathroom and kitchen area. This was the first time in twelve years that I and all my things were in the same place. Unpacking, I realized I had saved a lot of stuff that I now wanted to give away.

With my house purchase came a big surprise. "I bought a house in Cooperstown," I shared with my cousin Sally via text. She replied, "Oh, you know, that is where grandma visited." I texted, "What!?" Her reply was startling, "Yes, to visit family in Fly Creek." I stared down at her text, a bit incredulous, thinking, 'Fly Creek is only ten miles northeast from me, how is that possible?' "So, who was in Fly Creek?" I ask, imagining an obscure relative my grandmother wanted to track down for the sake of going on a road trip. "Our great-great-grandfather and grandmother are buried in the Fly Creek cemetery. Grandma's father was born in Middlefield, also close to you, I think." Close to me, I thought. It was directly across the lake from me, and I had thought about purchasing a house there.

Then I put a call in to my cousin Denise; I proposed, "You know, every family needs at least one member who cares enough to do the ancestral digging. Sally thinks we have relatives buried up here. Let's try to find our family tombstones when you get here. A woman in my ceramic class gave me some potential leads."

"Sounds good to me, let's do it before the kids arrive," she suggested. And so it was. In October of 2018, I was gifted with a visit from my cousin Denise and her daughter Mia, along with Mia's husband Alex and their children. Mia had blossomed into a wonderful mother who Denise and I both admired. Alex was a successful entrepreneur who loved food, music, outdoors, and just about everything in Life. Lilly was a thriving first grader who took good care of her younger twin siblings, now two years old, exploring, and climbing up stairs. Sadly, Jaime was missing our family adventure, busy as he was writing his short stories while living in Tijuana, Mexico.

"The president of the Fly Creek Historical Society suggested we start with the Presbyterian cemetery. It's across from the Fly Creek Historical Society and former Grange," I said.

"Sure, whatever you think," said Denise. A short fifteen-minute drive later, we were standing at the cemetery's entrance. In my hand was a printed copy of the ancestry.com family tree that Sally had diligently worked on for years.

"The tombs look really old; some we won't be able to read. Let's divide ourselves up. I'll start looking on this end and you on that end," Denise suggested. I walked to the south end of the cemetery and approached the first tall tomb I saw.

"I found them!" We couldn't believe it.

The tall tomb read, "Joshua Byard, Died February 25, 1867, Aged 57 Years. Mary, His Wife, Died June 24, 1861, Aged 66 Years." "So, this is grandma's father's father, right?" Studying the chart, Denise says, "It seems so." Our great-great-uncle, James Jackson Byard, was buried close by, along with others who weren't on our printout. The following day, we took the kids to the cemetery, snapping family photos to send back to Sally, which she would no doubt upload to ancestry. com. As we were driving out of the cemetery heading toward town, Denise, who has a great sense of humor, began to wave at people as we drove by, quipping, "I am saying hello, they may be our cousins."

I recounted my coming home story that Sunday during my presentation at the Opening of our Light of Heart Sanctuary. There in the pews were Mia and her family. I was thrilled that Lilly could be there so she could come to know me in that way, as a role model for her own becoming. We can't have too many of those. The sanctuary looked beautiful. The outdoor handicap access ramps, the bathroom, the podiums, and the altar space had all been repainted. Our new logo was the dove carrying an olive branch, as embossed on the tin-lined altar alcove that we'd had refurbished by a local artist. The image is from Genesis in the Old Testament; it comes from the story of Noah's Ark and represents the peace that comes when the flood waters of emotion subside. I shared how my church had helped my emotional waters to subside, a healing vision we now held for the sanctuary. The pews were filled, and we felt satisfied with our kickoff.

Unbeknownst to me, the river had carried me back home, both physically and to a place within myself, a place of self-love and a recognition of our divine design—our innate cosmic nature. Perhaps I felt not unlike Dorothy in *The Wizard of Oz* when she landed back in Kansas. Having retrieved her heart, brain, and courage, and now aware of the magical powers of each, she felt more integrated, whole, and grateful. Her feelings of separateness, of being the orphan who felt she did not belong, had been transformed. Also, Dorothy's adventures are the journey of the heroine, the adventurer, the community builder, as Jean Houston describes her in her book *The Wizard of Us*; and the fact is that the Wicked Witch of the West did more to expand Dorothy's soul than all the other characters.

I held a women's retreat in my new home that year. There, happily sitting on my own couch, I shared my thoughts about wholeness with our ten guests. Andrea's mother, Michelle, was one of them. I began with a quote from the twelfth century Persian poet Rumi—one reflecting a truth that had brought so much relief, joy, and peace into my life, a truth that had sent me on a quest to know more:

"My soul is from elsewhere—I'm sure of that. And I intend to end up there."

Yes, we return to where we began. I don't fear that day, nor do I long for it as I did when Alex died. I now imagine it to be a grand celebration of having overcome substantial adversity while discovering who I Am along the way.

Fifteen homes, eight cities, and twelve years ago, unshackled from years of intense caregiving and mental restraints, I sold my home and put my few belongings in storage for what I estimated would be six months, to finish my dissertation. But I never could have predicted what transpired. Hidden deep within was a seeking, a longing, to know Paula, all aspects of her. As I found beauty within myself, the outside world shifted. It too became more beautiful, supportive, and nurturing. Along the way, I became the person I was destined to become from the beginning. I found her in Tedlock's book, Villoldo's classes, in the stones on Martha's Vineyard, in the jungles of Peru, and in the Native American sweat lodge. I was a destined to be a healer and even a writer—who came to find her Self and help others discover their own Light, their own divinity, their own truth.

Impelled, however, by my perceptions of lack, not unlike Jung's Orphan archetype, my journey was challenging. I kept seeking a place where I would be nourished and find peace of heart, where I could be myself and my knowing would be accepted and acknowledged. I kept circling back to my nuclear family in the hopes that safe place could be with them, only to be repeatedly reminded that my path was destined to be different. Also, like the orphaned child, I found my way not through guidance but much on my own, through trial and error. This includes the writing of much of this book. Going it alone is arduous. In lieu of a mentor, my clients have often been my teachers. In those intimate moments during healing sessions, their stories felt like mine. As I helped heal their wounds, I healed my own. Their longings and desires triggered buried parts of myself that I could no longer deny. Revealing my shadows—the hidden aspects of myself—made room for the Light.

In all of my doing, I often forgot to take care of myself, resulting in downward spirals, dark entities, and losing sight of my own goals. I came to realize that Awakening is the easy part. More difficult is to keep the fire burning. Community is required to sustain Life—it has always been required.

My journey home was a gift from my daughter, a mutually agreed upon soul contract. Regardless of this knowing, there are moments when I wish it all had been different, that Alex could be here physically sitting next to me, having a cup of tea, perhaps, talking about her brother, politics, spirituality, and her latest hairdo. I still wish we could go shopping, to a good movie, to the beach, which she loved, and do mother daughter things together. It would mean more than I can say to hear her hearty laugh and see her blue eyes twinkle; to listen to how she is with herself; and to feel her hand in mine.

However, we chose a different kind of life together. She visits me in my dreams and during energy medicine sessions; we meet on mountaintops and through the intuitive eyes of mediums and psychics. And all the while, we are able to live from our best cosmic selves, clearing out karmic dust along the way.

Alex empowered me with her life and then again with her death. She was the daughter who never gave up on me—who conjured up a way to summon Bert Farr from his small town in Georgia to South Florida, to arrive on the eleventh anniversary of her death. I live in gratitude to her. I am grateful to the daughter who appears as Dorothy on her bicycle with our cat Sam as Toto and her brother as the Tin Man, the little girl who breaks the news to her mother that the Wizard is Fake and that she is the Wizard. She led me down the yellow brick road to decipher its meaning until I too became Dorothy, put on my red slippers, and found my way back to Self. She was the voice that whispered, "The girls are here," as she so lightly tapped me on the shoulder. Yes, that little girl. I am grateful for her sacrifice, her love, and her life. She gave me back mine. She gave me a life—a life worth living, a life where magic is real, the Wizard is fake, and we are all innately worthy of all that Life has to offer.

P.S.

I HOPE THAT MY LIFE STORY was inspiring and perhaps even life changing for you. In my experience, writers want to connect with their readers—and I am no exception. I would like for this experience to be as interactive as possible. Along these lines, you have a standing invite from me to share your stories of love, the afterlife, and ways in which magic is real to you on my Facebook group page, www.facebook.com/paula.petry11. For your interest, as a special bonus feature, I've also included real-life photos under "Memories" on my website: paulapetry.com.

I welcome all reader feedback. Please share your thoughts and feelings—you can email me at paula@paulapetry.com—and post a review on Amazon. Future readers will appreciate your effort.

Thank you for reading!

Acknowledgements

M Y GRATITUDE FLOWS ABUNDANTLY TO all the individuals who have helped me along my awakening path.

All my appreciation and love to those who supported me during the darkest days of my life. To my psychologist Dr. Rose Morgan for her steady presence, compassion, and insights—helping me begin to heal from the inside out. Psychiatrist Dr. Floyd Rosen for his deep listening, caring, and his healing words. I am forever appreciative to Reverend Burt Blomquist and the congregation of the First United Methodist Church of Coral Gables for their uplifting services and honoring of my daughter's life. My thankful heart is extended to Dr. Terri Urbano. Her professional ethics and empowering ways were just what I needed.

My life transformed from the ordinary to the extraordinary the day I met grief psychologist and medium Bert Farr. There are really no words to express the amount of gratitude I have for this friendship, his gift of mediumship, and his generous heart. The Four Winds Society gave me a map into the invisible world and the gifts of sight and healing. I will be forever grateful to Linda Fitch for her teaching and leading us up the sacred mountain Salkantay, and to founder Alberto Villoldo for his sacrifice and his excellent writings and teachings. Hours and hours of shamanic journeys with Dr. Hank Wesselman and his beautiful teachings and writings enriched my shamanic path, for which I am indebted.

The list of personal friends who have contributed their help along the way is extensive. All my love to Susan Duwa, who has put wind underneath my wings since 1986, when she came to Miami to mobilize parents to help other parents. Forever grateful for the spiritual wisdom and friendship of Helen Masin. Sonja Bogensperger for sharing her yogic practices, our daily chants, and her encouragement when skies were grey. My beloved Brazilian Voices, Inc., particularly Loren Oliveira, for their unyielding support and Dr. Eugene Ahn for being a cheerleader for all of us. My YPO sisters, particularly Lurenda Turner and Marianne Kircher for their comradery and support of my work. My deep felt thanks to Patricia San Pedro and Dr. Donna Surges Tatum, whose friendship, insights, and encouragement sustained me during my long bouts of not feeling up to the task. Jeanie Scarzafava, who invited me into many women's circles as I settled into my new home in upstate New York.

I am abundantly grateful to The International Women's Writers Guild for their writer's workshops, conferences, and talented and generous members. I have deep gratitude for Cathleen O'Connor, my editor, who skillfully brought my book across the finish line. I am forever appreciative of her editing skills and intuitive gifts.

My editor Jane Kinney Denning, for supporting the acquisition of my book and helping me through the process as a first-time author.

Finally, I give thanks to my parents; their sacrifices and hardships were many. I appreciate everything they did to make my life more plentiful.

About the Author

D R. PAULA PETRY'S JOURNEY OF self-discovery, healing, and personal empowerment began with the birth of her daughter, Alexandra, who was born with Spina Bifida. Complicating things, the birth and earliest care took place in the Dominican Republic, where in 1984, the lack of adequate healthcare and skilled providers forced Paula to pave a new path not only her daughter but for many others. She became a strong advocate for children with disabilities, forming what is now one of the leading parent advocacy organizations in the country. She brought that knowledge and her passion for family-centered care services to her faculty position at the University of Miami, School of Medicine, Department of Pediatrics, where she worked for over a decade preparing pediatricians to work with children with special health care needs.

Alexandra's death at age twelve brought great loss, suffering, and new beginnings. On her journey to healing, Paula studied energy medicine, sound healing, and the expressive arts, which she now blends together in retreats, workshops, and individual shamanic healing sessions. Her passion is to help women awaken to their inner truth and power, a theme and focus of her book, *A Mother's Courage to Awaken: Hope and Inspiration from My Daughter's Journey in the Afterlife.* Paula is a founding member of the Lightwork Education & Wellness Center, a virtual elementary and middle school; there she advises and teaches her *Medicine Wheel & Me* curriculum to teachers, students, and parents. Paula resides in Cooperstown and is a co-owner of the Light of Heart Sanctuary, the former St. Matthew's church, near Sharon Springs, New York.

Mango Publishing, established in 2014, publishes an eclectic list of books by diverse authors—both new and established voices—on topics ranging from business, personal growth, women's empowerment, LGBTQ studies, health, and spirituality to history, popular culture, time management, decluttering, lifestyle, mental wellness, aging, and sustainable living. We were recently named 2019 *and* 2020's #1 fastest growing independent publisher by *Publishers Weekly*. Our success is driven by our main goal, which is to publish high quality books that will entertain readers as well as make a positive difference in their lives.

Our readers are our most important resource; we value your input, suggestions, and ideas. We'd love to hear from you—after all, we are publishing books for you!

Please stay in touch with us and follow us at:
Facebook: Mango Publishing
Twitter: @MangoPublishing
Instagram: @MangoPublishing
LinkedIn: Mango Publishing
Pinterest: Mango Publishing
Newsletter: mangopublishinggroup.com/newsletter

Join us on Mango's journey to reinvent publishing, one book at a time.